IMAGES
of America

HISTORIC FAULKNER COUNTY

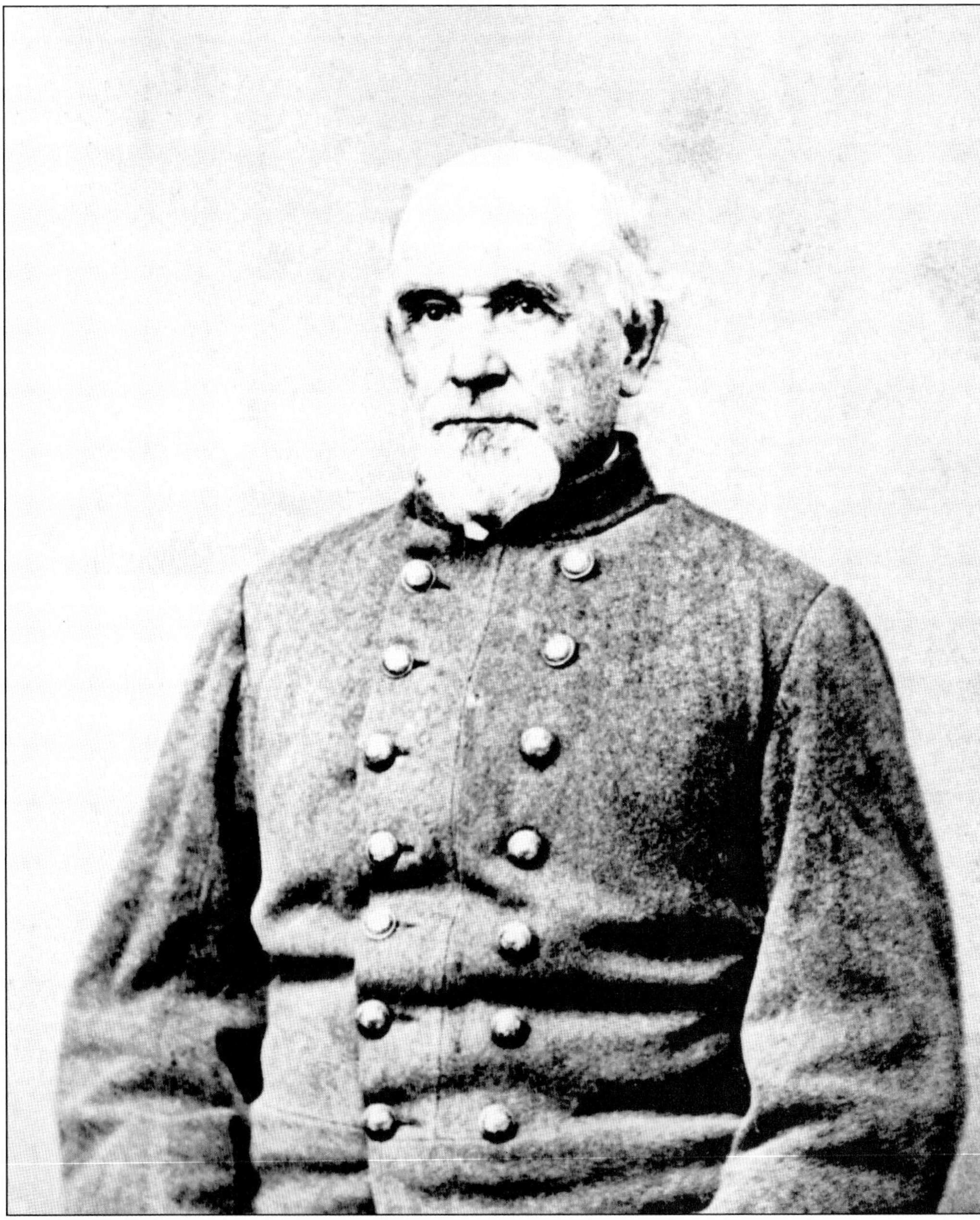

COLONEL SANFORD C. FAULKNER. This photograph of Colonel Faulkner was taken at about the time Faulkner County was named in his honor. (J.N. Heiskell Collection, UALR Library Archives.)

IMAGES
of America

HISTORIC FAULKNER COUNTY

Paulette H. Walter and Alan C. Paulson

ARCADIA PUBLISHING

ISBN 978-0-7385-0007-2

Published by Arcadia Publishing
Charleston, South Carolina

Printed in the United States of America

Library of Congress Catalog Card Number: 99-63436

For all general information contact Arcadia Publishing at:
Telephone 843-853-2070
Fax 843-853-0044
E-mail sales@arcadiapublishing.com
For customer service and orders:
Toll-Free 1-888-313-2665

Visit us on the Internet at www.arcadiapublishing.com

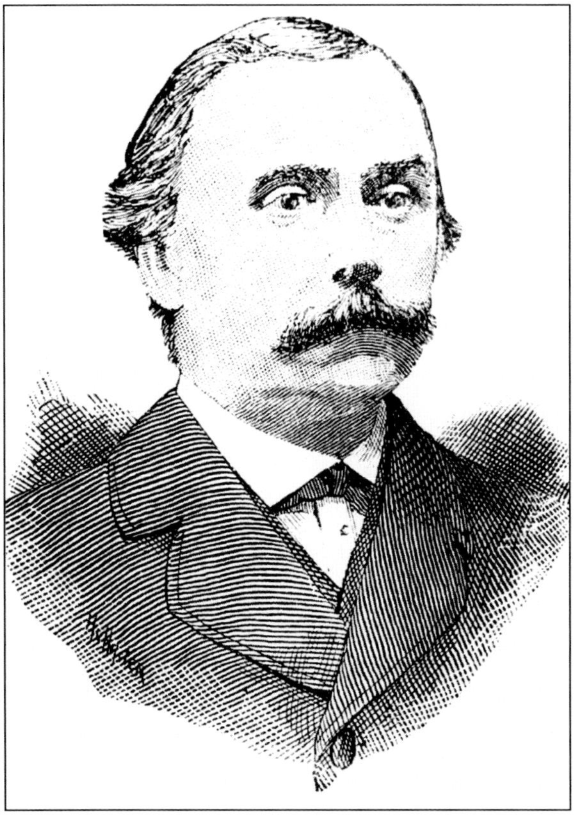

COLONEL ASA P. ROBINSON. Robinson founded Conway along the railroad line he built. (J.N. Heiskell Collection, UALR Library Archives, HEIS JNH.)

CONTENTS

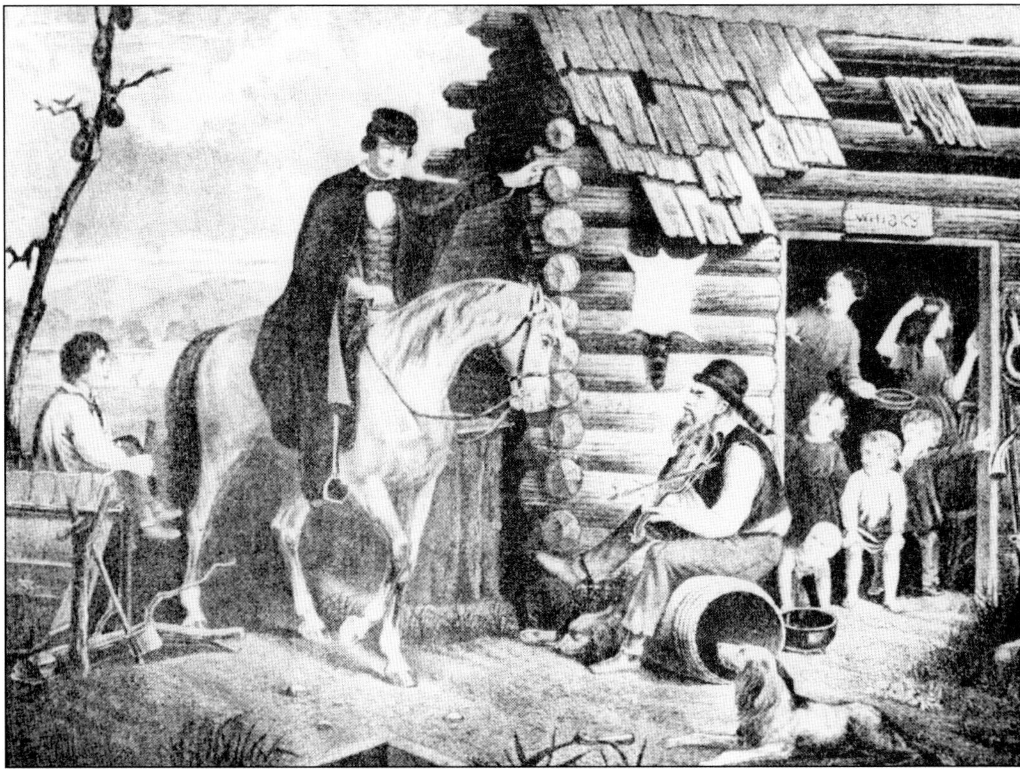

THE ARKANSAW TRAVELER BY ARTIST EDWARD PAYSON WASHBURN. *The Arkansaw Traveler* depicts the story of the fiddle tune that made author Col. Sanford C. Faulkner famous. Written in the 1830s, the tune tells the story of a weary traveler encountering a backwoods family in Arkansas Territory. The hilarious story was loosely based on Faulkner's experiences while accompanying several friends through "Arkansaw." (Special Collections, University of Arkansas Libraries, Fayetteville.)

About the Authors

Polly Walter has taught journalism at the University of Central Arkansas since 1990. Before that, she taught at the University of Alaska and worked as photograph editor and associate editor for *Alaska* magazine, *Alaska Journal*, and *Alaska Geographic*. She subsequently served as production manager and photograph editor for *Mushing* magazine. A veteran journalist, her work has appeared in dozens of books, magazines, and newspapers such as the *Fairbanks Daily News-Miner*, *The Pioneer All-Alaska Weekly*, and the *Anchorage Daily News*. More recently, she edited and did most of the photography for the highly acclaimed book, *Roadside History of Arkansas* (ISBN 0-87842-335-4), which was written by her husband, Al Paulson.

Al Paulson is an author and journalist specializing in the realms of history, science, and technology. Voted Alaskan Writer of the Year in 1977, he has written hundreds of magazine articles and several books. He has also worked as a biologist, conducting scientific research from the Arctic to the South Seas.

Walter and Paulson are currently collaborating on several books about Arkansas and Alaska. Both are members of the Ozarks Writers League.

Introduction

The land now known as Faulkner County has seen the ebb and flow of history since long before Europeans began to explore the eastern edge of the continent. Arkansas rivers functioned as the superhighways for impressive Native-American cultures with large communities and well-developed agriculture. The Arkansas River, which runs along the western edge of Faulkner County, remained a primary thoroughfare after settlers followed the first European explorers into the heart of Arkansas and points west.

Just below a horseshoe bend on the Arkansas River, an eddy provided a place where keelboat crews could rest for a time or await higher water before poling their boats farther upriver. These men worked hard and they played hard, too. When anchored for a time, they tended to pull out their jugs and "suck up whiskey like toads" or "have themselves a regular toadsuck." This turn of phrase would soon become a focal point of local lore.

Congress established Arkansas Territory in 1819, and within a few years, a new postal road crossed the river at this eddy on the Arkansas. Here, a ferry operator ran a small skiff that could carry a single horse and rider. Soon the crossing was known as Toad Suck Ferry. By 1830, a tavern at the spot catered to anyone traveling by trail or river.

As demand increased over the years, the ferries, which were owned by private citizens, got larger and more sophisticated. The last ferry was owned by Dave Ward (who went on to found one of the largest school bus factories in the country), Paul Van Dalsem (who was a representative in the Arkansas legislature), and Guy "Mutt" Jones (who was a colorful senator in the legislature, a flamboyant orator, and a true friend of Faulkner County). These three partners tried to get the state government to buy a new ferry for Toad Suck in the 1940s but failed. Jones spent the next several decades trying to persuade various government entities to upgrade the crossing. Jones finally got the federal government to foot the bill, thanks to some fancy politicking by Sen. Wilbur Mills, who was chairman of the Ways and Means Committee in Congress. Toad Suck Ferry Lock and Dam was completed in 1969. This proved to be the culmination of Mutt Jones's long quest, since the lock and dam included a bridge over the Arkansas River.

The first community of consequence in the area was established just upriver of Toad Suck, at the mouth of Cadron Creek. The first settlers to the area came in 1808 and homesteaded along the shore, across the river from the mouth of Cadron Creek. Several years later, John McElmurry platted a town called Cadron in the hills around Cadron Creek. The settlement lay on the border between the Osage and Quapaw Indian nations. The settlers got along fine with the Quapaws, but the Osages were another matter entirely. So McElmurry built a blockhouse that served as a home for his family and as a fortified refuge for his neighbors. Jonas Menifee bought a quarter interest in Cadron, a small community two miles north of the Cadron town site now bears his name.

In 1820, the territorial legislature voted to move the Pulaski County seat from Arkansas Post to Cadron, where court was held in the local tavern. But the political winds changed quickly. Two years later, the county seat moved to Little Rock and the little settlement at Cadron began to drift away on the wind. Cadron's epitaph was written soon after Pres. Andrew Jackson got Congress to authorize the relocation of all Native Americans living east of the Mississippi. The route of the Native-American trek westward came to be known as the Trail of Tears.

The proverbial nail in Cadron's coffin came in 1834, when low water on the Arkansas River forced a band of relocating Cherokees ashore at the old Cadron town site. Already weakened by measles, fatigue, and a poor diet, the Cherokees were devastated by a cholera epidemic. The families spread out into the surrounding woods in a vain attempt to escape the pestilence. Soon graves littered the forest, marked by simple headstones and footstones of native rock. Cedar Park now occupies the old townsite, where a bronze plaque lists the names of those who died at this place along the Trail of Tears.

The area remained something of an agricultural backwater through the cotton boom of the antebellum years as well as during the Civil War. It was the coming of the railroad that really stimulated the economy of the land that would become Faulkner County.

Soon after the end of the Civil War, the United States experienced an euphoric time of railroad-building and economic expansion. Due to fluctuating water levels, the Arkansas River had never provided a reliable route for river-borne freight upriver of Toad Suck, so building a railroad between Little Rock and Fort Smith was long overdue. Beginning in 1869, a civil engineer named Asa Robinson laid out the route and ramrodded the construction of the Little Rock & Fort Smith Railroad. Robinson fell in love with a stretch of open prairie dotted with clusters of trees along the right-of-way several miles south of Cadron. Here, he established Conway Station, which was named after the first LR&FS locomotive (which was named the *Conway* in honor of a prominent family that had given Arkansas two governors). Naming engines and Pullman cars was a common practice of the day. Nearby Mayflower, for example, was named after the Pullman car that served as the mobile headquarters for the railroad during construction. The cable address for telegrams going to the mobile headquarters was *Mayflower*; the name stayed behind when the Pullman moved on as the track laying progressed northward.

The railroad gave Robinson the deed to a square mile of land in lieu of salary on July 6, 1871. He filed a plat for a town named Conway in August. The town got a big boost two years later, when Conway Station became the temporary county seat for the newly established Faulkner County. The town around the station began to thrive, and Conway soon became the permanent county seat.

While most counties are named after politicians or war heroes, Faulkner County was named after a fiddle player. Col. Sandy Faulkner had served as an ordnance officer of the Confederate army, but his real claim to fame was a fiddle tune he wrote in the 1830s called the "Arkansaw Traveller." The tune and its story of a weary traveler encountering a backwoods family in Arkansas proved remarkably popular for 50 years. Several notable paintings subsequently depicted the story. Colonel Faulkner fell on hard times in his later years, forcing him to work as doorman at the hotel where politicians stayed when the legislature was in session. Despite his fallen fortunes, Faulkner remained the quintessential Southern gentleman. Since he was liked by everyone, naming the new county after Sandy Faulkner in 1873 proved to be an extremely popular idea. Colonel Faulkner died a year after receiving this honor.

Acknowledgments

We would like to thank Desmond Walls Allen of Arkansas Research for suggesting this project and subsequently providing invaluable assistance and photographs. Jimmy Bryant, archivist at the University of Central Arkansas, made this project possible with his enthusiastic and generous support. We also drew upon his research on the Women's Army Auxiliary Corps. Others who provided important help include Ken Mathis, John and Betty White, Bill Alderson, Susan Allen, Henryetta Vanaman, and the staff of the Arkansas History Commission.

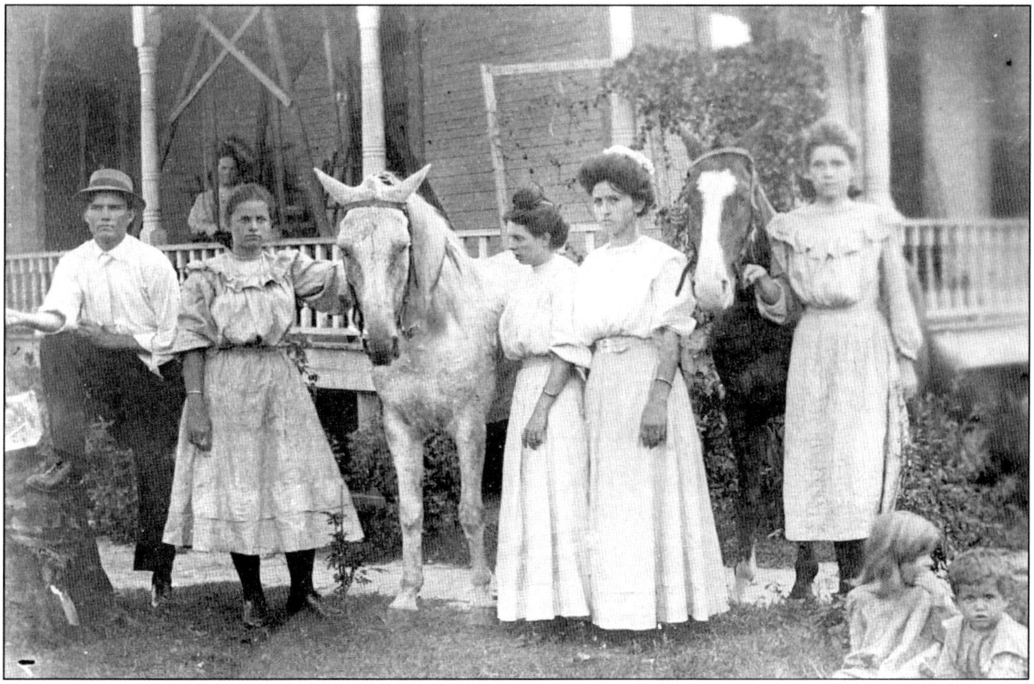

Family with Horses in the Front Yard, c. 1910. (UCA Archives.)

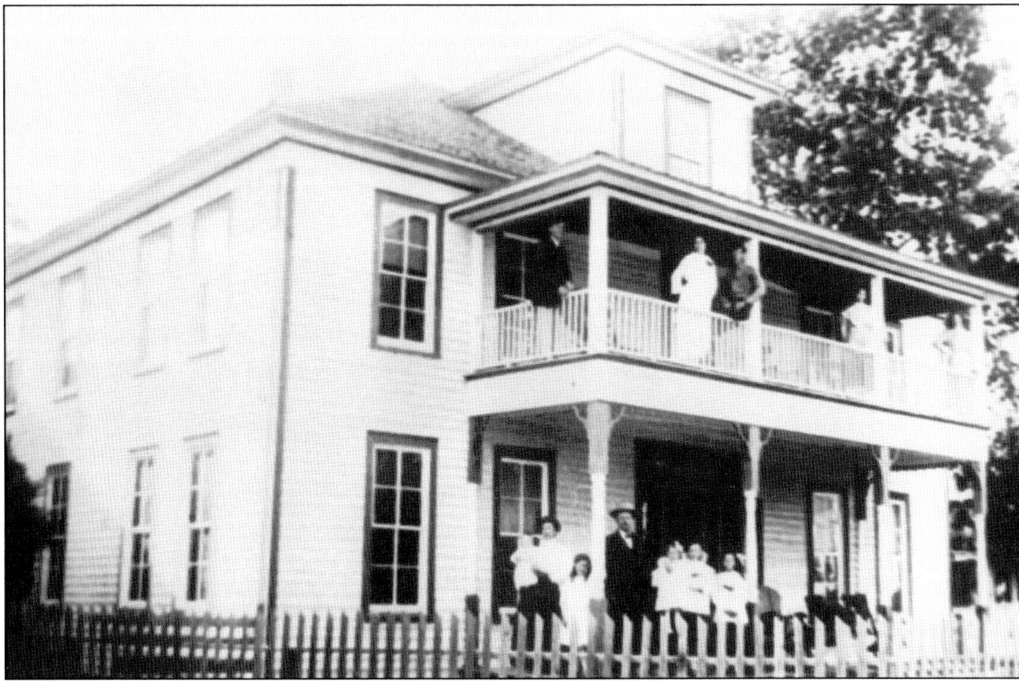

Ledrick Family, c. 1916. The family members appear in front of Mayflower Hotel in the community of the same name. The name Mayflower appeared in 1871 at Twenty Mile Camp as the name for the Pullman car that served as the mobile headquarters for the Little Rock & Fort Smith Railroad. *Mayflower* was the cable address for telegrams going to these temporary headquarters; the name stayed behind when the Pullman moved on and the track laying progressed northward. (UCA Archives.)

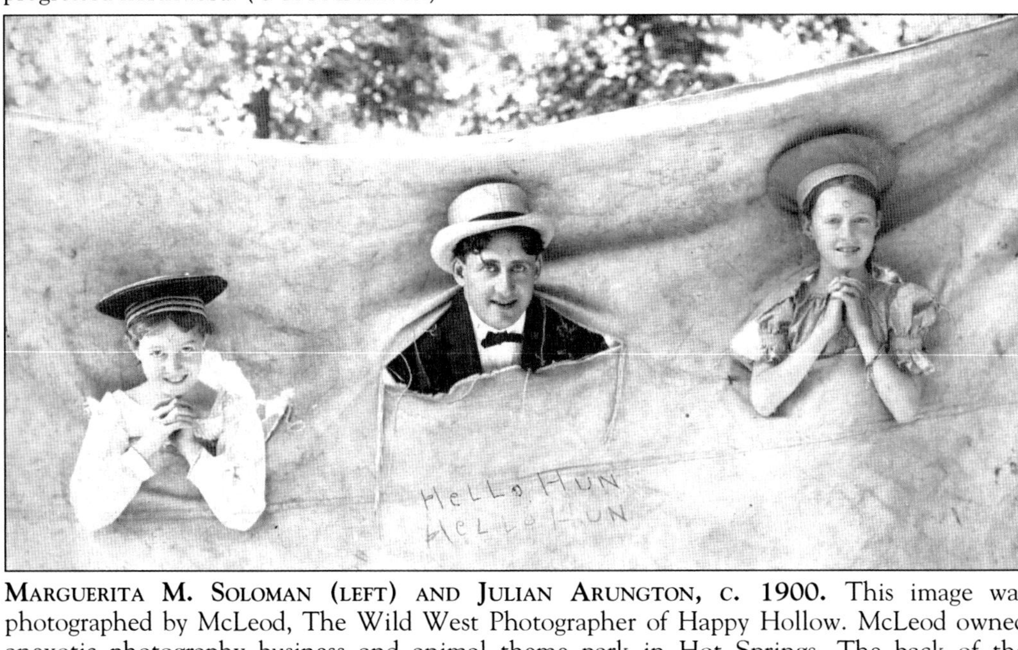

Marguerita M. Soloman (left) and Julian Arungton, c. 1900. This image was photographed by McLeod, The Wild West Photographer of Happy Hollow. McLeod owned anexotic photography business and animal theme park in Hot Springs. The back of the photograph is inscribed "To Miss Annie from Julia." (UCA Archives.)

One

The Early Years

From the days of the earliest pioneers, farming provided the principal economic activity on the land that became Faulkner County. Early settlers raised cattle and grain, but cotton came to dominate the local economy by 1860. Cotton production ceased during the Civil War and rebounded slowly, as did the rest of the economy. The coming of the railroad in the early 1870s precipitated tremendous economic growth by stimulating the birth of the timber industry and by providing transportation of farm goods to market. Farming flourished in Faulkner County. By 1880, cotton production exceeded antebellum levels. Other local farms began shipping fruits and vegetables to lucrative city markets. Thanks to the railroad, Conway became the transportation and trade center for the burgeoning commerce of the area.

As the fortunes of raising cotton began to decline, Conway began to broaden its economic base and soon became known as a college town. The young community founded by Asa Robinson got its first college in 1890, when the Rev. Alexander Miller moved Hendrix College from Altus to Conway. Seven towns courted the college, but Conway got the nod when local residents pledged $55,000 to help build the campus about a mile north of Conway Station. Such generosity set the stage for Conway's extraordinary support for higher education over the next century, even through the depths of the Great Depression in the 1930s.

Conway got a female-only college two years after Hendrix moved to Conway; this addition proved especially popular among the all-male student population at Hendrix. The Central Baptist College for Women remained an important part of the community for a half century.

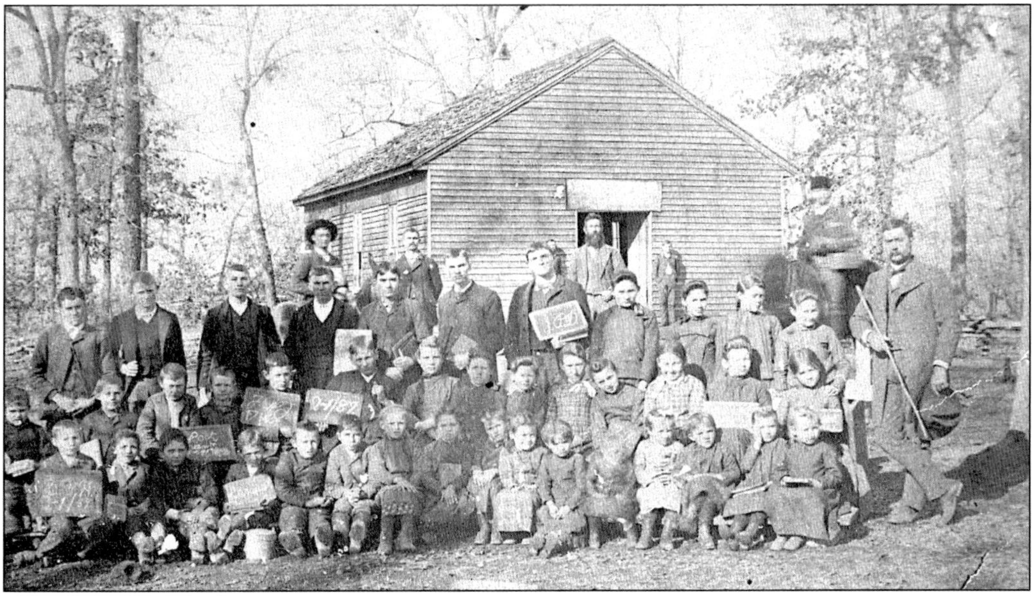

Center Point School and Students. Center Point was originally known as Boardmanville. It was named for Albert F. Boardman, who owned a blacksmithy and gristmill there. His wife, Daisy Mills Boardman, was the local postmistress; another Boardman ran the local cotton gin. (UCA Archives.)

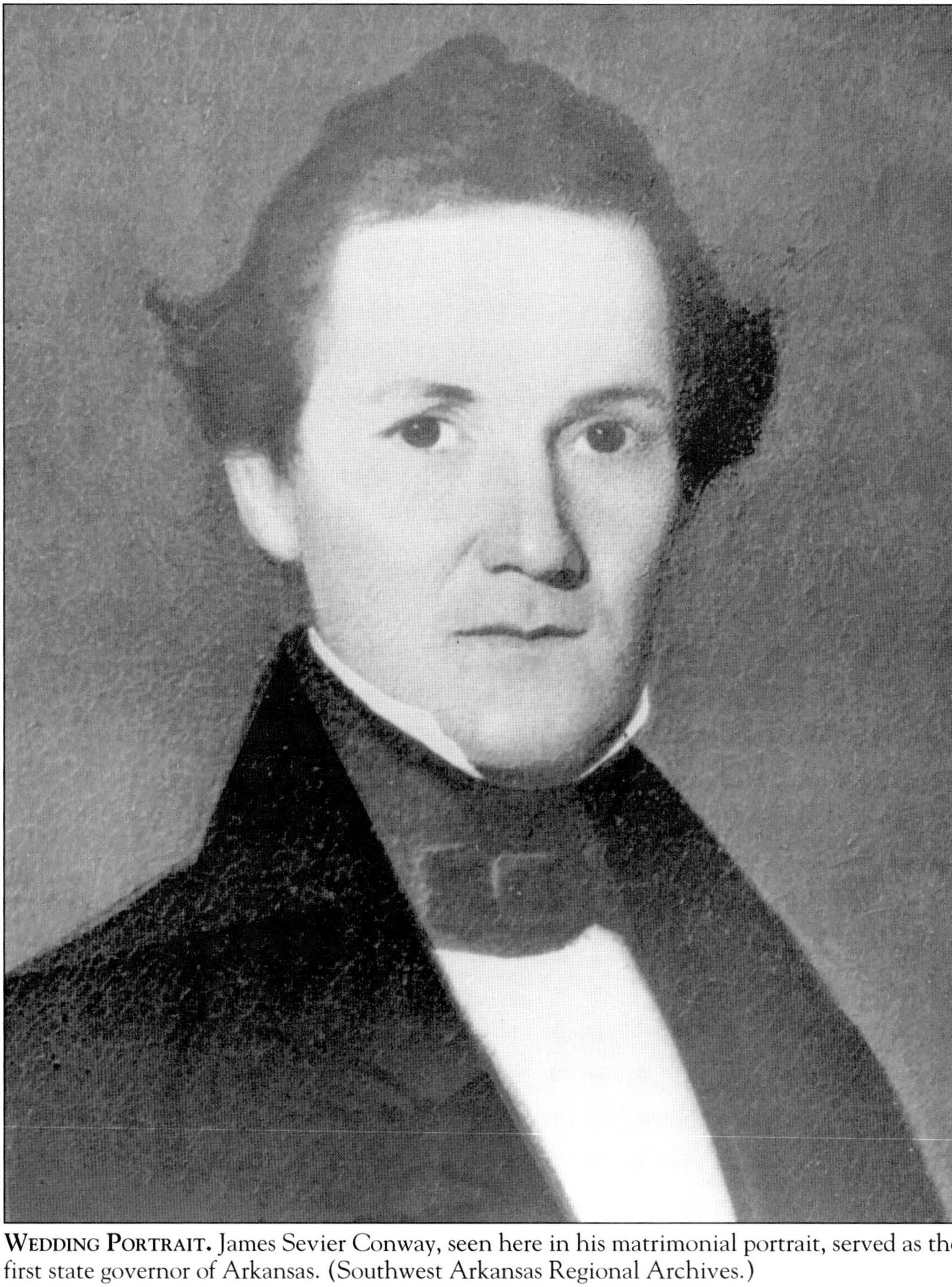

WEDDING PORTRAIT. James Sevier Conway, seen here in his matrimonial portrait, served as the first state governor of Arkansas. (Southwest Arkansas Regional Archives.)

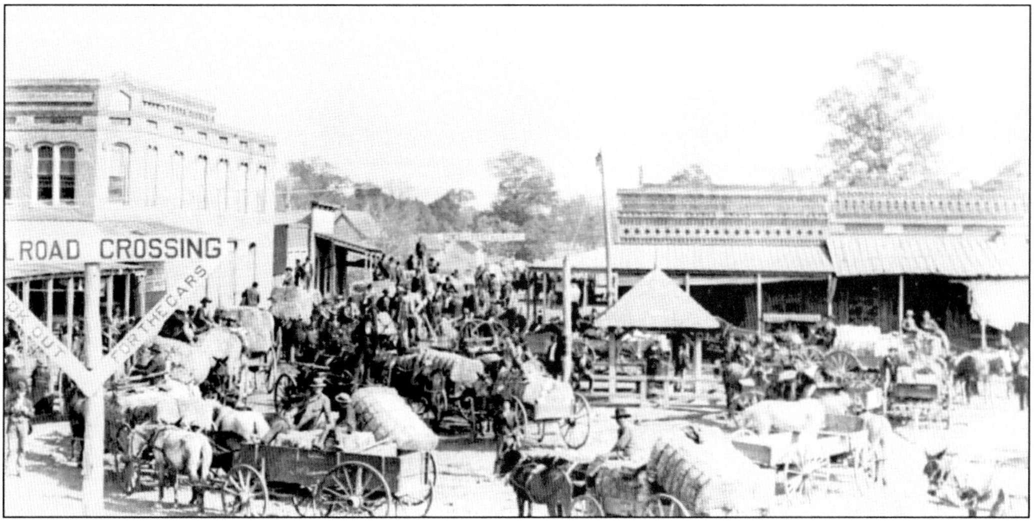

DOWNTOWN VIEW OF FRONT AND OAK STREETS, LOOKING EAST DOWN OAK STREET. Farmers bring cotton to market, *c.* 1886, in Conway. Note how the town has changed in the center of the photograph. The Halter Building replaced the structure in the right of the image, while the McNutt Building (now the Toadsuck Square Building) replaced the structure in the left of the photograph. (UCA Archives.)

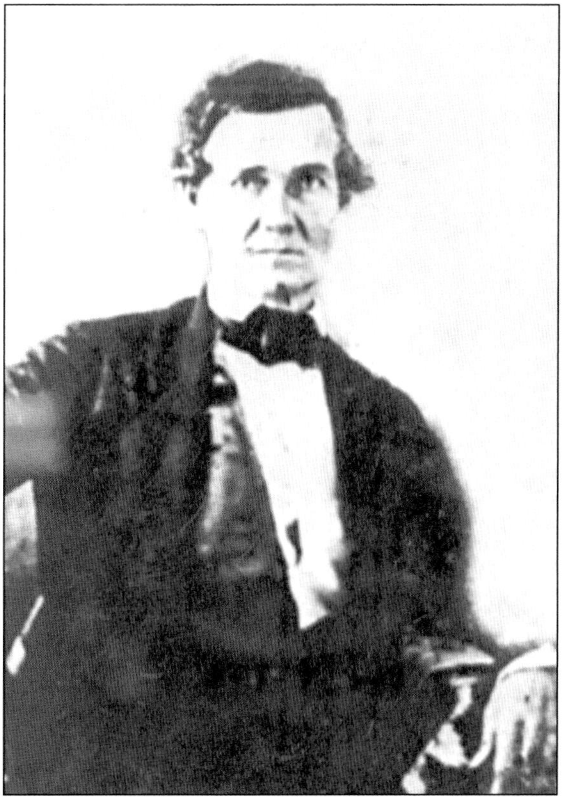

FIRST STATE GOVERNOR OF ARKANSAS JAMES SEVIER CONWAY, *c.* 1860. (Southwest Arkansas Regional Archives.)

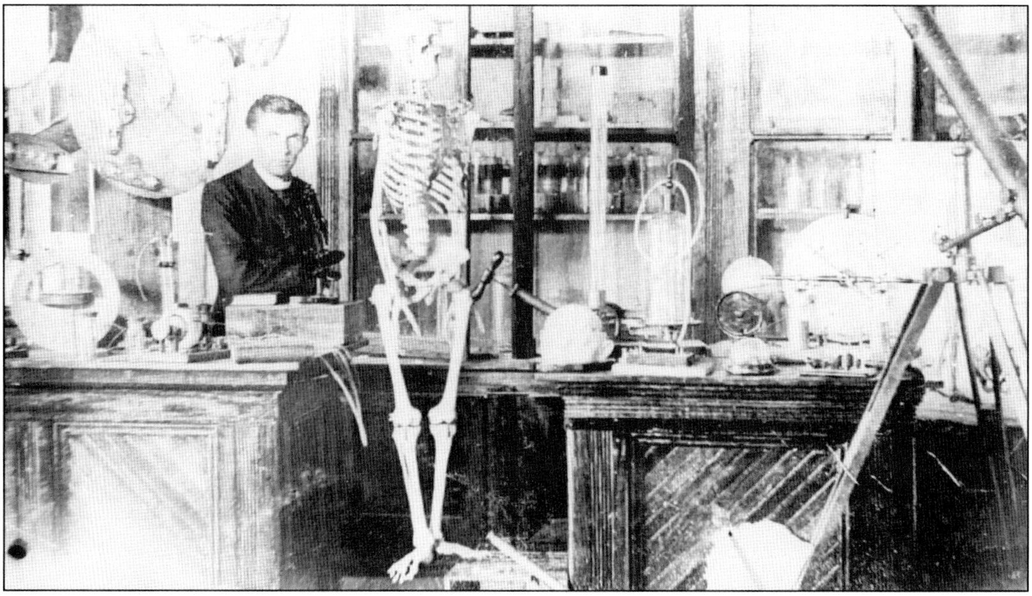

PROF. GEORGE H. BURR. Burr stands in the Hendrix College science laboratory next to a skeleton in this 1892 photograph. In 1891, the innovative professor installed the second telephone system (arguably, the first "real" phones), by running a line from his home on Davis Street, north of Mill Street, to the college. He then joined forces with George Coale Millar in 1899 to establish the first practicable telephone exchange in Conway. This exchange included 28 subscribers. Professor Burr soon sold his half of the business to Mrs. Perminter. (UCA Archives.)

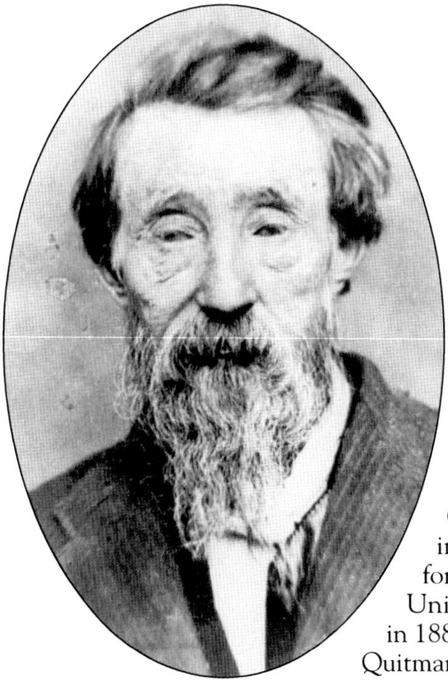

DR. JOHN JAMES HARTON. Local residents asked Dr. Harton to stay behind to look after the village when all the men of military age left to join the Confederate army. When the Union army moved into the area, soldiers tried to arrest the doctor's son for questioning, but he managed to escape through Union lines. This photograph of Dr. Harton was taken in 1885; Harton lived on North Cadron Creek near Quitman. (UCA Archives.)

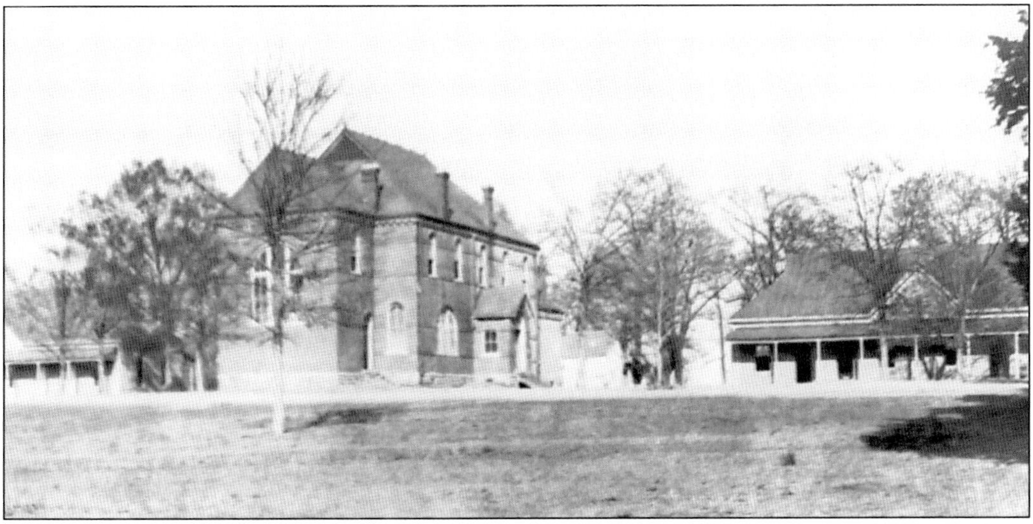

ORIGINAL THREE HENDRIX COLLEGE BUILDINGS. Hendrix College moved into these three structures in Conway from the Altus campus in 1890. The photograph was taken in the 1890s, looking east from Washington Avenue. The central building housed the dining hall, classrooms, and offices. The smaller flanking buildings were the North and South dormitories, and the structures continued to be called "North" and "South" long after they had been converted to other uses, which included music classrooms, a campus post office, and student recreational facilities. (UCA Archives.)

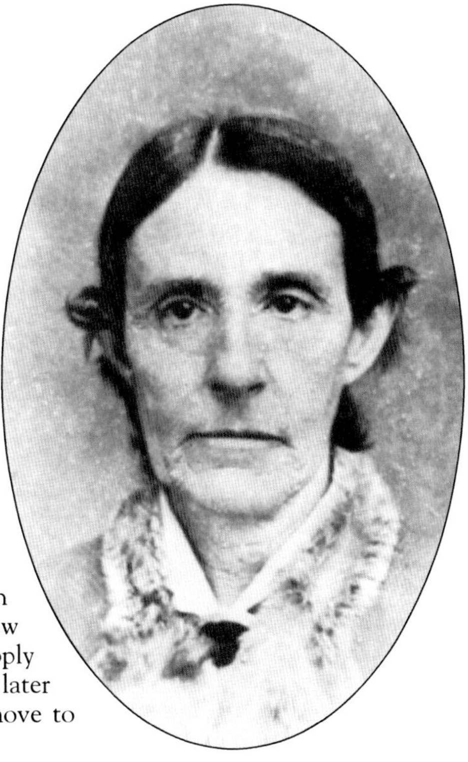

ELIZABETH GOODEN LOVE HARTON, C. 1885. Elizabeth married Dr. John Harton, who established a medical practice in Quitman, in the 1840s. Her son Nathaniel came to Conway Station along the new railroad to open a general mercantile and farm supply store with partner W.W. Martin. Both men would later prove influential in getting Hendrix College to move to Conway. (UCA Archives.)

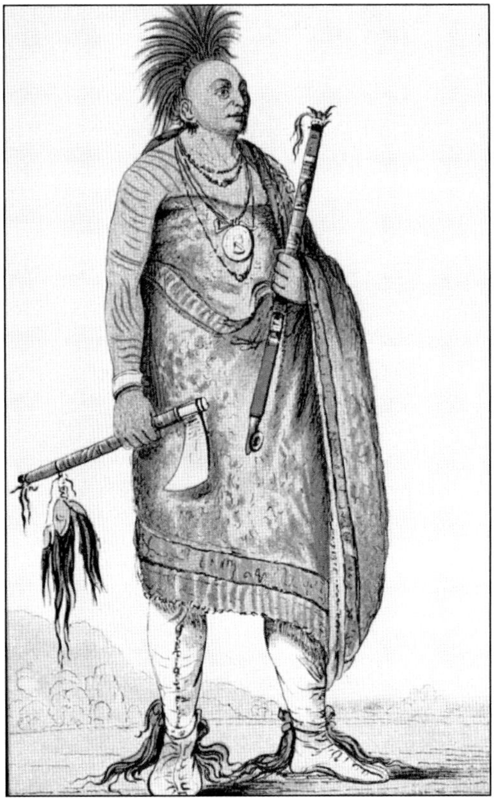

Osage Indian Chief Tchong-tas-sab-bee (Black Dog), in Painting Created by George Catlin at Fort Gibson. The Osages were the tallest race of men in North America; Black Dog was seven feet tall. The early French explorers referred to the Osages of Arkansas as "Les Beaux Hommes" or "The Handsome Men." The Handsome Men did not get along well with the Anglo settlers at Cadron. (UCA Archives.)

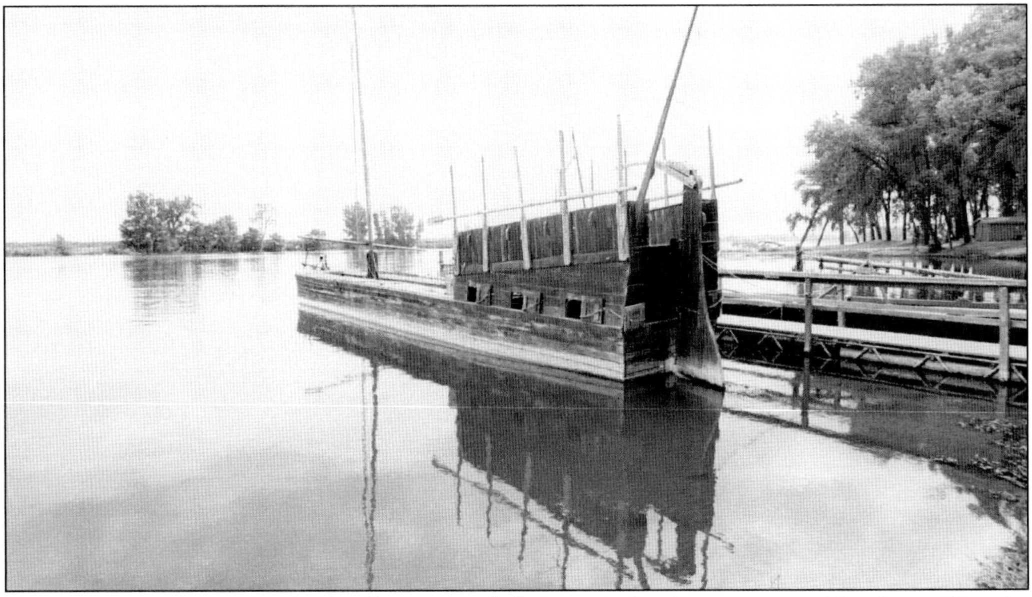

Utilitarian Keelboat. The keelboat provided a means for the economical hauling of freight upriver or downriver before the invention of the steamboat. The keelboat featured a round bottom, a keel, and a pointed bow, which enabled the crew to maintain a straight course as they poled the craft upstream. Barring snags or low water, a good crew could push a keelboat about ten miles upstream during a long day of back-breaking labor. (Photographed by Polly Walter.)

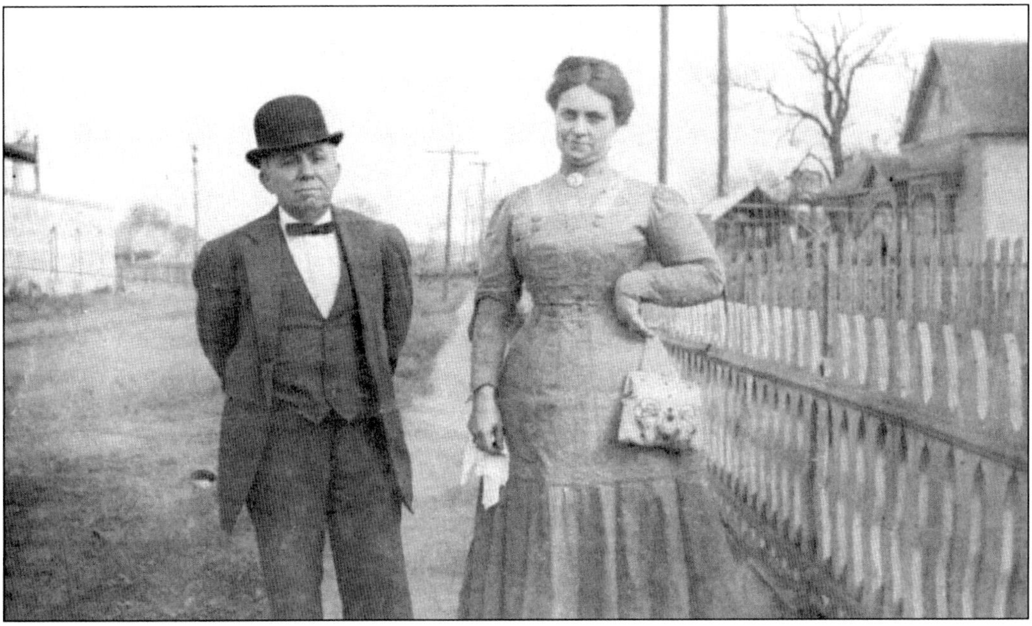

SAM AND MINNIE MERRIMAN HEILIGERS IN FRONT OF THEIR HOME ON NORTH FRONT STREET, C. 1898. Their 1882 marriage license was the first one issued by the newly established Faulkner County. They were married at the Merriman house in Little Rock; when they returned to Conway to start their life together, the whole town turned out to greet them at the train station. Sam ran a grocery and provision business. Their daughter, Mary Adams, who was known as Minnie Merriman, was the first white girl born in Conway. (UCA Archives.)

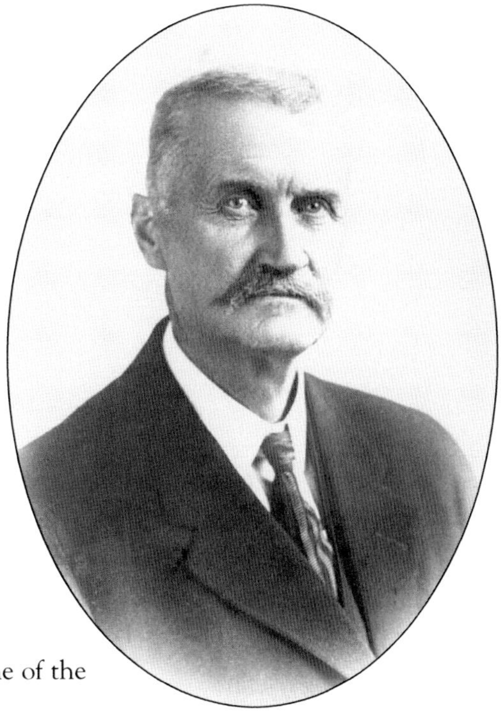

DR. GEORGE SNYDER BROWN. Dr. Brown was one of the first physicians in Conway. (UCA Archives.)

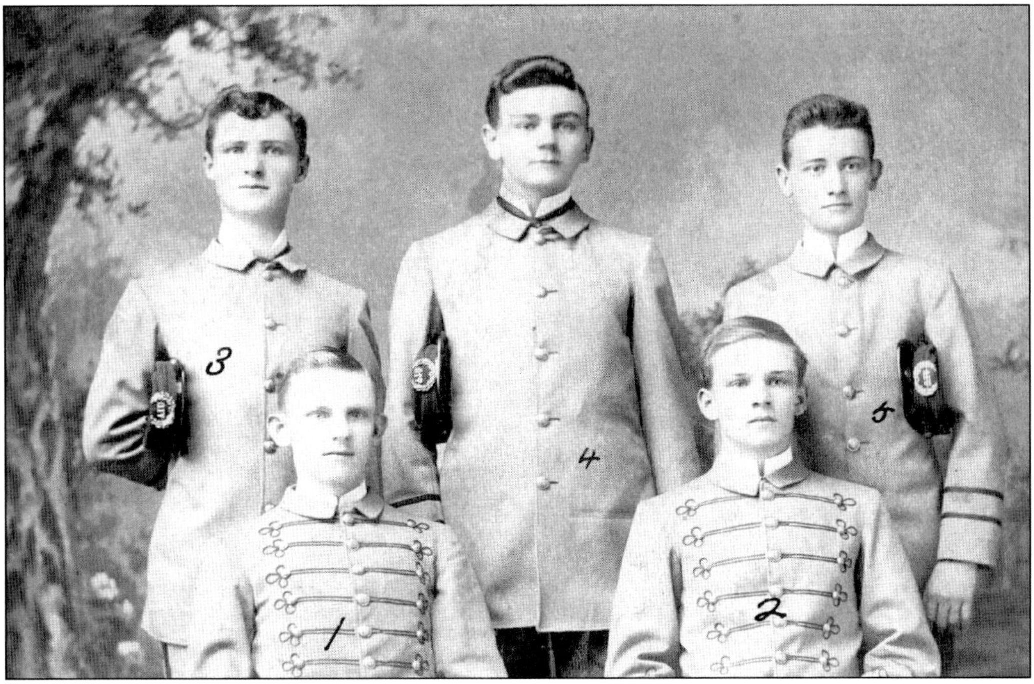

ROTC STUDENTS AT THE UNIVERSITY OF ARKANSAS AT FAYETTEVILLE, c. 1891. Shown here, from left to right, are as follows: (front row) Earl Smith of Conway and Russell Rock; (back row) Ed Bruat of Conway, James A. Clifton of Conway, and Mr. Marshall. (UCA Archives.)

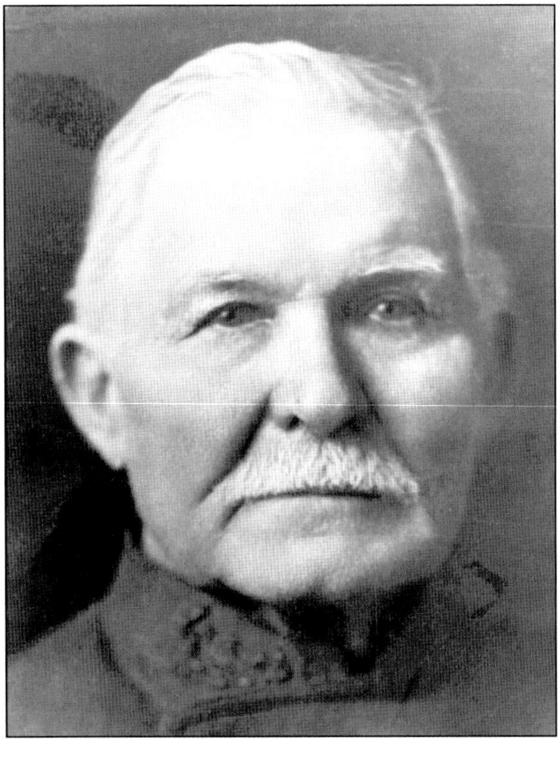

COL. GEORGE WASHINGTON BRUCE, c. 1890. Bruce served in the Confederate army and survived battles at Savannah and Manassas. Once a prisoner of war (taken by the Federals), he subsequently moved to Conway Station and became the best criminal lawyer in the state. He also served as a Conway alderman, state representative for Faulkner County, and mayor of Conway. Bruce Street, an arterial in Conway, was named after the colonel. (UCA Archives.)

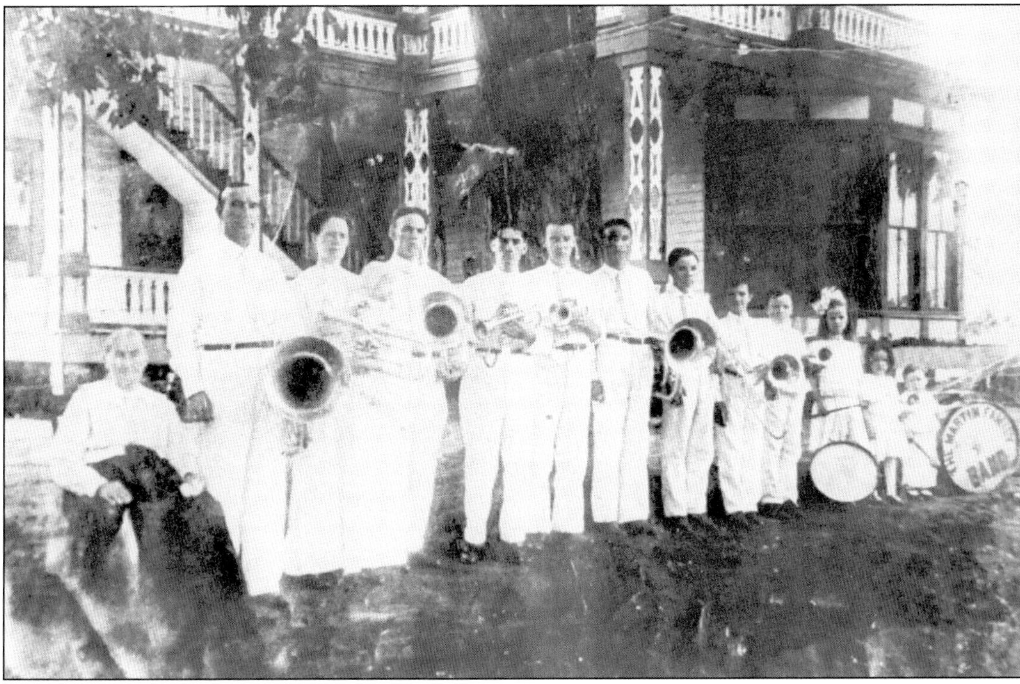

The Martin Family Band of Faulkner County. Charlie W. Martin taught his children to play musical instruments; the family performed at picnics, state fairs, and other social occasions. When Charlie's wife died, he married her 19-year-old cousin, Mable Bates, who raised C.W.'s six boys, in addition to another five children they had together. Community bands were common during the late 19th and early 20th centuries. (UCA Archives.)

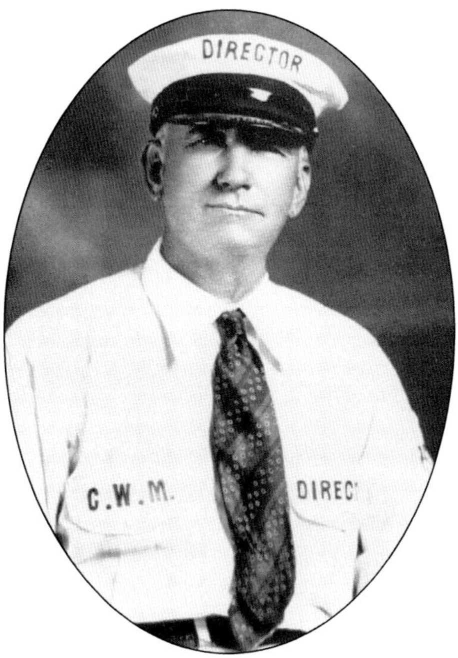

Charlie W. Martin in Uniform. (UCA Archives.)

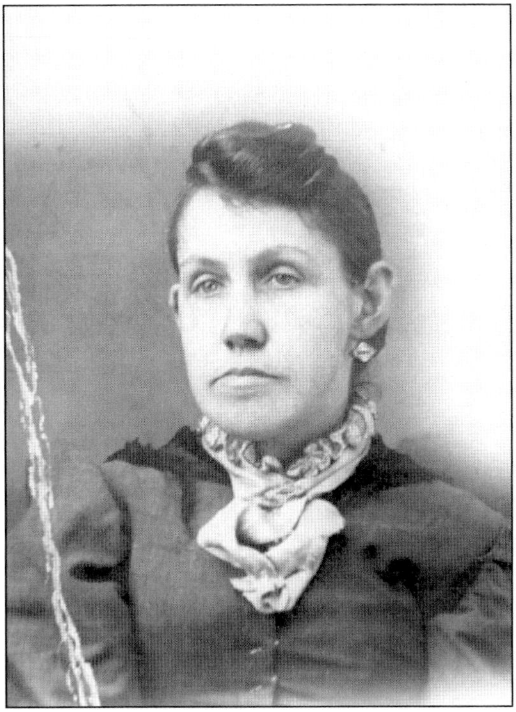

Mary Randall Berry, Wife of Lemvel Brook Berry. Mary moved to Beryl in Faulkner County from Virginia in 1888. She was the postmistress at Justice, and subsequently, at Berry Gap in 1903. She was also the grandmother of Doris Berry, who married Curtis Dolan. Mary Randall Berry died in 1931 and is buried at Oaklawn Cemetery. (UCA Archives.)

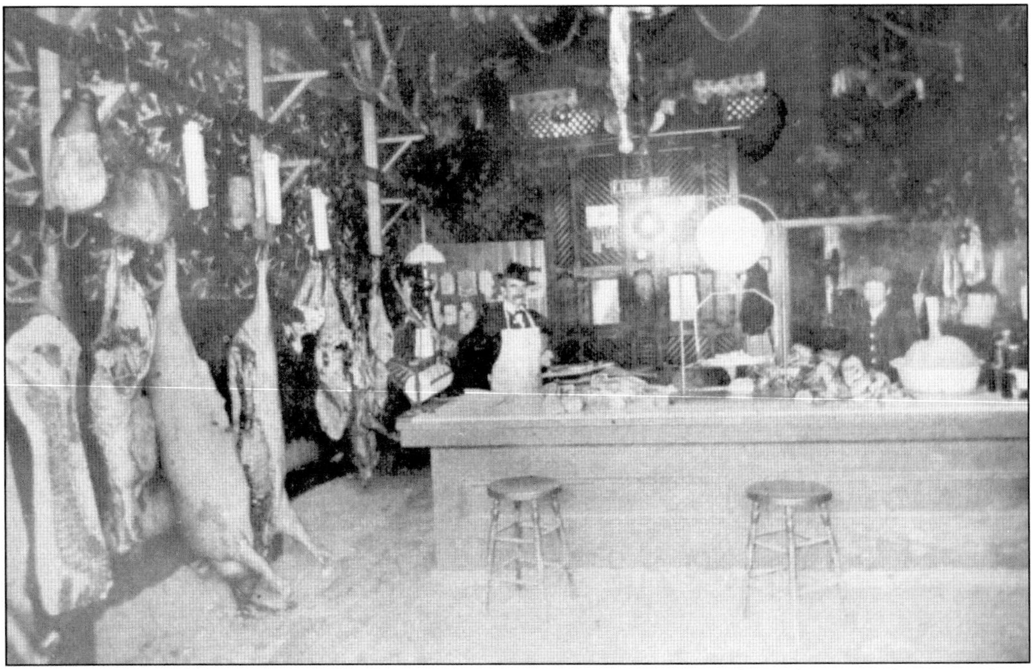

Interior of Erbacher Meat Market in Conway. The date this photograph was taken remains unknown. (UCA Archives.)

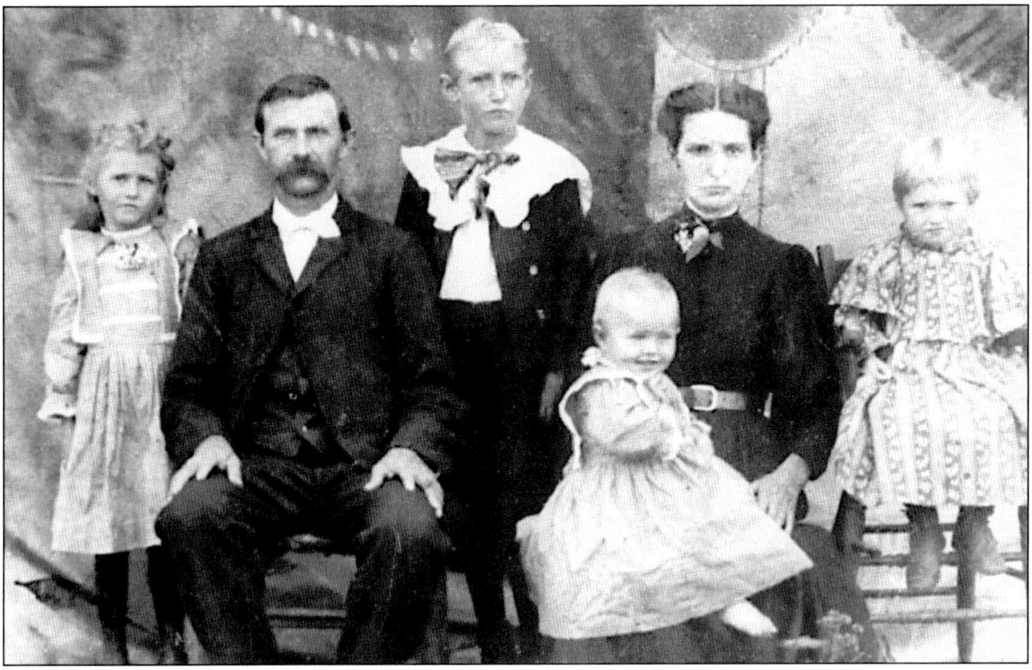

Early Settlers of the Pickles Gap Area. Settlers seen here, from left to right, are as follows: Lillian Blackwell Frigatt (wife of John Frigatt), Richard David Blackwell, Thomas Edgar Blackwell (standing), Nancy Louise Mabry Blackwell (wife of Richard), Cora Blackwell(on Blackwell's lap), and Gertrude Blackwell Day Fulmer. Cora Blackwell worked for many years at Frauenthal & Schwarz in Conway. (UCA Archives.)

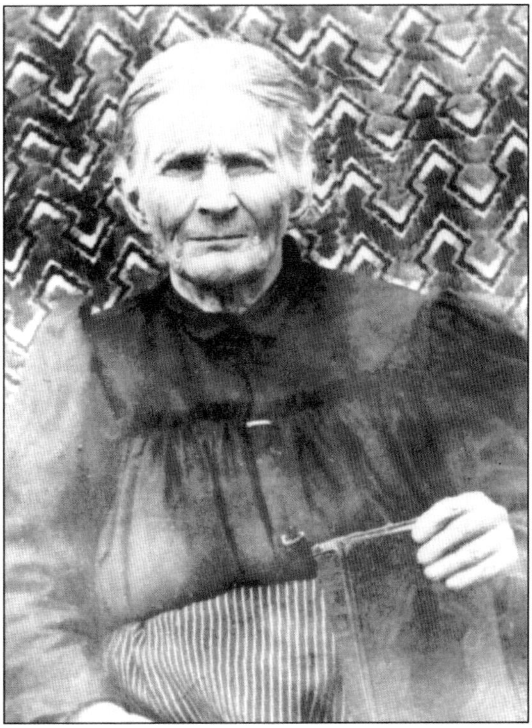

Evaline Bagley Glover of Faulkner County (1826–1898). Her husband, August L. Glover, came to Faulkner County with his family as refugees from Union General William Tecumseh Sherman's infamous March to the Sea through Georgia. After their home in Georgia was destroyed, the family hid in caves before beginning their trek to Arkansas. This photograph was taken c. 1890. (UCA Archives.)

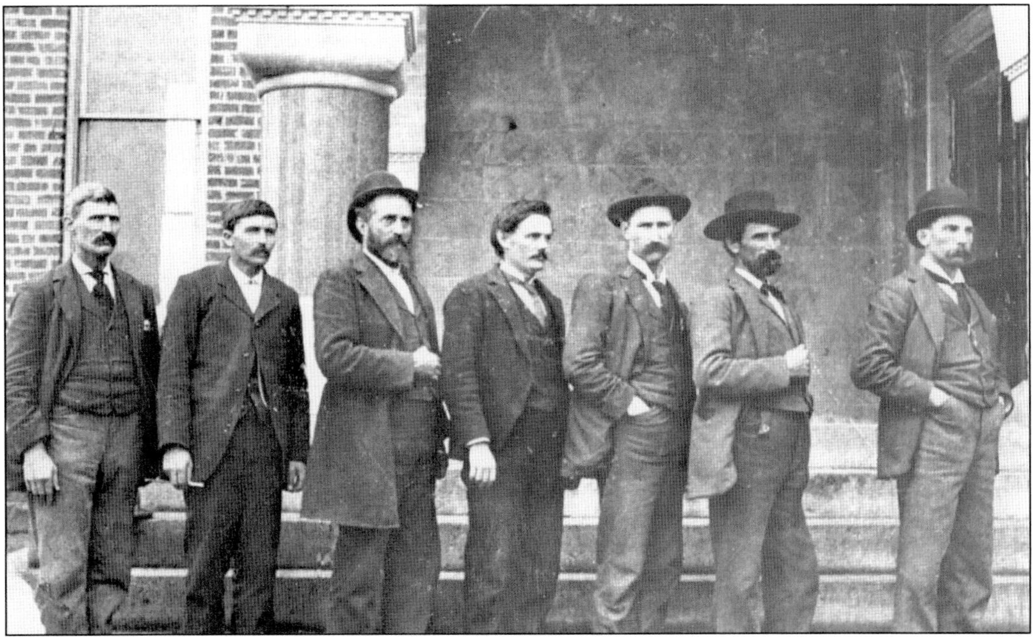

Political Leaders of Conway from 1894 to 1897. Seen here, from left to right, are W.R. Wilson, R.S. Maddox, Judge G.W. Rice, Ike Campbell, J.N. Cornell, Edward Erbacher, and H.B. Ingram. G.W. Rice was a Faulkner County judge from 1894 to 1898. (UCA Archives.)

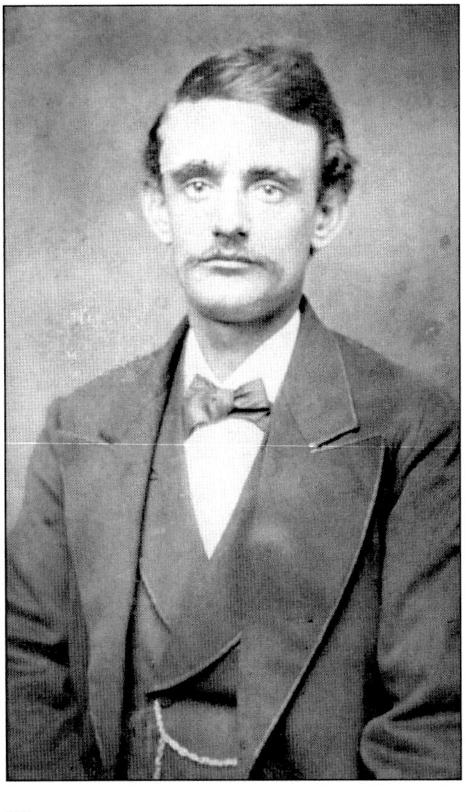

A.C. Hoss, c. 1878. Heir of Gov. John Sevier, Hoss was a member of the Conway School Board when this photograph was taken. (UCA Archives.)

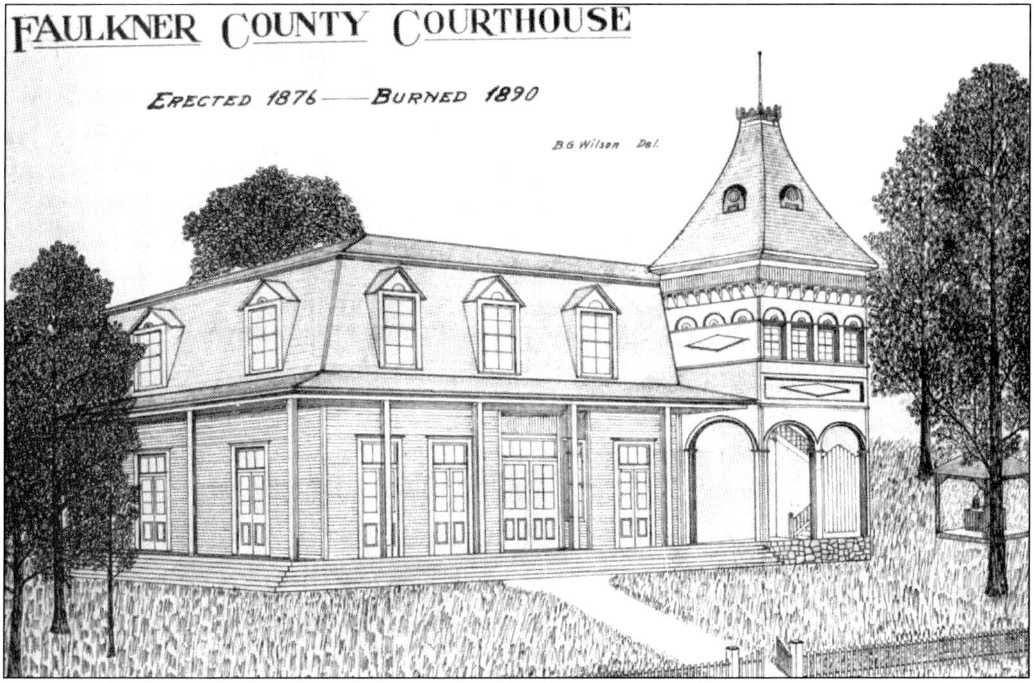

THE FIRST FAULKNER COUNTY COURTHOUSE. The courthouse, built in 1876, was destroyed by fire in 1890. (UCA Archives.)

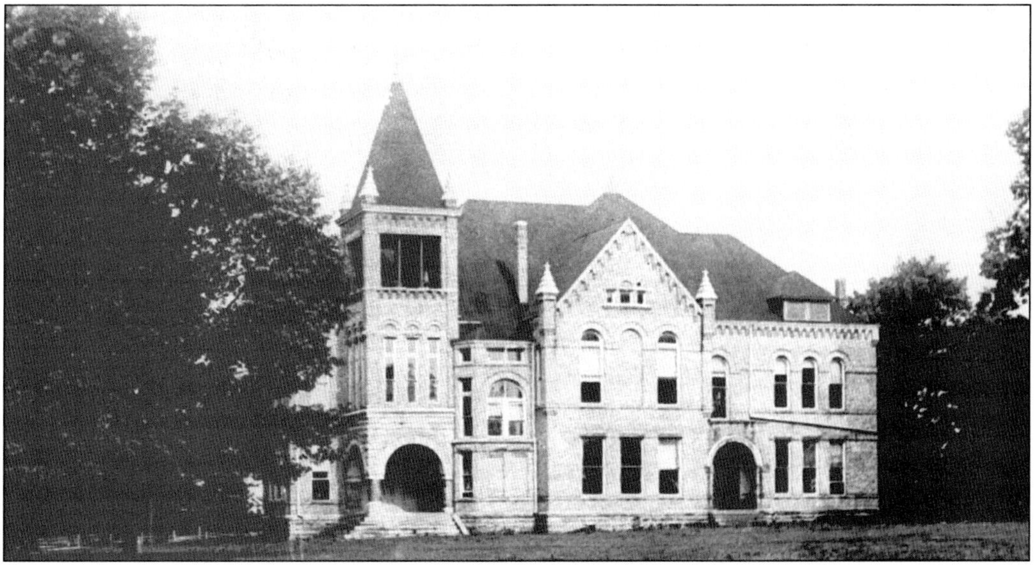

SECOND FAULKNER COUNTY COURTHOUSE IN CONWAY. This second courthouse was photographed in 1893. (UCA Archives.)

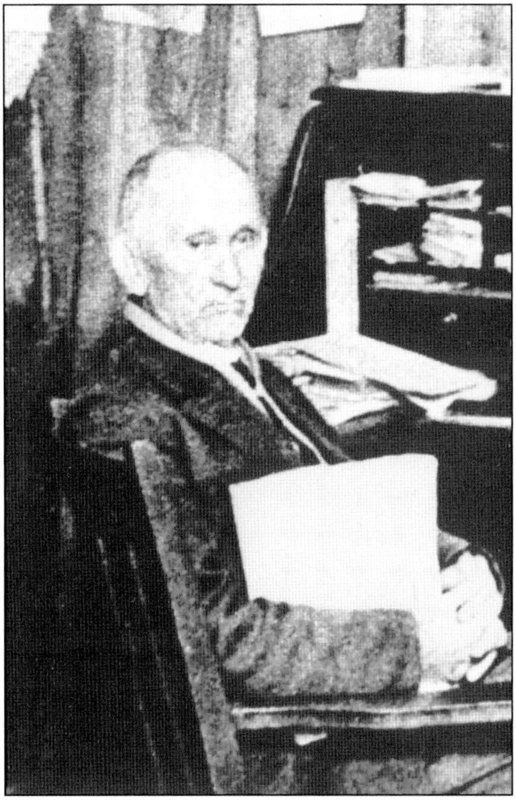

P.H. Prince, c. 1888. He moved to Arkansas in 1874 and bought a small farm near Conway. Having earned a law degree in Kentucky, he began practicing law and soon had the largest clientele in the county. P.H. Prince was a Faulkner County judge from 1888 to 1890. The street that runs past Conway High School was named after the judge. (UCA Archives.)

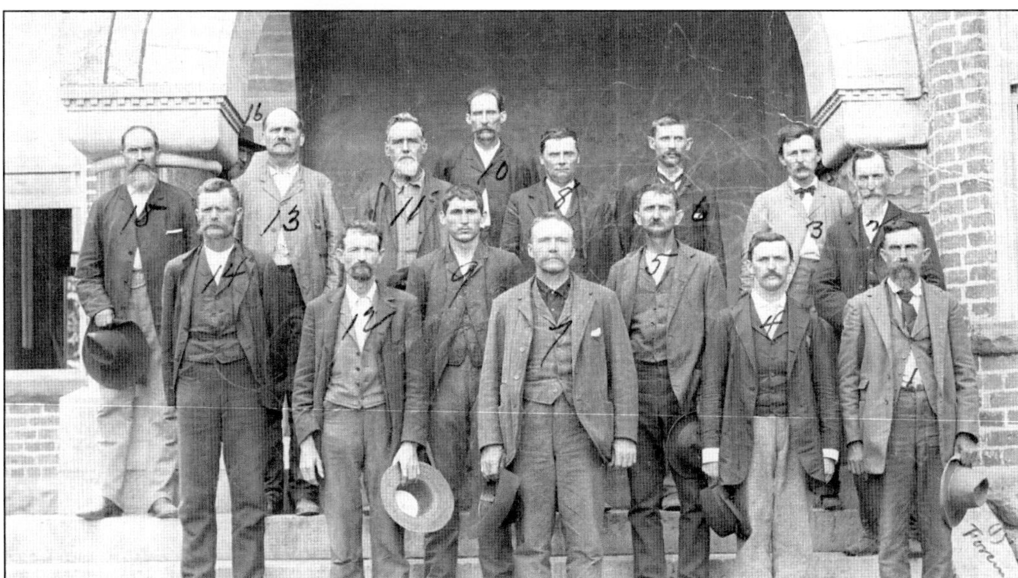

Portrait of 1895 Grand Jury in Conway. Seen with the following identifying numbers are S.S. Wilson (13); J.M. Roberts (14); J.B. Ball (15); A. Shoulders (10); James McLuer (11); J.S. Lattimer (12), W.H. Shannon (7), Thomas Farris (8), L.E. Pearson (9), E.E. Jones (4), D.M. Chivers (5); J.L. George (6); J.M. Gentry (1); J.A. Madden (2); and D.O. Harton (3). (UCA Archives.)

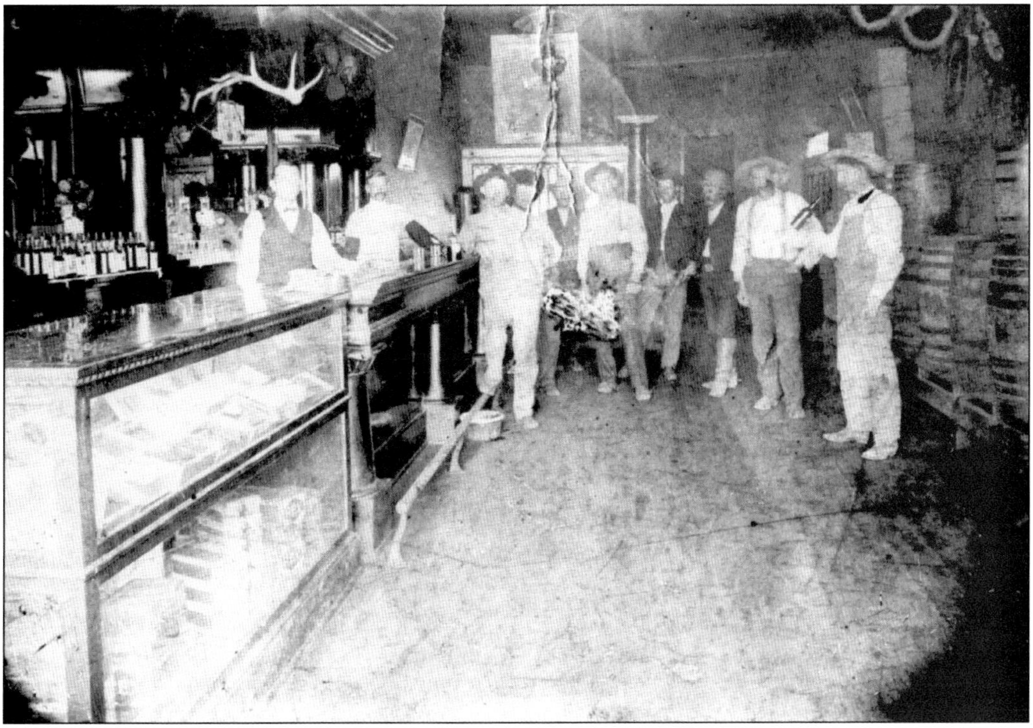

INTERIOR OF A SALOON IN CONWAY, C. 1888. (UCA Archives.)

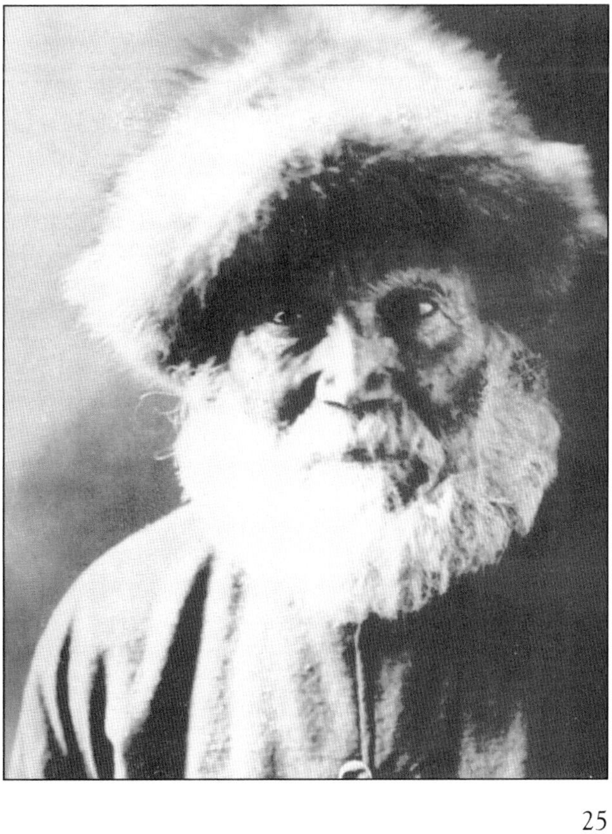

HOMESTEADER. This man is wearing a coonskin cap and a homespun jacket. (UCA Archives.)

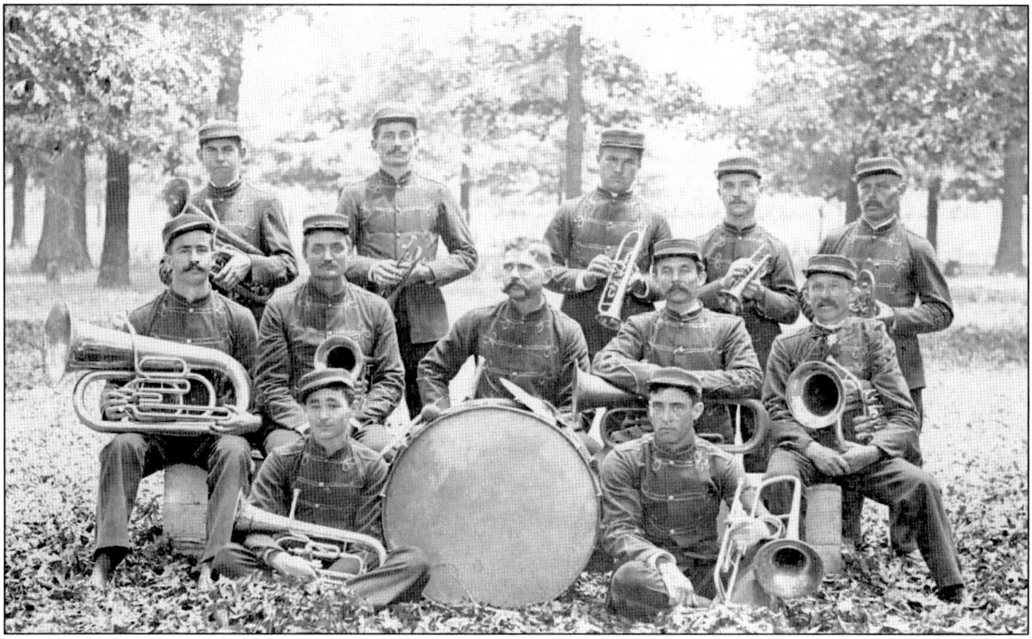

CONWAY CITY BAND IN 1895. Band members seen here, from left to right, are as follows: (front row) unidentified and Hugh Pence; (middle row) Casper Dum, unidentified, Bailey Wilson, unidentified, and bandleader Ed Shrol; (back row) Henry Erbach, Joe Enderlin, Albert Lackowsky, Philip Yaeger, and August Hein. (UCA Archives.)

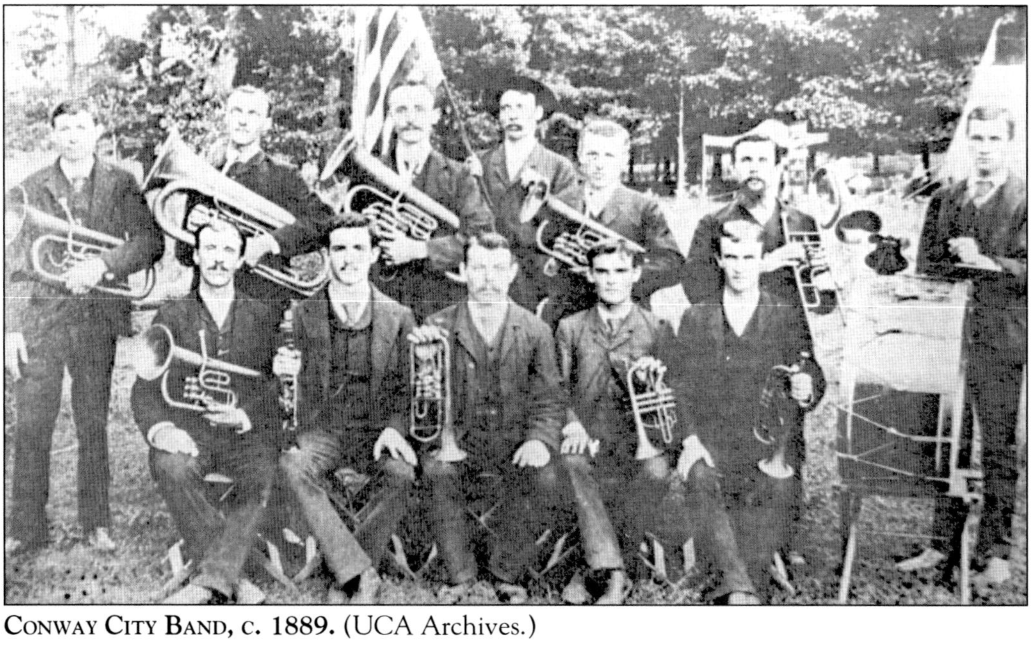

CONWAY CITY BAND, C. 1889. (UCA Archives.)

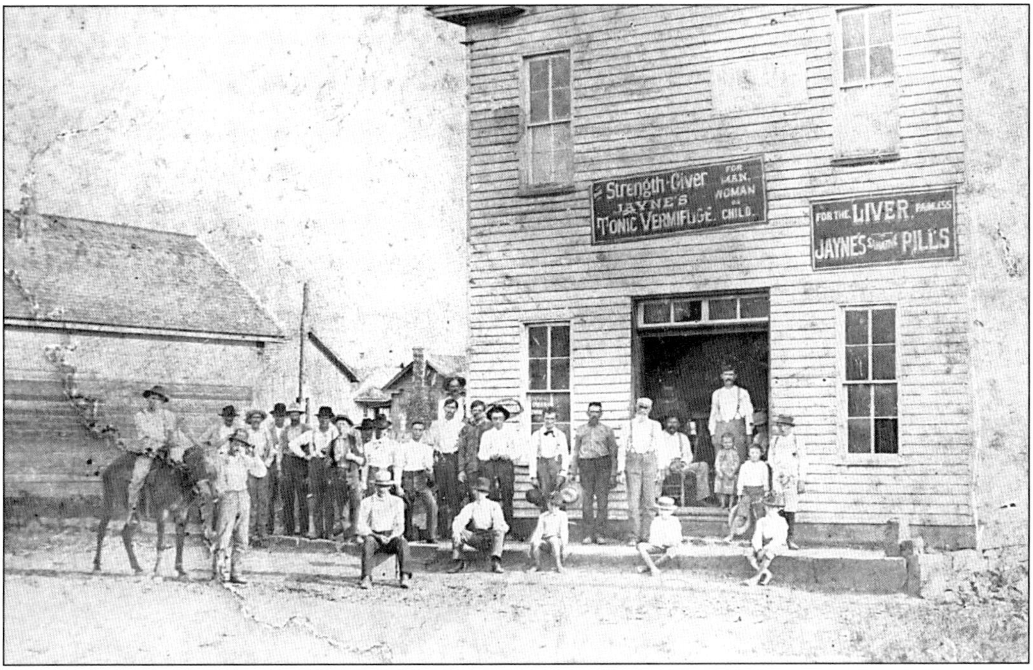

McCracken Drug Store with Advertisement for Jayne's Tonic Vermifuge and Samative Liver Pills, c. 1900. Located in Greenbrier, the store owned by Jasper McCracken was probably the first drug store in Faulkner County. (UCA Archives.)

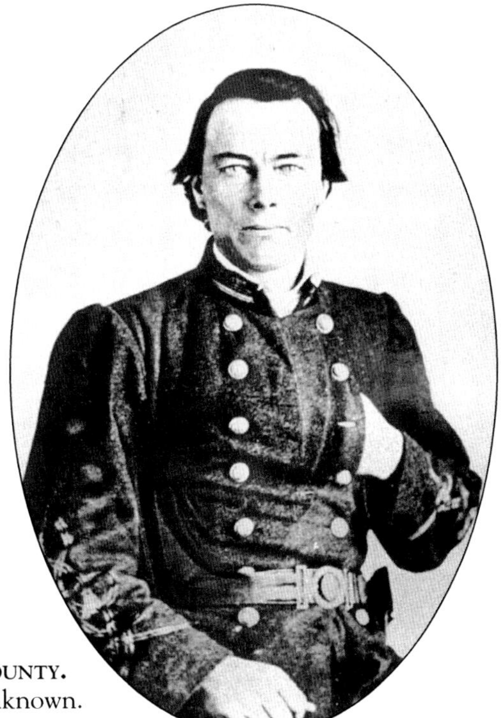

Confederate Captain from Faulkner County. The date of this photograph remains unknown. (UCA Archives.)

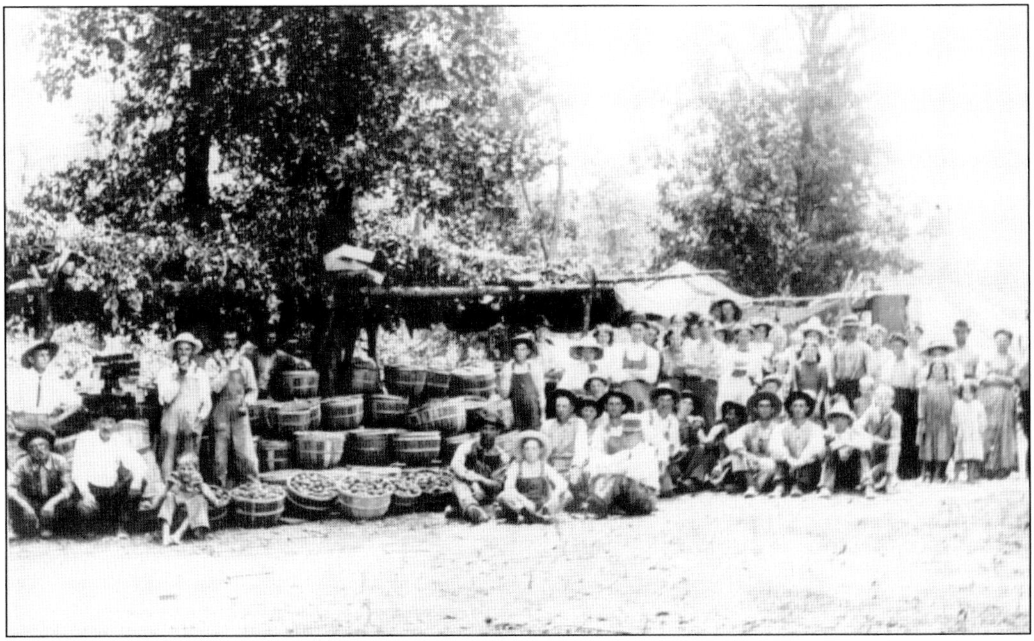

Peach Harvest on Round Mountain in Faulkner County, c. 1900. According to local legend, Round Mountain got its name when surveyors, who were laying a route for a telegraph line, found the mountain too difficult to climb. After circling around the mountain, they discovered it was a solitary round mountain, rather than part of a mountain chain. (UCA Archives.)

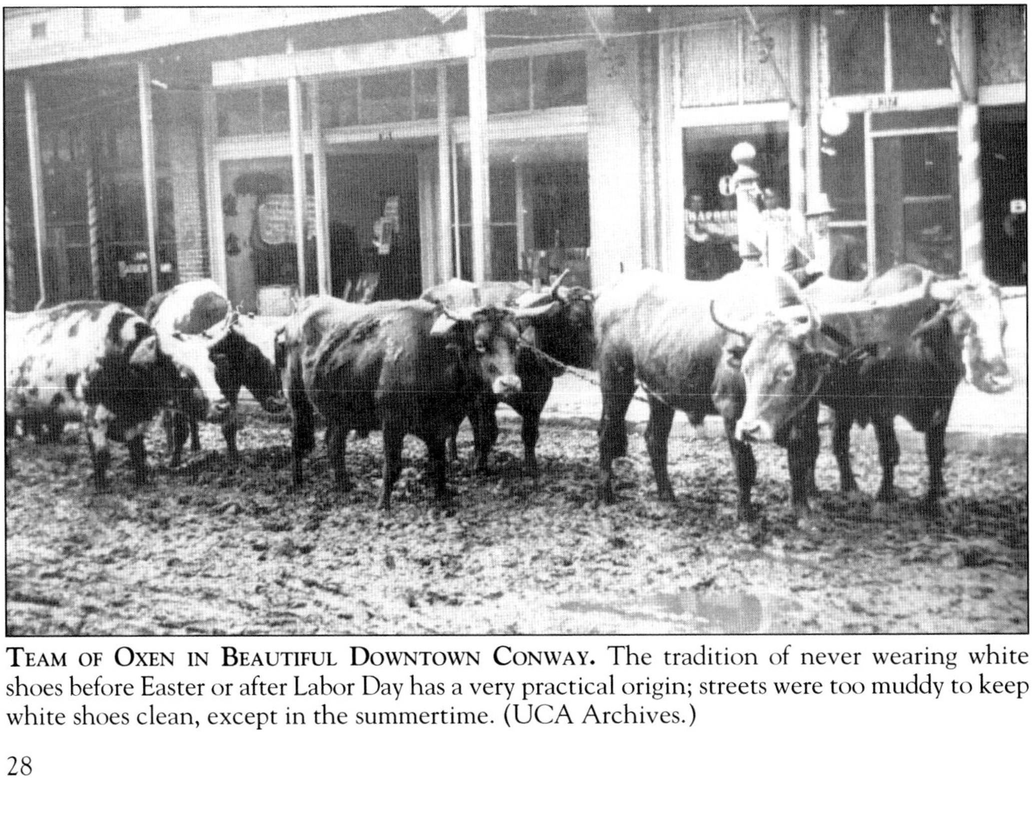

Team of Oxen in Beautiful Downtown Conway. The tradition of never wearing white shoes before Easter or after Labor Day has a very practical origin; streets were too muddy to keep white shoes clean, except in the summertime. (UCA Archives.)

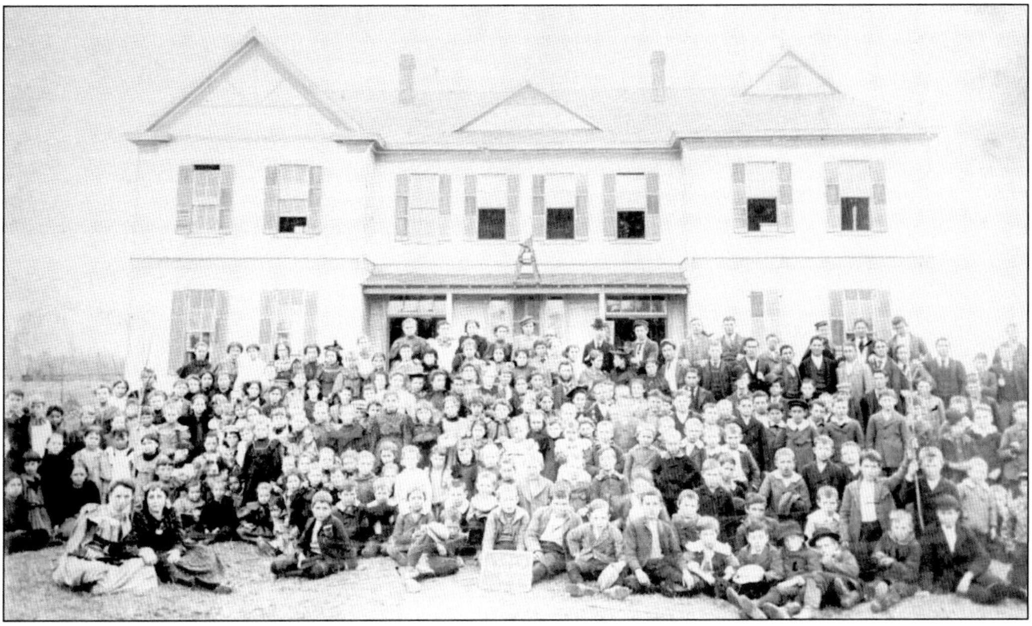

The Second Public School for Whites in Conway. The girl on the left is Gertie Douglas. The photograph was taken December 17, 1895. (UCA Archives.)

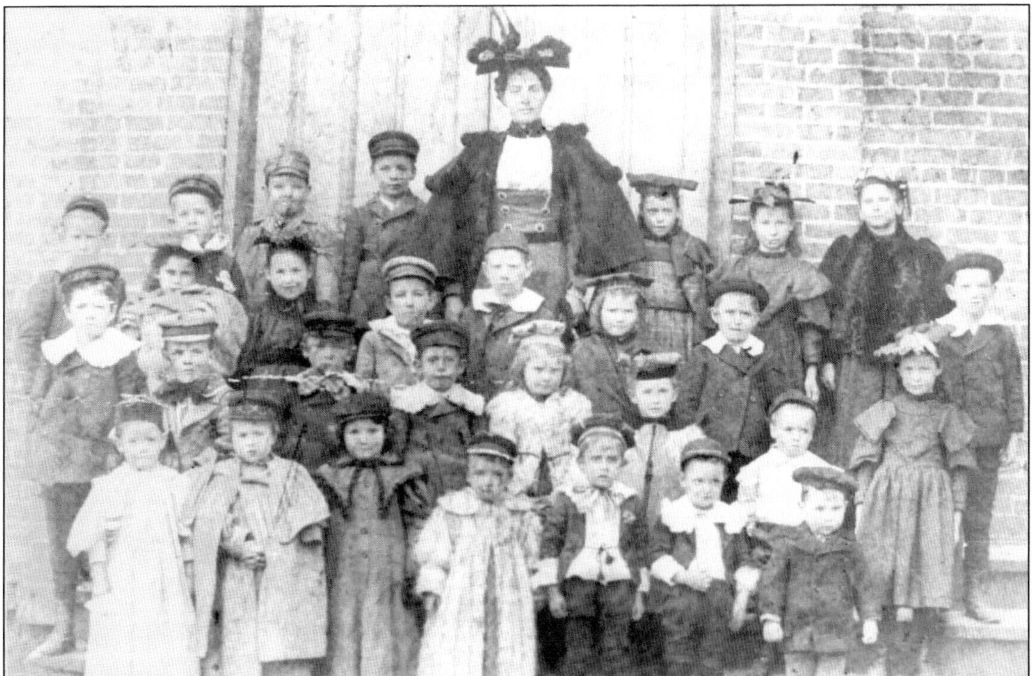

Children's Sunday School Class at the First Baptist Church in Conway, pre-1900. Evie Shaw is fourth from the left in the front row, and George Shaw is third from the left in the second row. The teacher, Fannie Dunaway Hogan Goodman, was about to lose her hat in the back row. Eno Hilliard is the boy in front of the teacher, wearing a cap; his sister, Mary Hilliard, stands in front of him. (UCA Archives.)

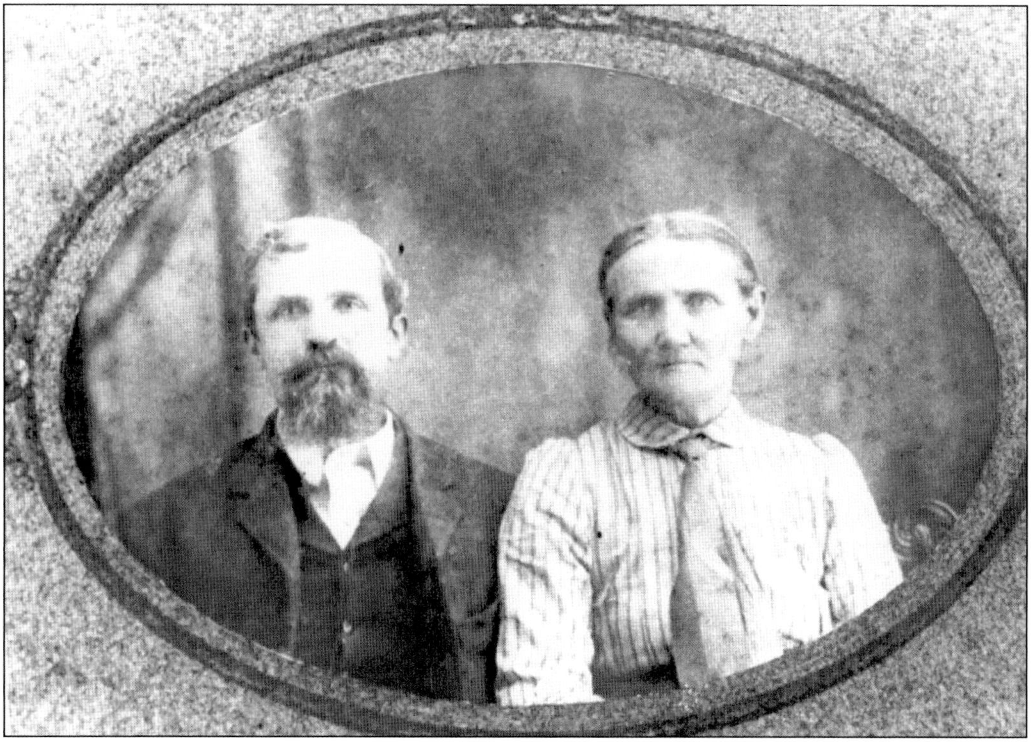

Alyes A. and Tennessee Jane Coples Parsens of Faulkner County. The date of this photograph is unknown. (UCA Archives.)

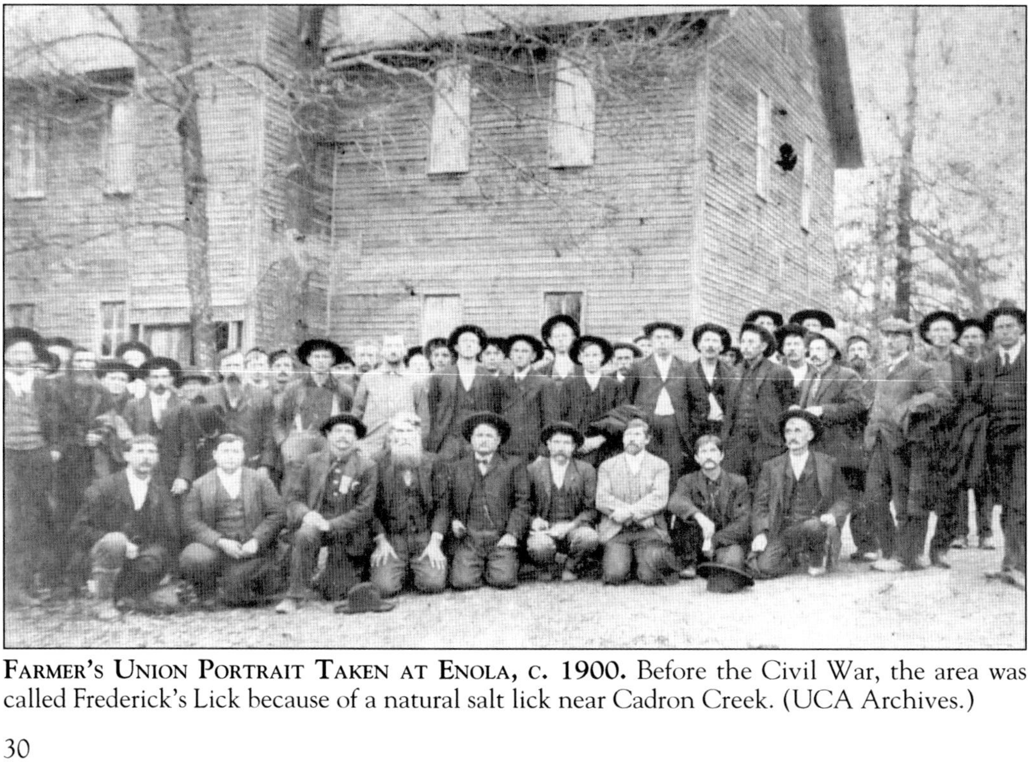

Farmer's Union Portrait Taken at Enola, c. 1900. Before the Civil War, the area was called Frederick's Lick because of a natural salt lick near Cadron Creek. (UCA Archives.)

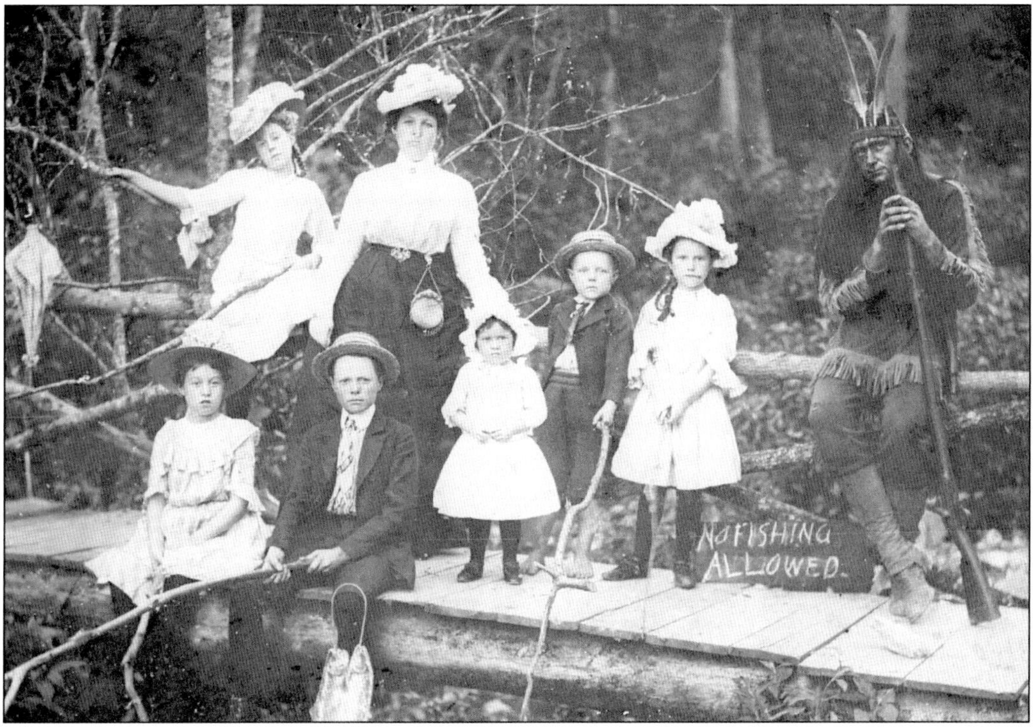

FAMILY PORTRAIT MADE BY McLEOD. He was known as the Wild West Photographer of Happy Hollow in Hot Springs, which has been a popular destination for residents of Faulkner County for more than a century. (UCA Archives.)

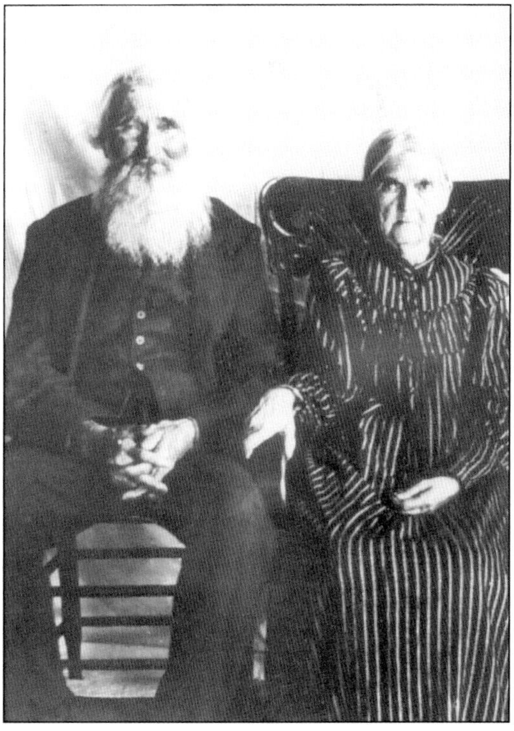

WILLIAM MARION BECKETT AND LUCINDA (MILES) BECKETT OF FAULKNER COUNTY, c. 1900. This couple had nine children. Mr. Beckett was a soldier in the 24th Alabama regiment in the Civil War and served throughout the war under Generals Lee and Johnston. The Becketts moved to Faulkner County in 1871 and settled about five miles west of Rosebud, where they lived until his death by heart failure. The Becketts were members of the Methodist Church; Mr. Beckett belonged to the Masonic Order and was an uncle to Mrs. J.H. Pritchard of Rosebud. (UCA Archives.)

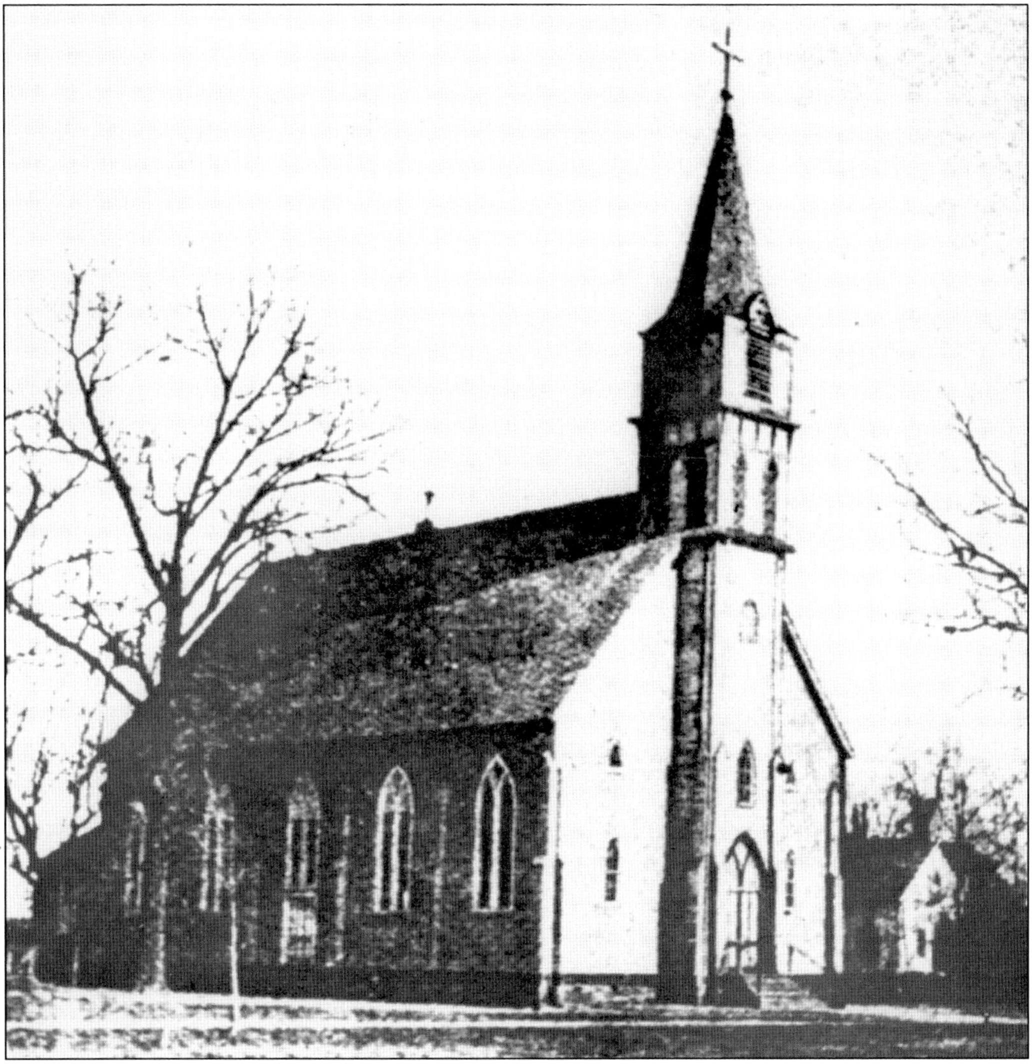

St. Joseph Church in Conway, c. 1900. The St. Joseph Parish dates back to 1873. Construction of the first church for the parish in 1879 was greatly aided by the Missouri Pacific Railroad, which donated the land in Conway for the church. This frame structure was destroyed by a storm in 1883. The church shown here was destroyed by fire in 1926; construction of a new church began in 1934. (UCA Archives.)

Two

GRASS-ROOTS GROWTH OF A COLLEGE TOWN

Conway got a state-sponsored college in 1908, when the University of Central Arkansas began life as the Arkansas State Normal School. Unfortunately, state funding fell far short of student needs, but the residents of Faulkner County provided strong grass-roots support through these difficult years. The college grew and changed its name to Arkansas State Teachers College in 1925. The school's bid for national accreditation failed, however, since it needed a new library. The legislature was unable to fund construction.

In typical Faulkner County fashion, the Hiegel Lumber Company provided the solution. Hiegel built the new library in 1929, with the understanding they would, eventually, be paid. The company waited without complaint for 17 years before they were reimbursed for their investment in the future of Arkansas. Generosity in support of Faulkner County's colleges has been the rule, not the exception, over the last century.

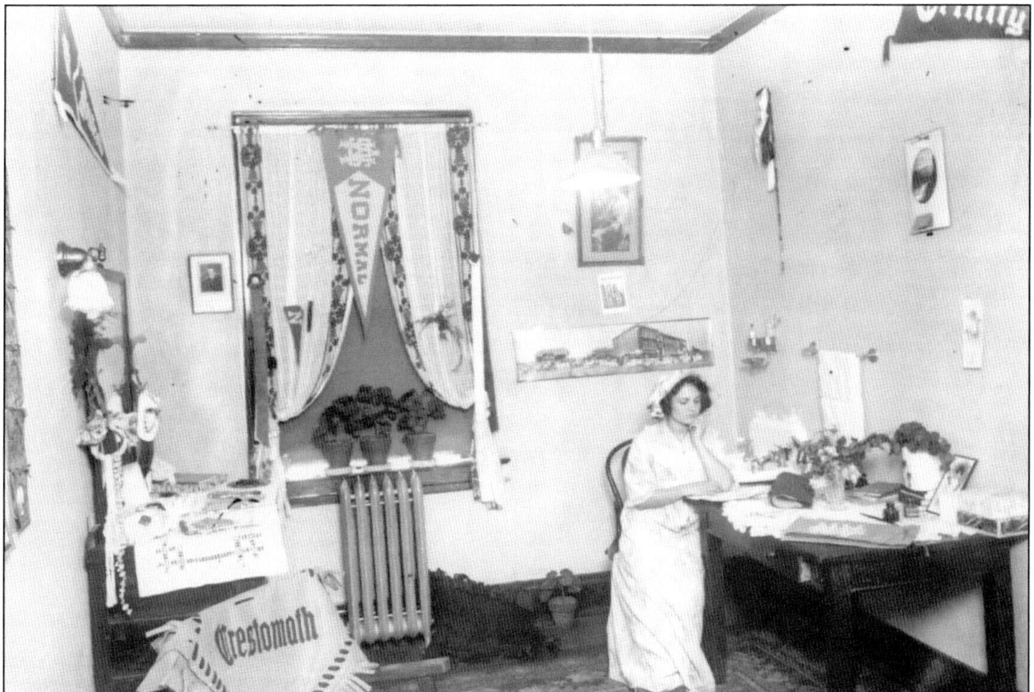

INSIDE A DORM ROOM AT DOYNE HALL, ARKANSAS STATE NORMAL SCHOOL, C. 1915. "Crestomath" was a women's literary society established in 1909. The name comes from a work of fiction in which a man named Math saves a woman named Cres from drowning. In gratitude, Cres pledged her love to Math. (UCA Archives.)

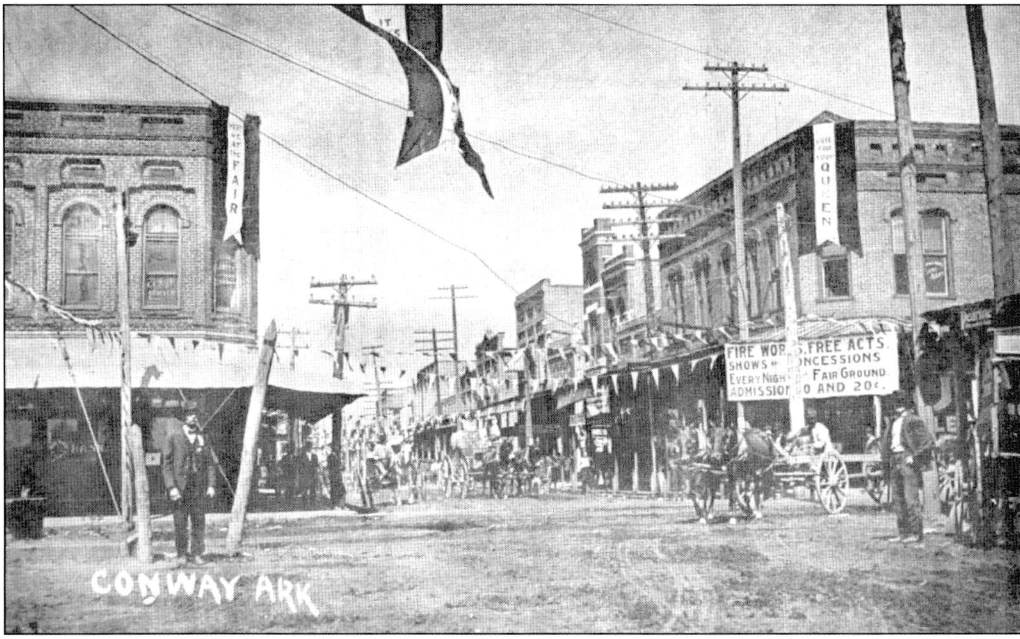

STREET SCENE IN DOWNTOWN CONWAY, C. 1900. This view looks north along Front Street. (UCA Archives.)

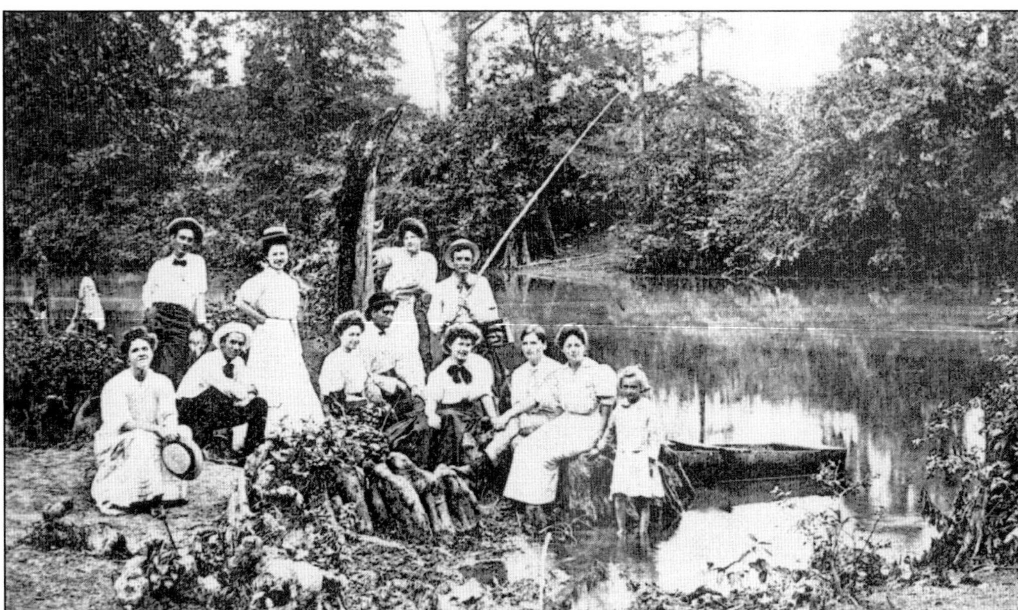

FAMILY OUTING AT GOLD LAKE IN CONWAY, C. 1900. (UCA Archives.)

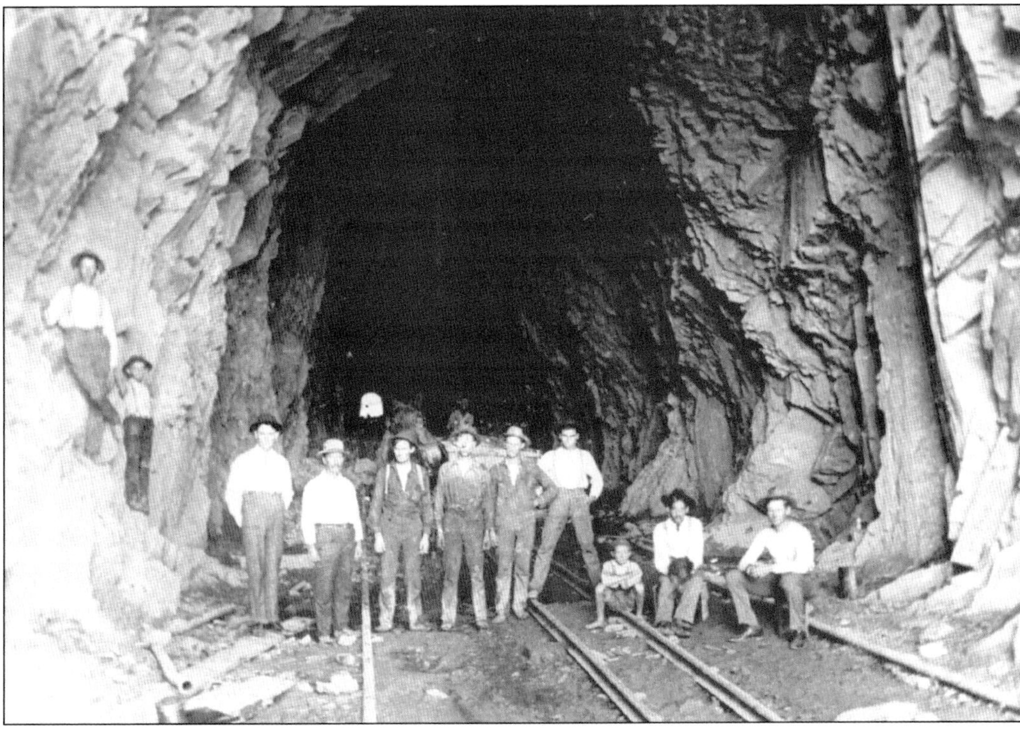

Railroad Tunnel Construction at Cadron Ridge, c. 1902. Pat C. Brian is the third man from the left with black hat and white shirt. (UCA Archives.)

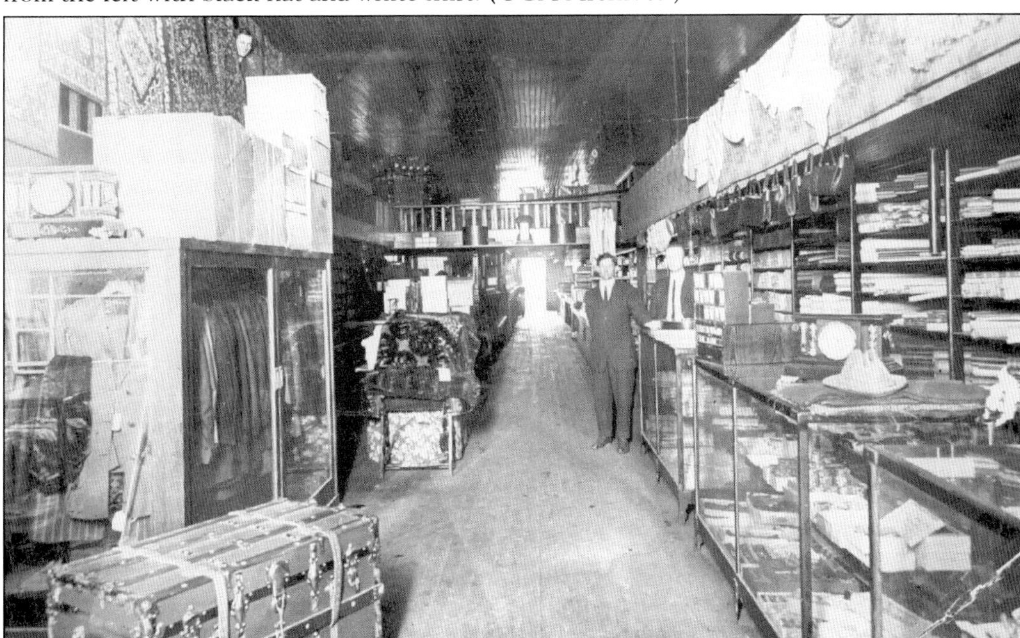

Interior of S.G. Smith's General Store, c. 1906. The store was located at Front and North Streets in Conway. Note the man peaking out from behind a Persian rug on the left wall behind some boxes. (UCA Archives.)

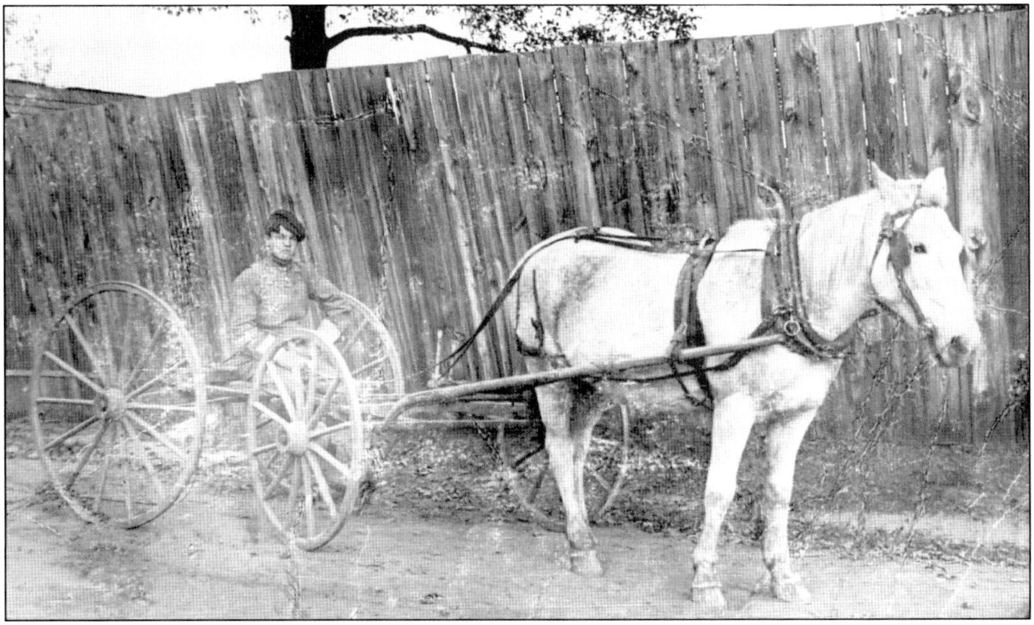

HIEGEL LUMBER'S FIRST DELIVERY WAGON. The wagon driver is Ben Gwin and the horse is a gray mare named Old Nellie. Hiegel Lumber Company, located at 800 Oak Street, would be an important fixture of Conway life until it closed its doors in 1998. A Walgreen drugstore replaced it.(UCA Archives.)

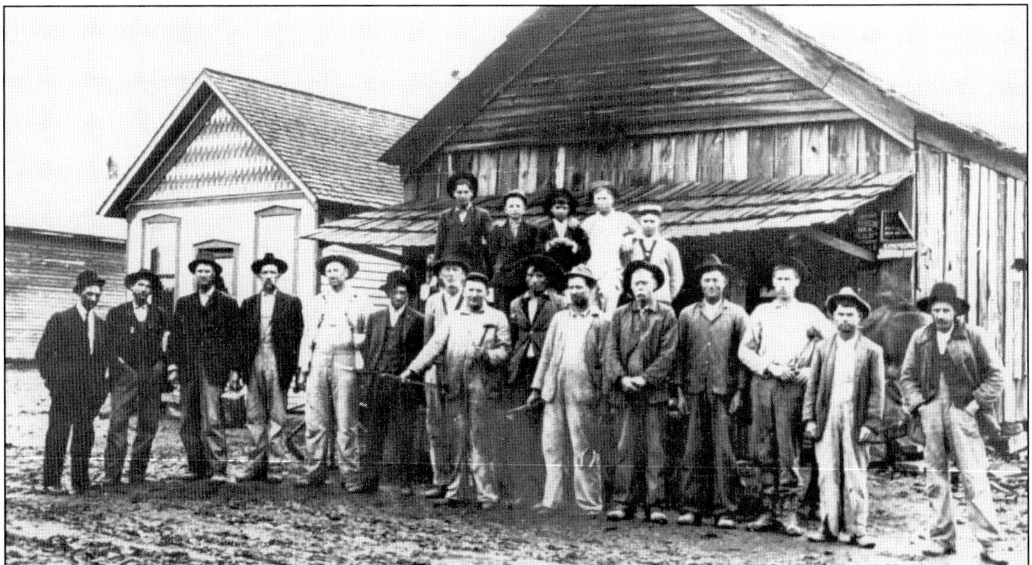

KELSO-WADDLE BLACKSMITH SHOP IN GREENBRIER, C. 1900. The people shown here are, from left to right, as follows: (front row) Dr. E.T. Williams, Will Brannon, Jim Taylor, R.B. Sims, H.L. Tyler, John Hollis, W.C. Kelso, T.C. Waddle, Isham Williams, Clyde Kelso, Jasper Snow, Tom Edwards, Tom Dickens, unidentified, and Jepp Dickens; (back row) Cecil McCall, Buck Waddle, Emmett Mobbs, Sherrill Benton, and Egbert Woolly. Clyde Kelso and Tom Waddle had a gristmill in the back of the shop; customers could have corn ground into meal while having work done at the smithy. (UCA Archives.)

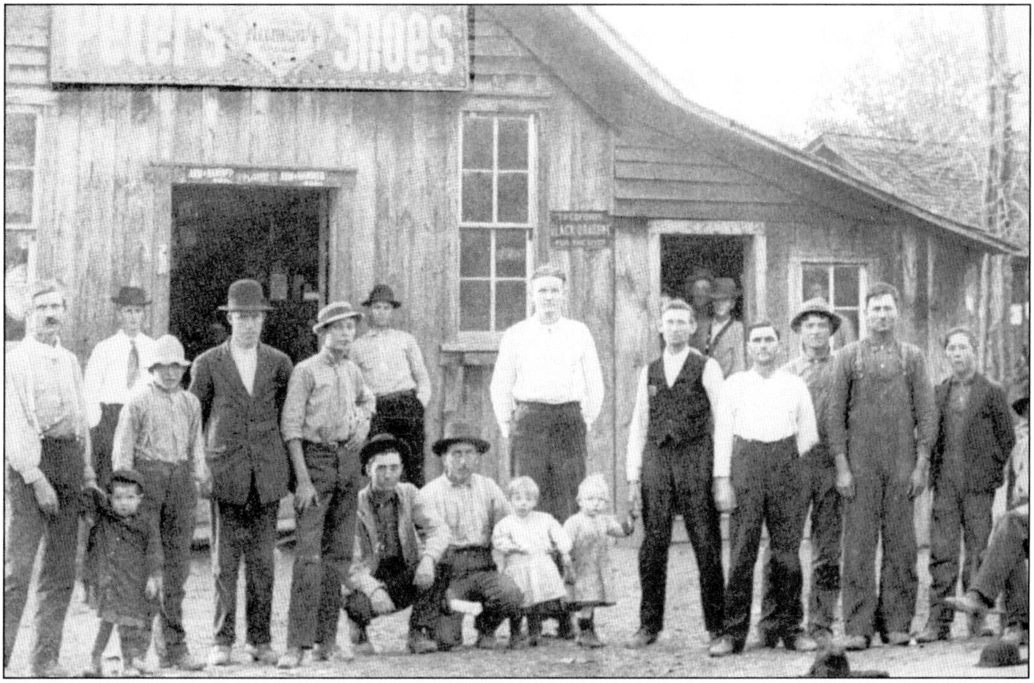

Hamilton Mobb's Store Advertising Peters Shoes in Republican, c. 1905. Originally called Cash Springs, the town's name had to be changed to Republican when the town applied for a post office in 1897; there was already another Cash Springs in Arkansas. (UCA Archives.)

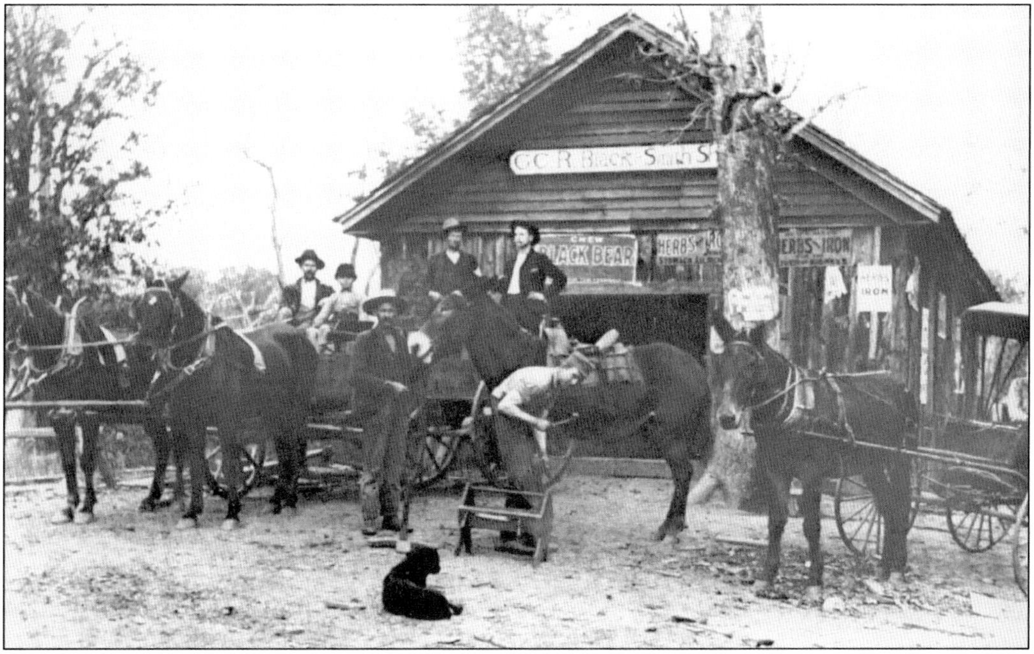

G.C.R. Blacksmith Shop in Republican, c. 1910. Included in this scene are Homer Harris, Oscar Lyons, Johnnie Finton, Carl Ward, Clifton Reynolds, George Reynolds, and Mary Reynolds Williams. (UCA Archives.)

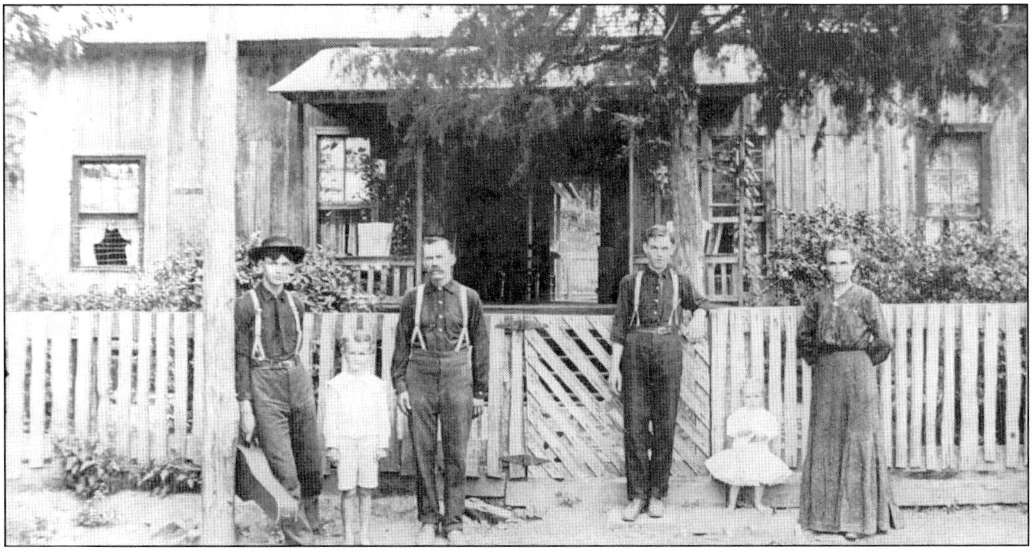

Family Portrait at Bud Bailey Home, c. 1907. Located at Hamlet, which was once known as Roden's Mill, the home was about eight miles east of Conway. Joe Roden built the one-room log house and kitchen before 1900 and died there in 1902. Roden was the first postmaster at Hamlett (note the spelling with two Ts). The Arkansas Highway Department decided this was not the correct spelling and used Hamlet with one "T" for its signs and maps; this spelling has been used ever since. Bud Bailey purchased and subsequently expanded the home for his family; the front room is the original log structure. The Bailey family, posed from left to right in front of the house are Frank, Coy, Bud, Joe, Florence, and Ina. Ina later became Mrs. George Watson and continued to live in Hamlet. The photograph was provided by Florence Bailey. (UCA Archives.)

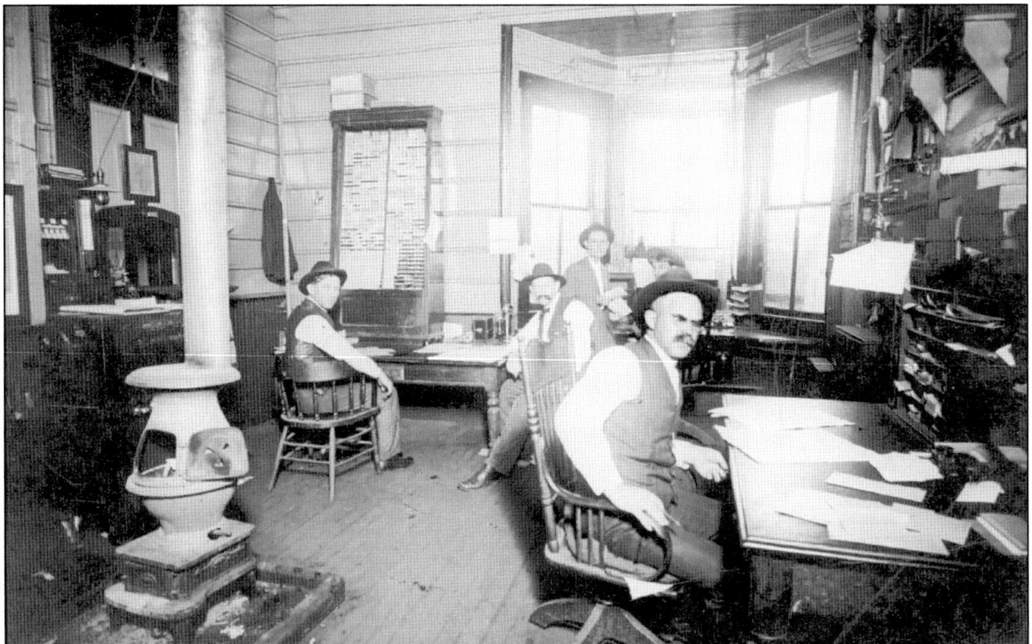

Interior of Railroad Depot in Conway, c. 1905. (UCA Archives.)

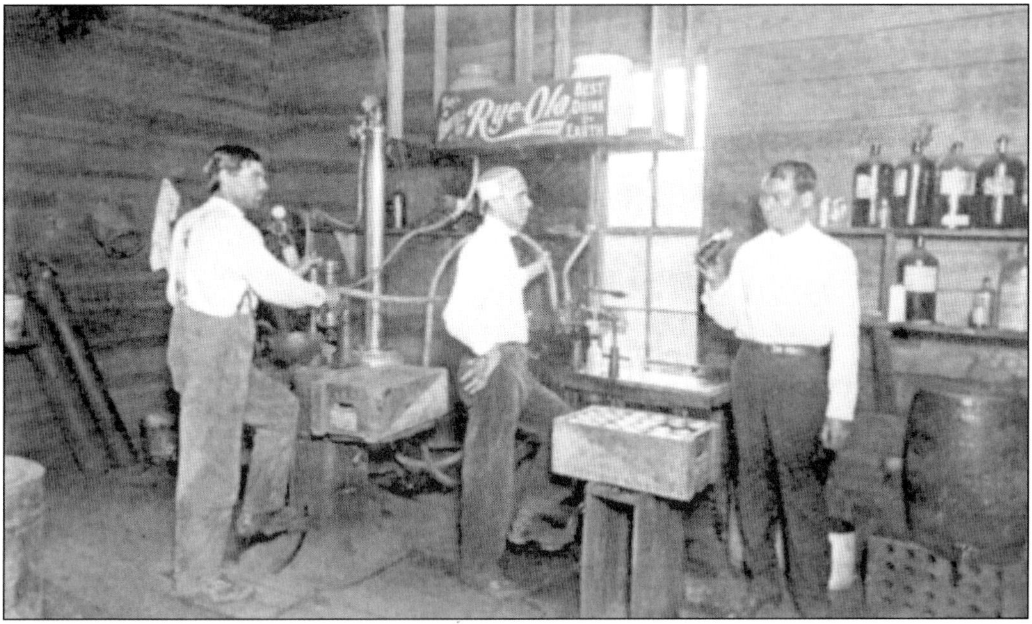

INTERIOR OF RYE-OLA BOTTLING WORKS. Rev. J.C. Dawson established this Conway bottling works in 1911. Located on North Front Street, this was the first bottling plant built between Little Rock and Fort Smith. Leigh Rotton, who worked at the plant, is in the center of the photograph, while customer Lee Mode is on the right. (UCA Archives.)

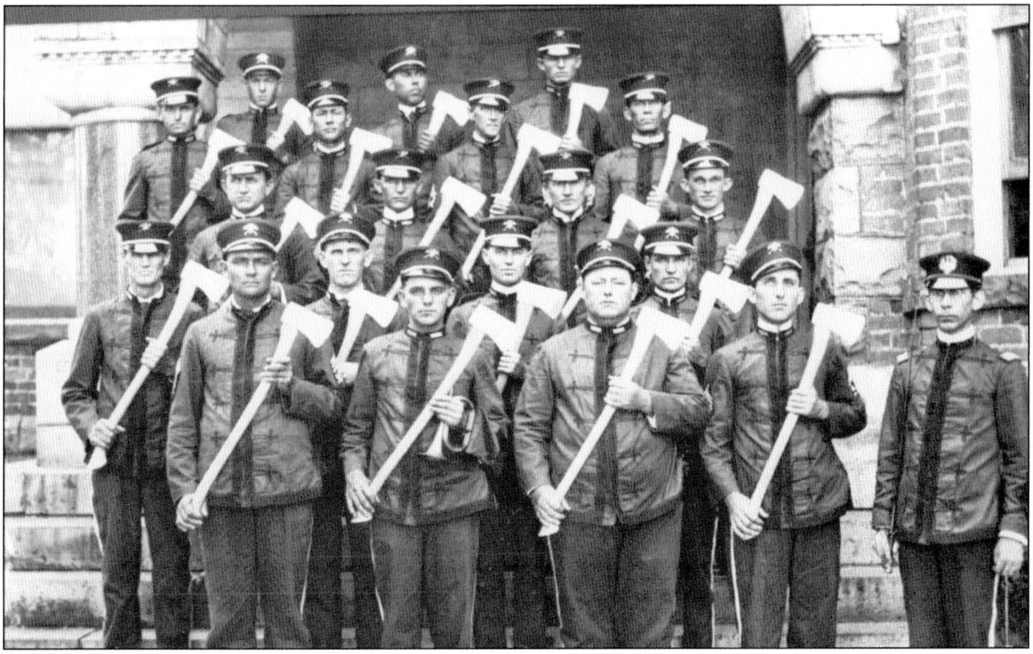

WOODSMEN OF THE WORLD (WOW) DRILL TEAM OF CONWAY CAMP NO. 35, C. 1910. WOW was a "fraternal benefit society" based on the local lodge system that was founded in 1890 by Joseph Cullen Root. One of the society's principal perks was the provision of insurance benefits for its members. WOW celebrated the 100th anniversary of its founding in 1990. (UCA Archives.)

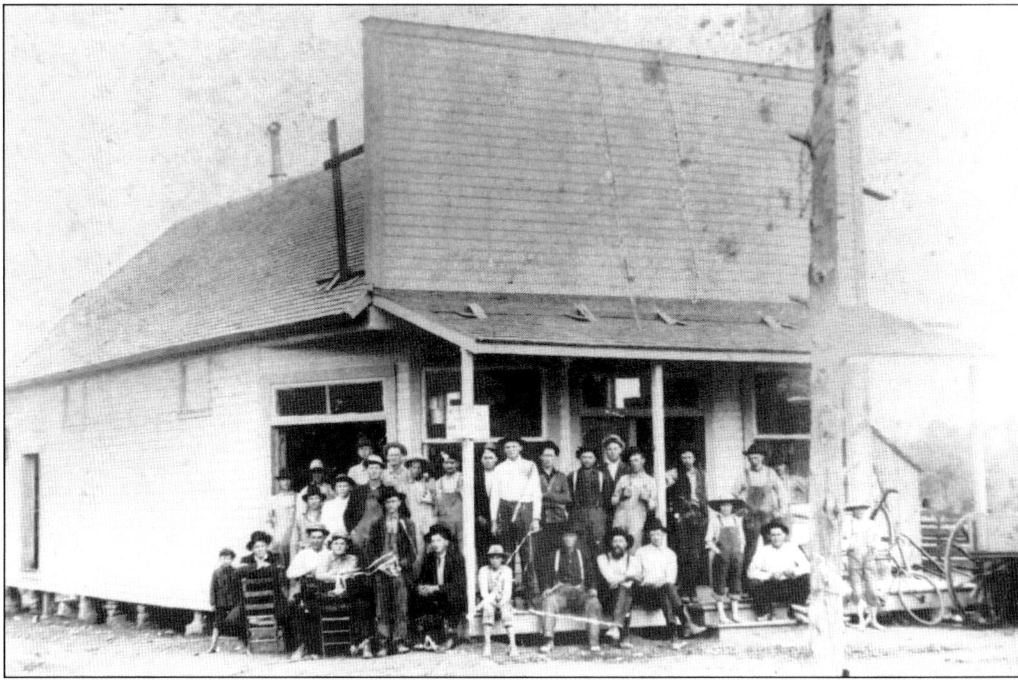

L.T. LASLEY STORE IN ENOLA, C. 1900. L.T. Lasley started a mercantile business at Enola in 1897, the year he married Agnes Mathews, and operated that store until his death in 1933. Lasley's home, store, and cotton gin were the first structures in Enola to have electric lights. (UCA Archives.)

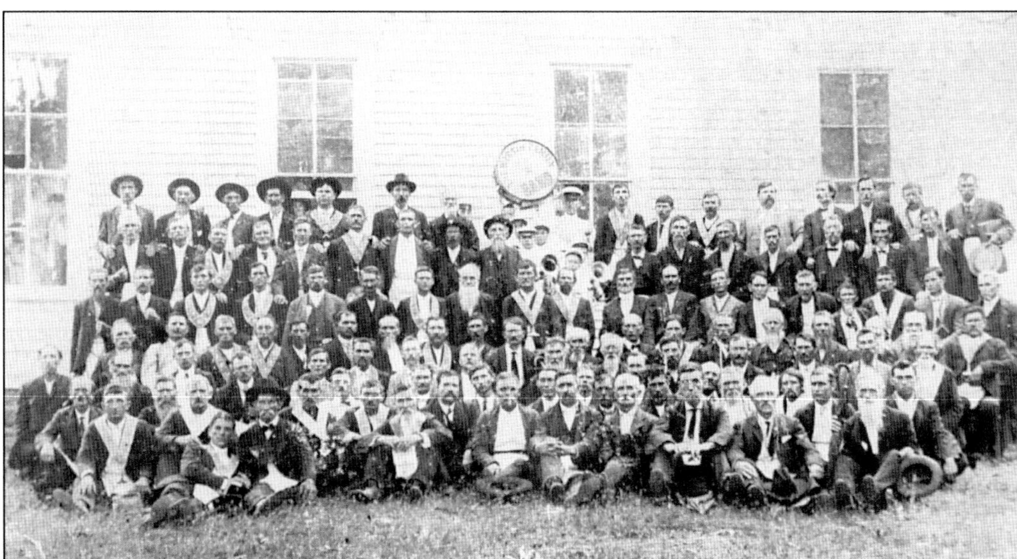

MASONIC GROUP AT QUITMAN, PRE-1910. The Holland Lodge, Free and Accepted Masons (F. and A.M.) was chartered in 1858. The town was named after General Quitman, who fought in the Mexican War and commanded the Southern Military District at the time the Quitman Post Office was established in 1848. While Quitman is located in Cleburne County, the town has always had very close ties to Faulkner County. (UCA Archives.)

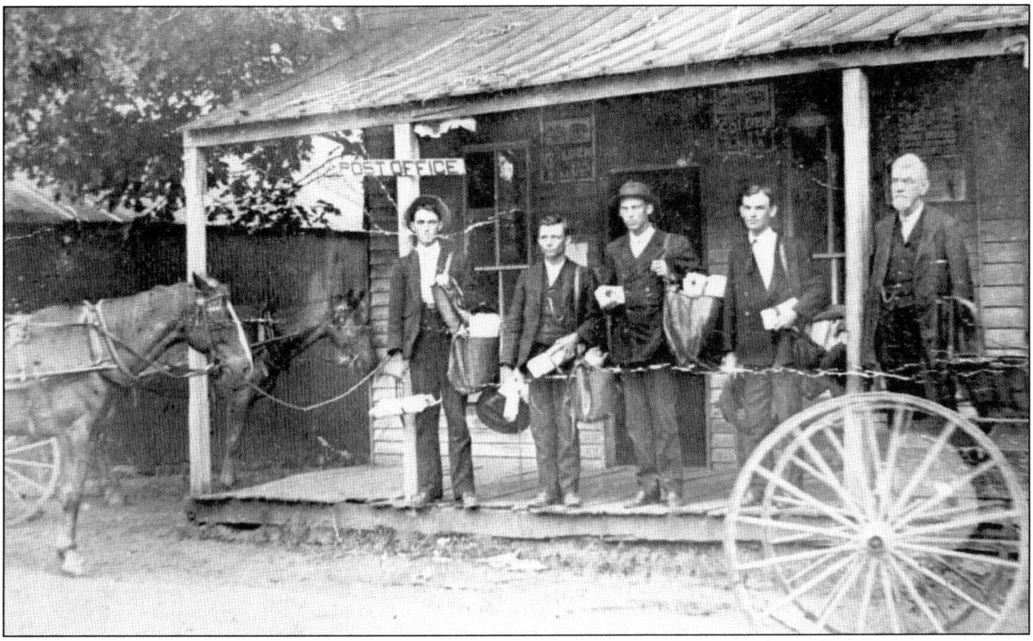

Vilonia Post Office and Mail Carriers, c. 1910. Early maps list the area as Cypress Township, but settlers named the place "Vilsonia" which means the "land with two valleys." A subsequent transcription error when local Masons applied for national affiliation inadvertently dropped the "s." Local residents accepted the spelling "Vilonia" rather than wading through the bureaucracy of trying to get their "s" back. (UCA Archives.)

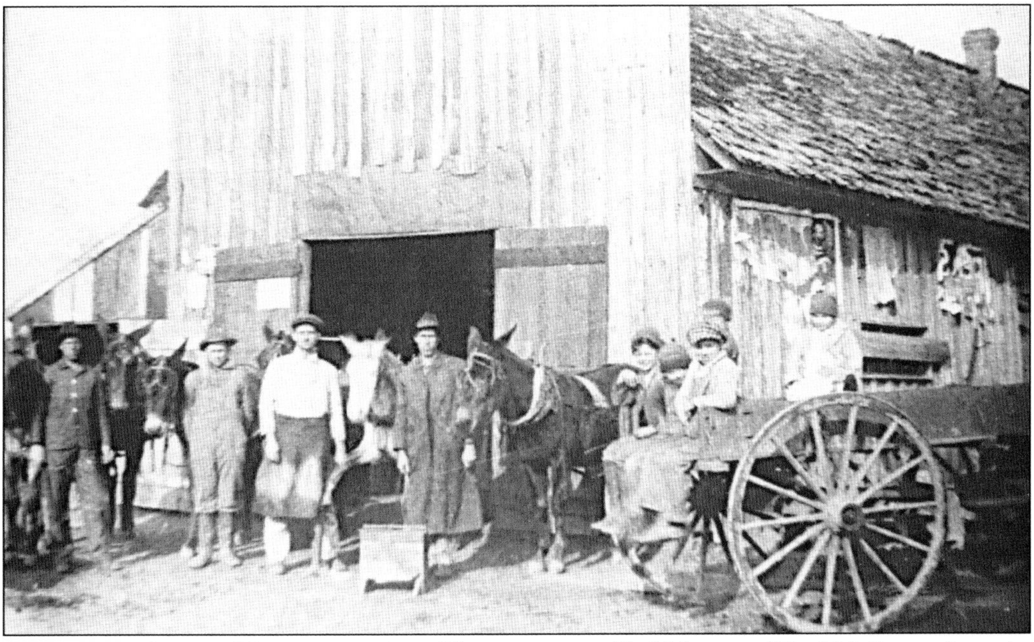

Blacksmith Shop in Vilonia, c. 1910. That same year, Earl Myatt and Dr. J.H. Downs brought the first horseless-carriages—automobiles—to town. As automobiles, trucks, and tractors began to replace the horse and mule, smithies would become less important in the daily life of small towns throughout America. (UCA Archives.)

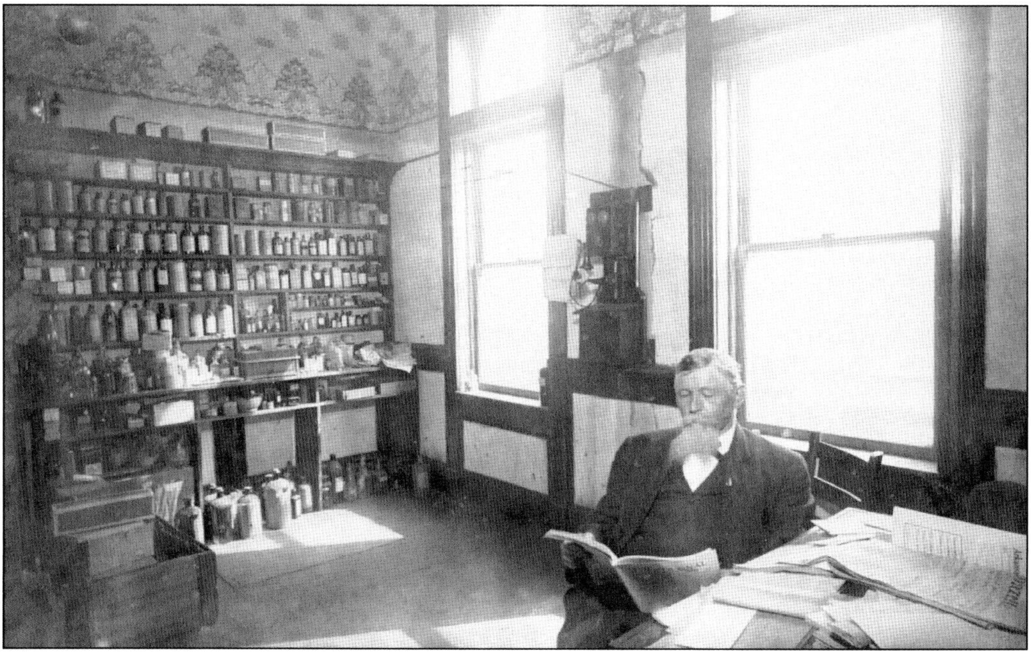

Dr. George Dickerson's Office in Conway, c. 1910. The office was on the second floor of the Halter Building, according to Mrs. Rubye Boydston of Conway, who furnished the photograph. Dr. Dickerson's son Cecil and grandson Cecil Jr. were also well-known Conway physicians. Dr. Dickerson had one of the first telephones in Conway; the founder of Conway, Col. Asa Robinson, could claim having the first phone in Conway since he installed two tin cups at either end of a 200-yard wire, which he strung between his home and the quarters of his servant, Uncle Ned. Prof. George Herndon Burr, who was a science instructor at Hendrix College, subsequently installed a real phone line from his home (north of Mill Street on Davis) to Hendrix in 1891. Professor Burr and G.A. Miller installed the first practicable telephone exchange in 1899. There were 28 original subscribers. Dr. Dickerson had phone number 1, while S.G. Smith's phone number was 2, the Bank of Conway was 3, Frauenthal & Schwarz was 11, Central College was 14, Martin & Harton was 18, and the *Log Cabin Democrat* was 21. These phone numbers were still used when the Bell Telephone Company took over local service. The newspaper's phone number was still 21 when Paul Faris came to Conway in 1928, and the *Log Cabin Democrat* kept their number until 1961, when Conway got dial telephone service. (UCA Archives.)

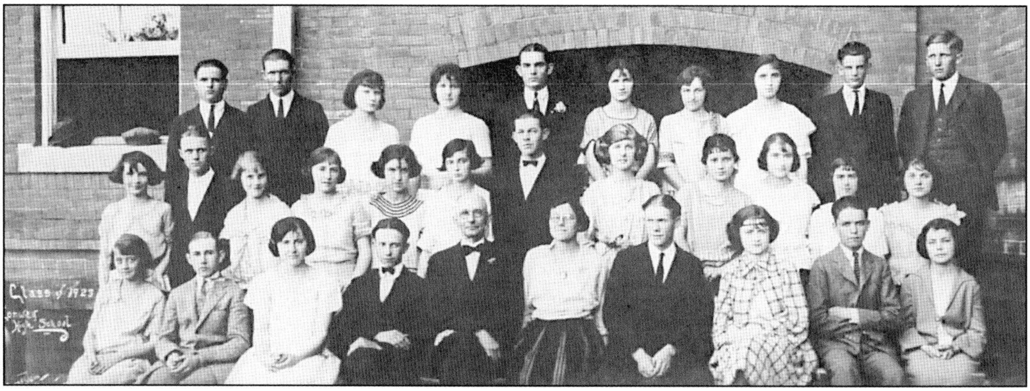

Conway High School Graduating Class of 1923. (UCA Archives.)

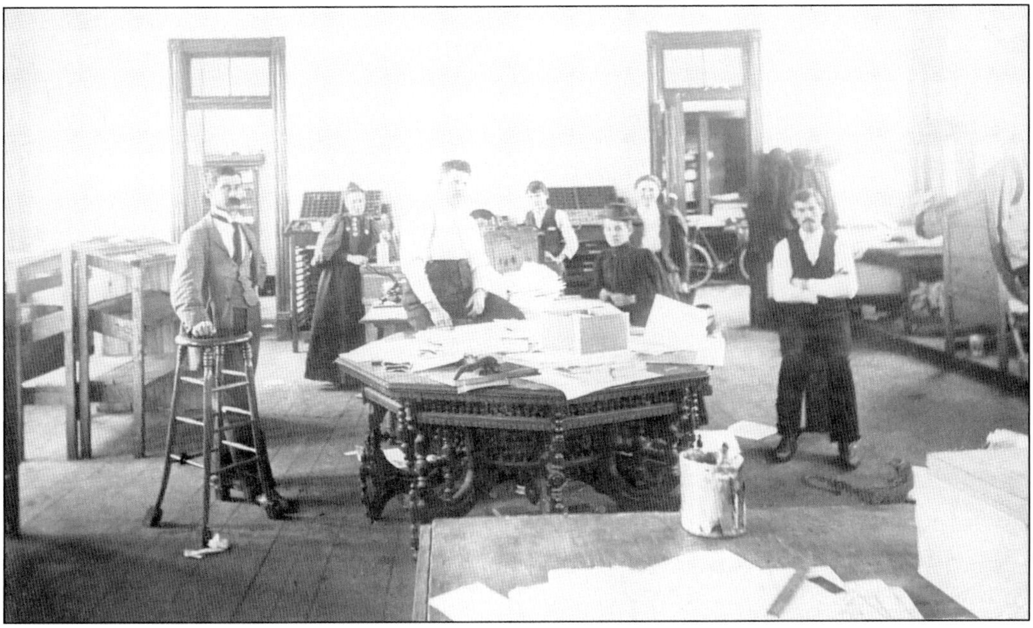

Interior of the *Log Cabin Democrat* Newspaper Office, c. 1910. People shown here, from left to right, are O.C. Ludwig, Milly Burnes, W.M. Carr, Frank Robins, Hattie Myrick, Mrs. W.M. Carr, and Will Farmer. (UCA Archives.)

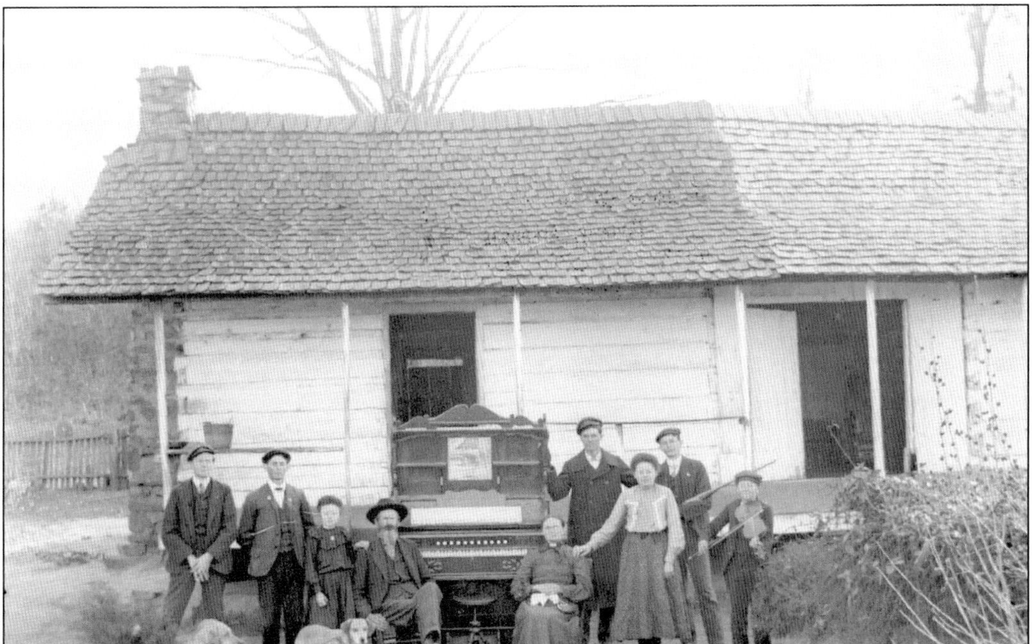

Family Portrait, c. 1910. This image was taken in front of the Will Russell home in Faulkner County. (UCA Archives.)

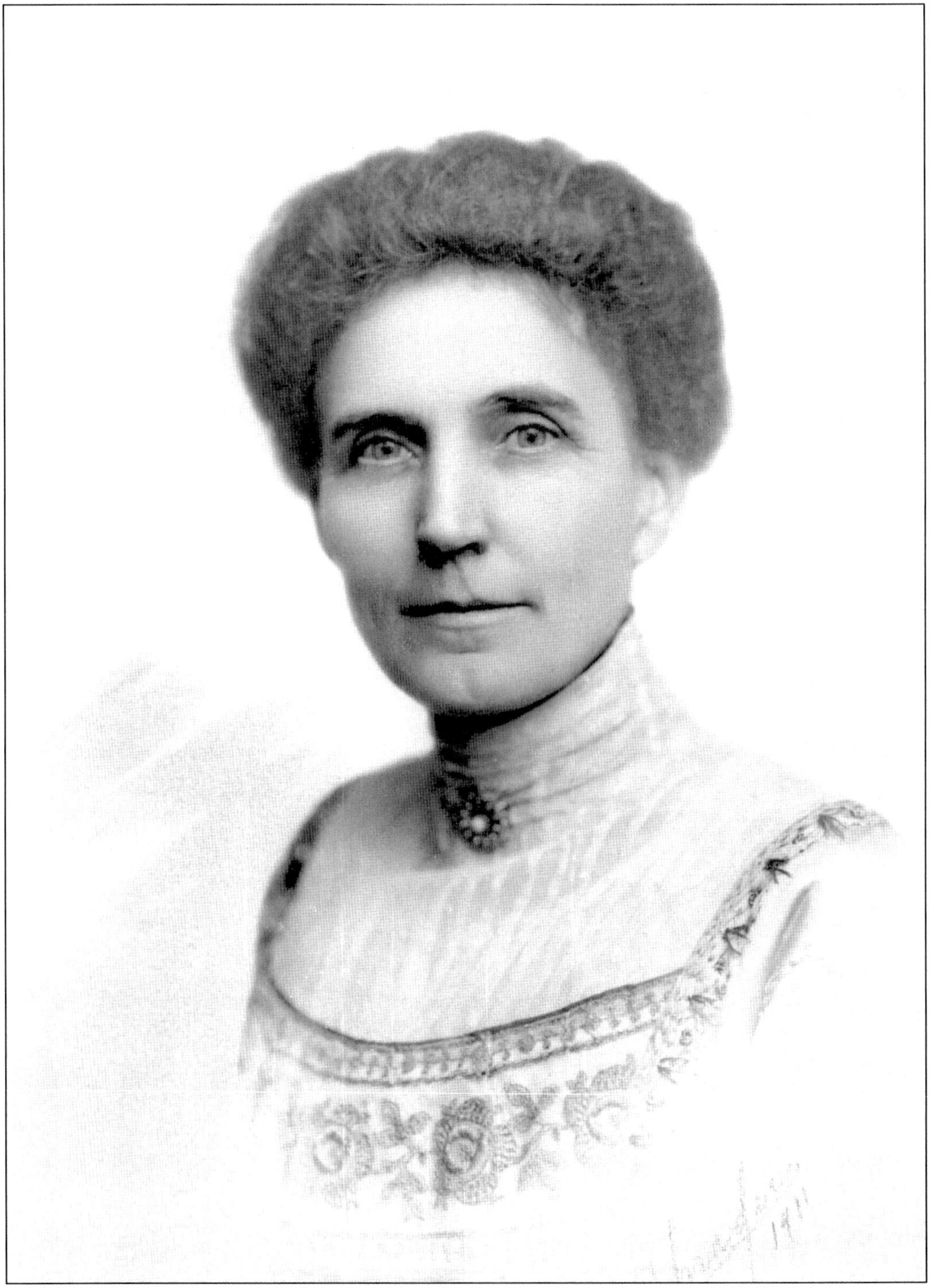

Louvenia Wallace Donaghey, Wife of Governor George W. Donaghey. They met at a Christmas party in 1879, when George was working as a carpenter in Conway. After a four-year courtship, they were married in 1883. Shrader photographed this image, *c.* 1910. (UCA Archives.)

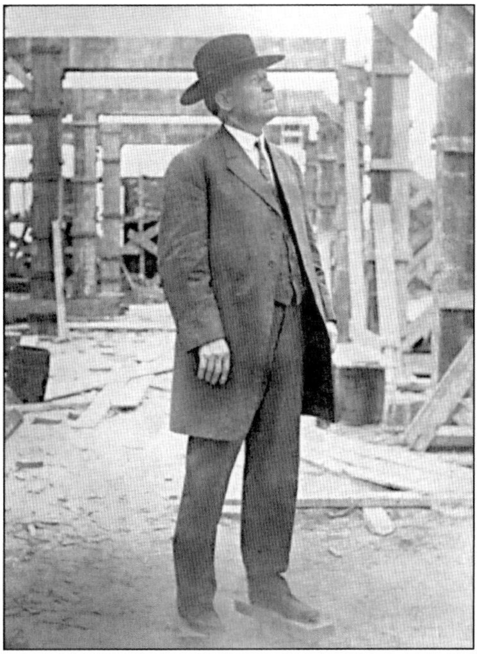

Governor G.W. Donaghey. Donaghey earned his living as a carpenter in Conway and went on to become a major contractor. He is inspecting work on the new state capitol building in Little Rock. The state government had outgrown its 1836 building, so construction of a new capitol began in 1899. (UCA Archives.)

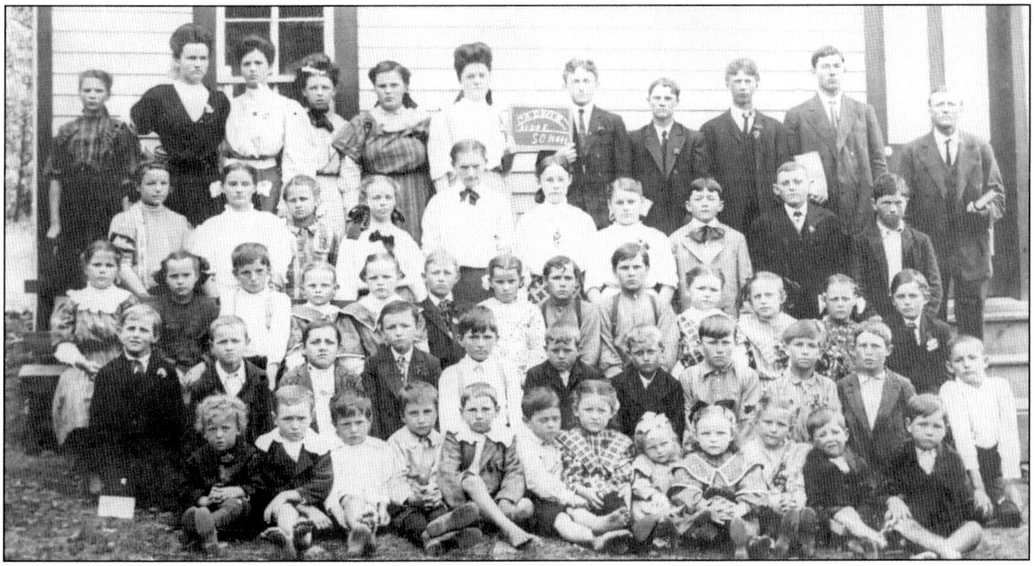

Group Portrait at Cadron Ridge School in 1908. Seen here, from left to right, are as follows: (first row) Dovie Aleur (Thomas), Nola Cry (Turner), Jeffie Richardson, Jennie Irby, Joe Cry, Leonard Turner, M. Snow, Otis Irby, and Clarence McRovane; (second row) Belle Irby, unidentified, Mary Mosley, Ovie Carden, Mary Ethridge, Belle Nixon, unidentified, Annie Evans, George Cry, Jobie Richardson, John Cry, and teacher Newt Jones; (third row) Belee Irby, Ovie Adams, Erie Irby, Lois Turner, Zerdic Turner, unidentified, Jennie Nixon, Ellis Adams, Carl Adams, Addie Turner, Mamie Richardson, Ovie Carden, and Ellis Irby; (fourth row) Elmer Turner, Dewey Allen, Roy Carden, Offie Turner, ? Atkinson, ? Etheridge, ? Etheridge, Arnes Atkinson, unidentified, unidentified, and ? Moatey; (fifth row) Lee Richardson, Jim Allen, unidentified, ? Atkinson, ? Irby, unidentified, ? Turner, Allie Turner, Lizzy Turner, Jerry Richardson, Berry Evans, and ? Wares. (UCA Archives.)

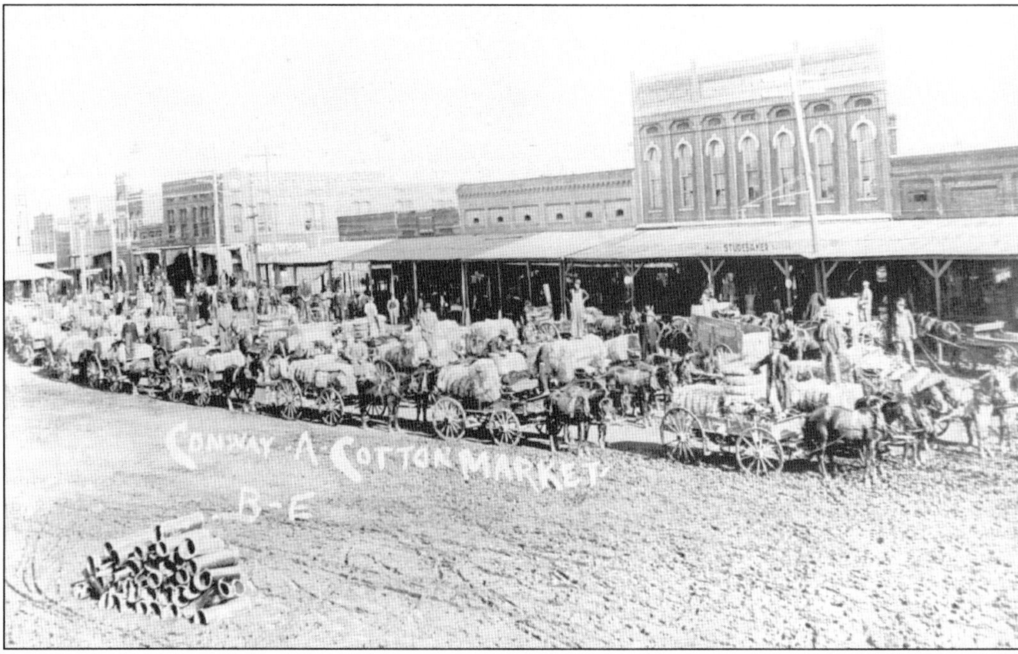

Open-Air Cotton Market and Stores along Front Street in Conway, c. 1909. At the far left is the intersection of Front and Oak Streets. Cotton buyers could usually be found scattered along the sidewalk. The center building belongs to Frauenthal & Schwarz, who were agents for Studebaker wagons and buggies. (UCA Archives.)

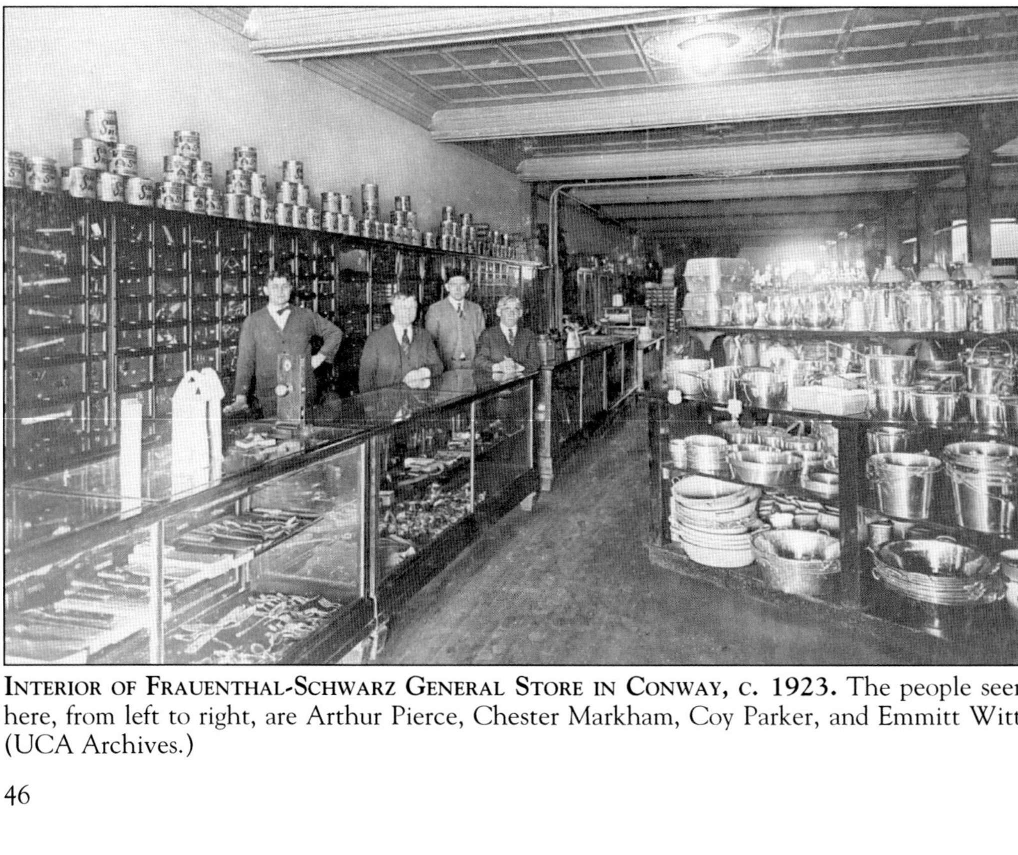

Interior of Frauenthal-Schwarz General Store in Conway, c. 1923. The people seen here, from left to right, are Arthur Pierce, Chester Markham, Coy Parker, and Emmitt Witt. (UCA Archives.)

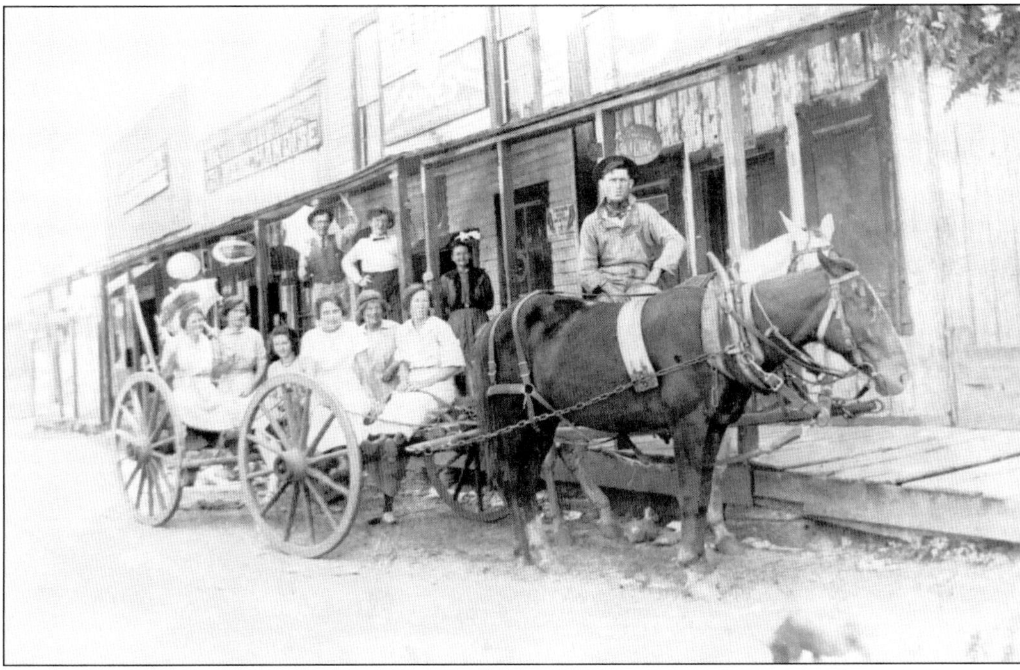

MAYFLOWER "GROUP DUTY," C. 1914. Will Nalor is sitting on the horse; Aunt Sally Carter is the elderly lady on the porch. The other ladies include E. Tew Boydson, Essie Taylor, and Florence McIntyre. (UCA Archives.)

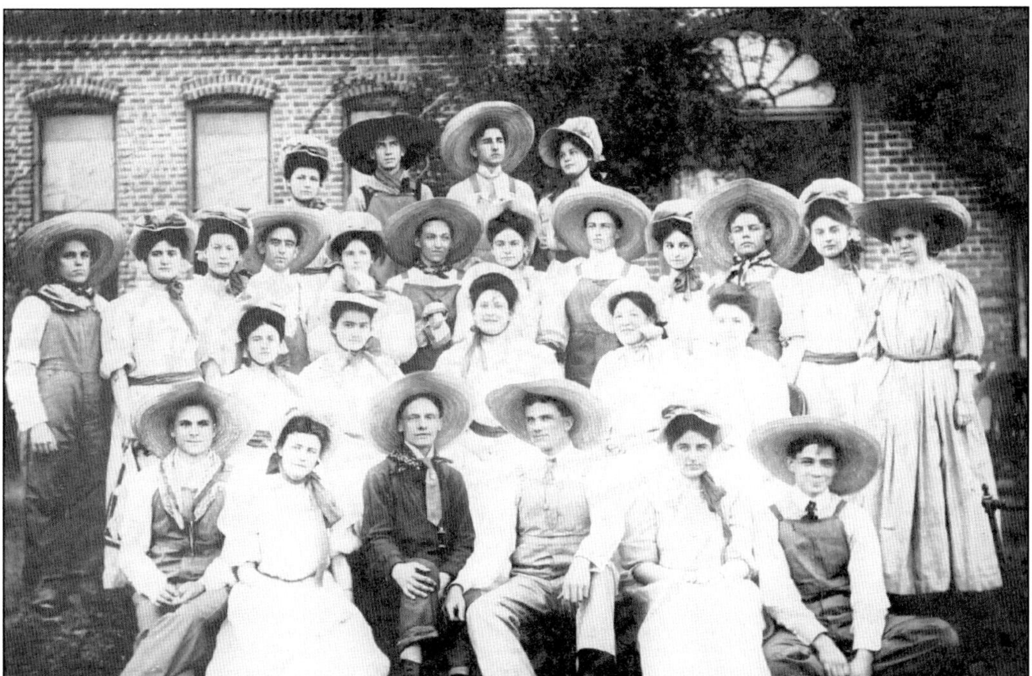

HENDRIX COLLEGE STUDENTS, C. 1910. (UCA Archives.)

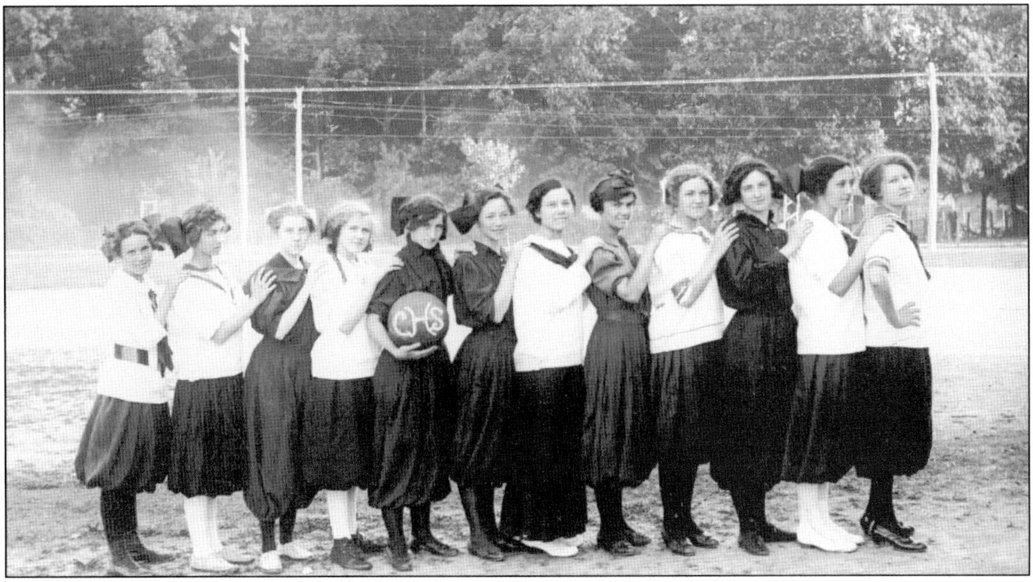

Conway High School Girl's Basketball Team, c. 1920. (UCA Archives.)

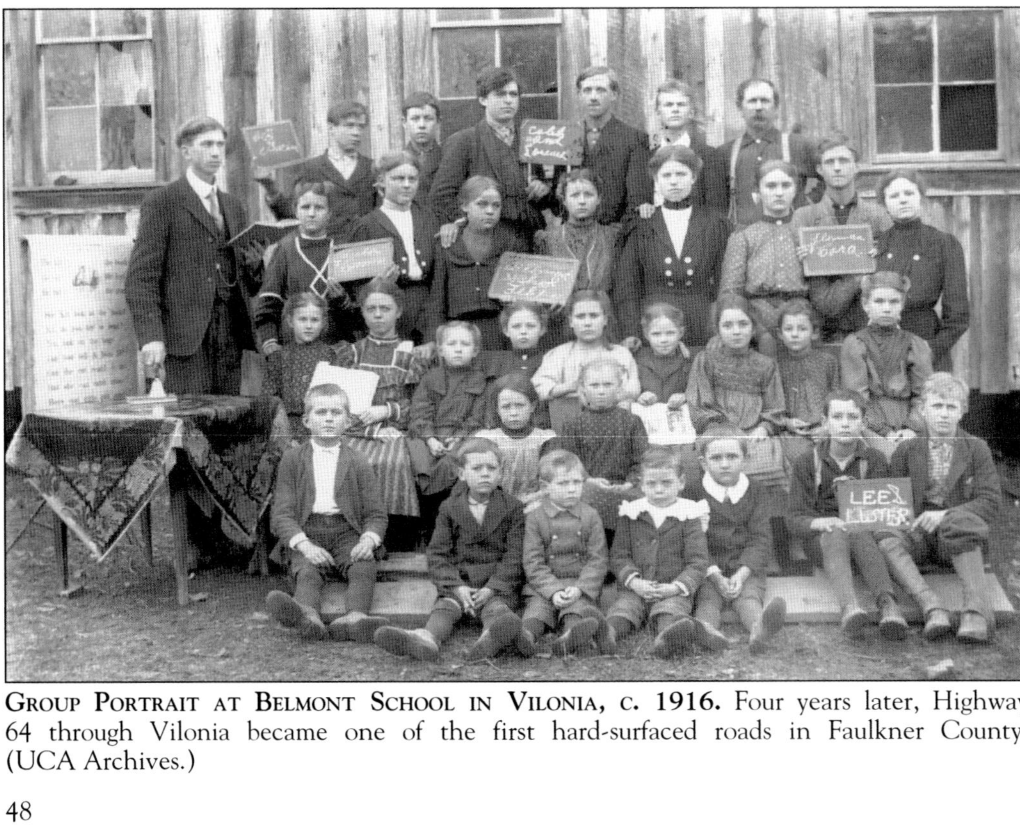

Group Portrait at Belmont School in Vilonia, c. 1916. Four years later, Highway 64 through Vilonia became one of the first hard-surfaced roads in Faulkner County. (UCA Archives.)

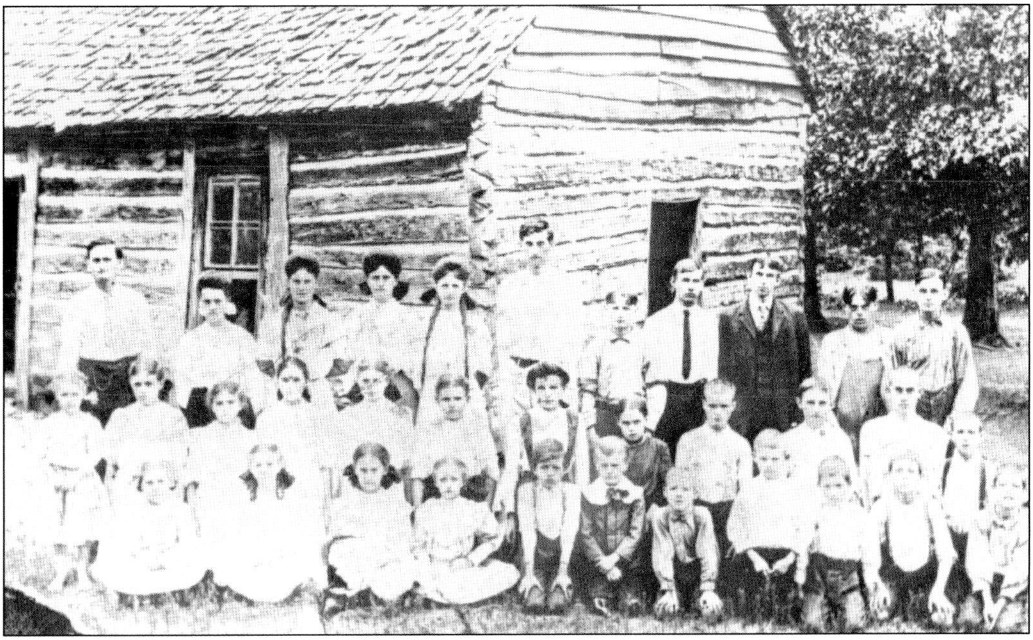

PICKLES GAP SCHOOL AND CHURCH, C. 1910. (UCA Archives.)

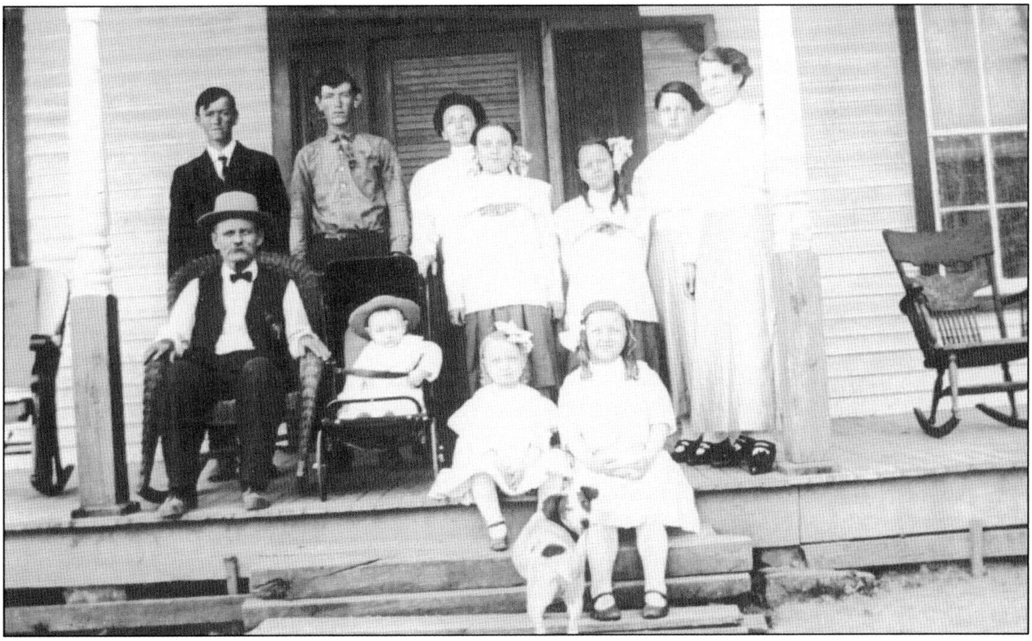

LEDRICK FAMILY PORTRAIT IN MAYFLOWER, C. 1915. These family members are shown on the front porch of a building that served as a combined residence and general store. (Arkansas History Commission.)

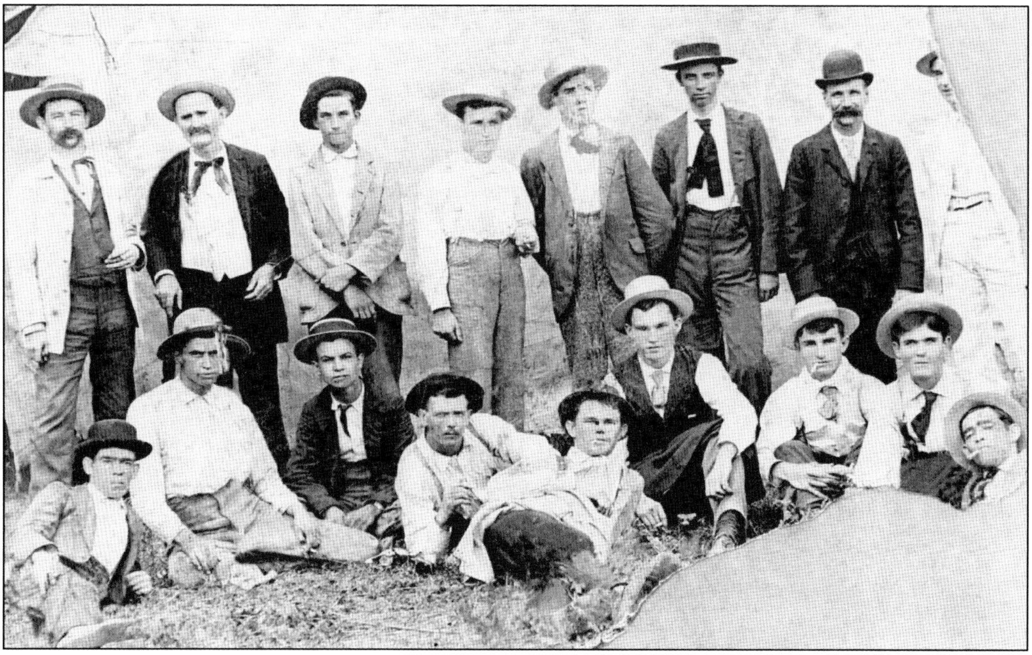

A Group Relaxing at Cascade Springs, c. 1895. This was an early settlement in eastern Faulkner County near El Paso. During the 1870s and 1880s, Cascade was a lively resort area with five to six mineral springs. The families of Myrtle E. Charles, Mabel Charles Serin, and Elfleda Charles Criswell lived there. Those photographed include Rod Dickerson, Newt Cole, Ed Witt, Wash Clibourn, Ralph White, Will Wilson, Peat Ingram, Albert Dollarhite, Burl Ingram, Roy Bruce, and Emitt Witt. (UCA Archives.)

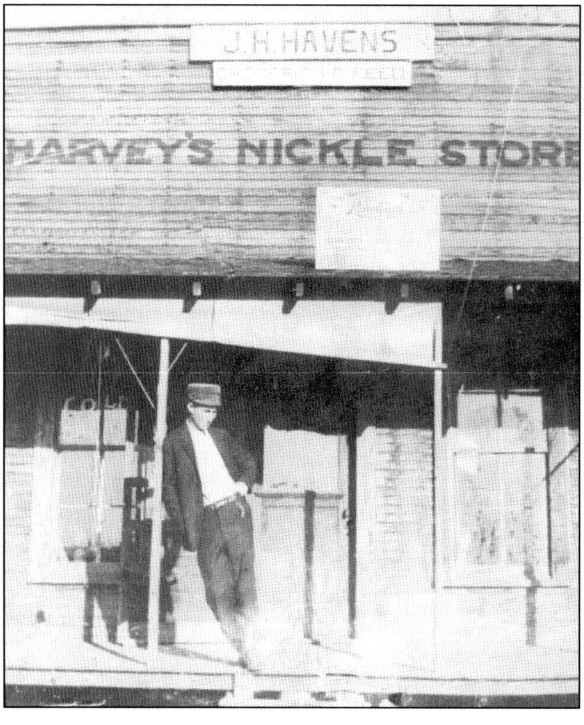

Harvey's Nickle Store at Cadron Gap on Old Highway 64, c. 1919. This photograph shows John Havens, age 19, who bought the store from J.H. Harvey Havens after graduating from college. The building remained at that location until about 1985, when Conway's North Fire Station replaced it. (UCA Archives.)

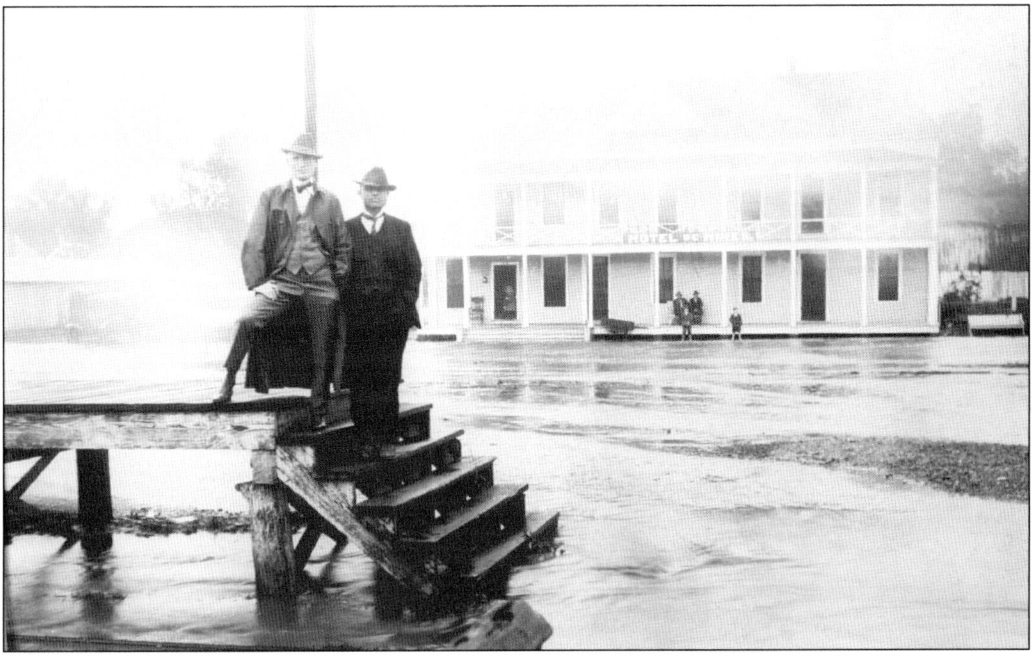

DOWNTOWN CONWAY DURING THE FLOOD OF 1920. Dr. J.Z. Bailey (left) and John Dunaway are standing on a railroad-loading platform. Railroad Avenue (later renamed Parkway) is behind the men; Main Street intersects Railroad Avenue to the left. The Hotel De Hines was destroyed by fire later that year. (UCA Archives.)

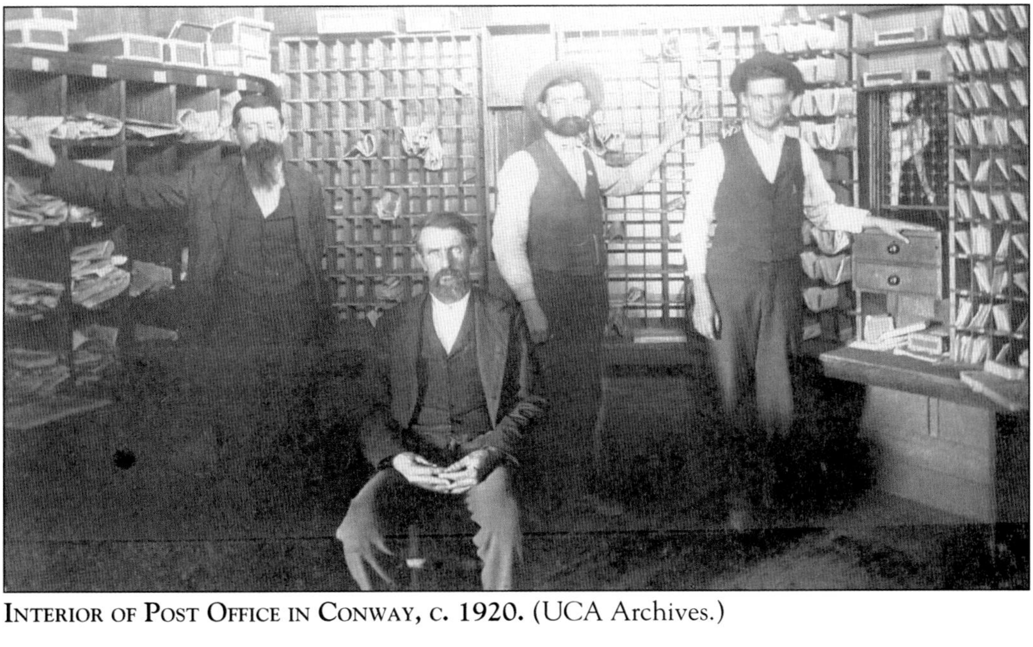

INTERIOR OF POST OFFICE IN CONWAY, C. 1920. (UCA Archives.)

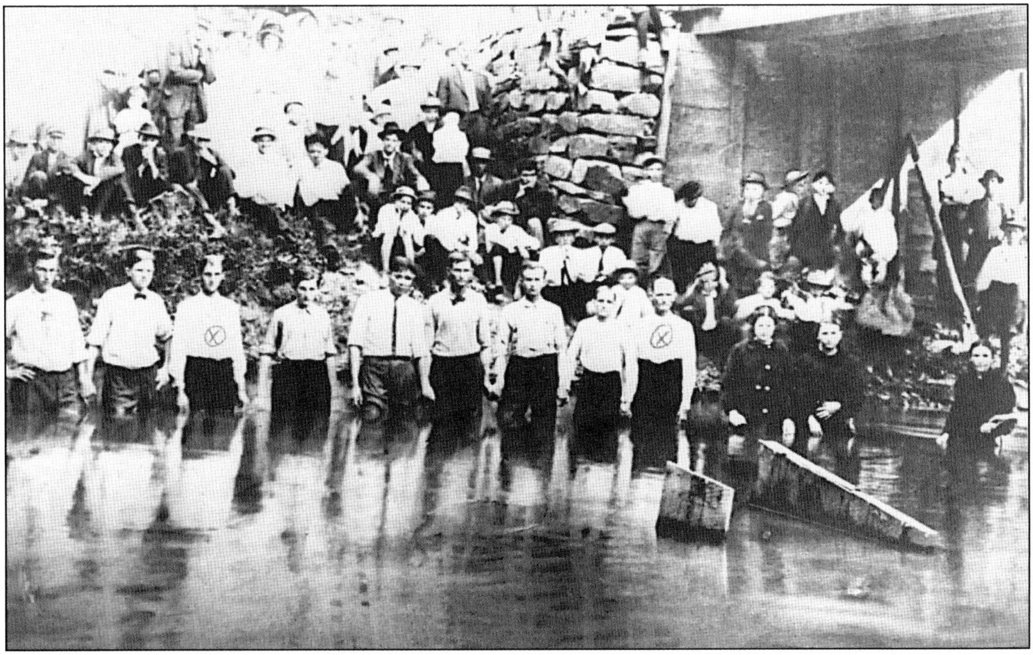

Baptism at Old Roden's Mill on Palarm Creek near Beryl, c. 1913. The mill was named after Joseph Roden, who fought with the 6th Arkansas Regiment until taken prisoner by Union forces in Louisiana. Roden subsequently married and established a farm, cotton gin, and corn and flour mill on Palarm Creek. He also became the first postmaster at Hamlet, a town named in honor of his wife's maiden name. (UCA Archives.)

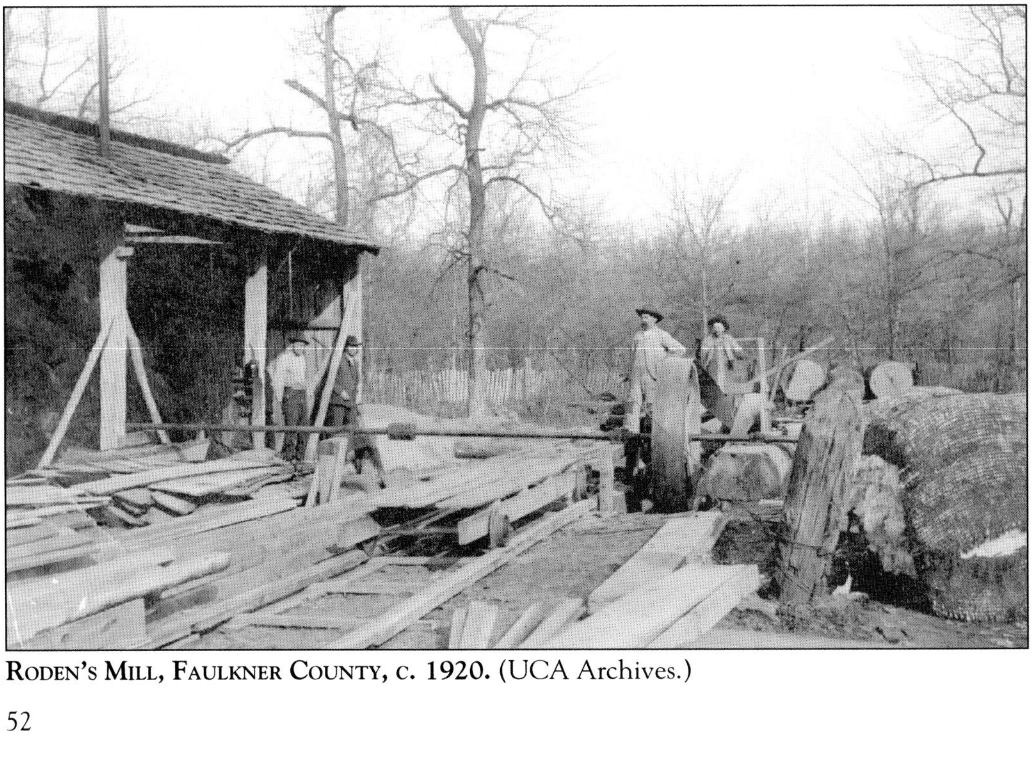

Roden's Mill, Faulkner County, c. 1920. (UCA Archives.)

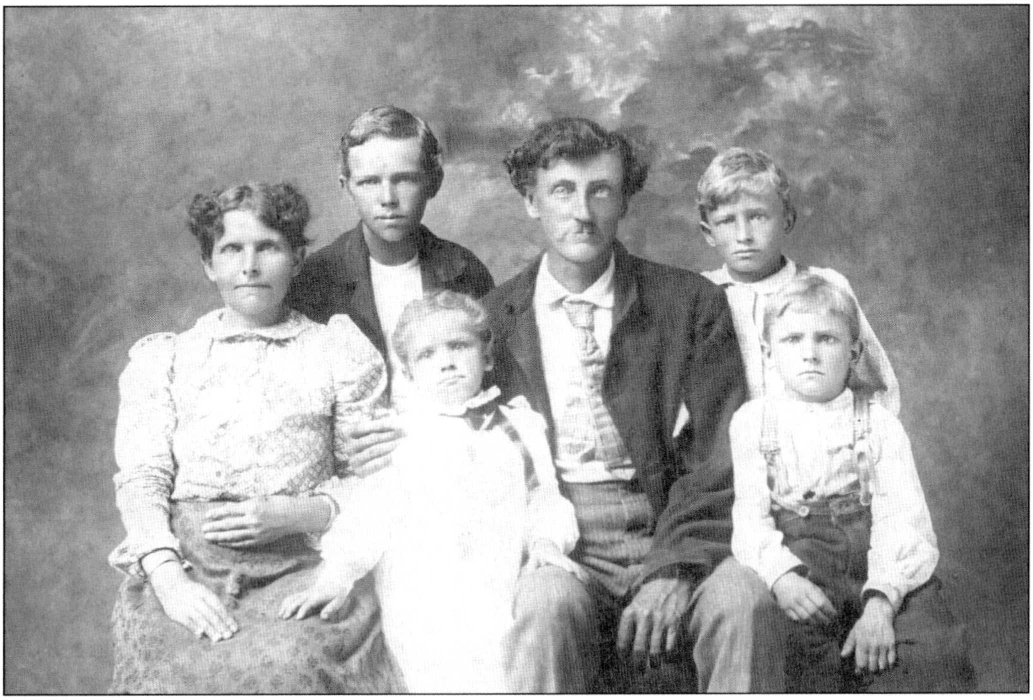

I.N. Fields Family of Faulkner County, c. 1915. (UCA Archives.)

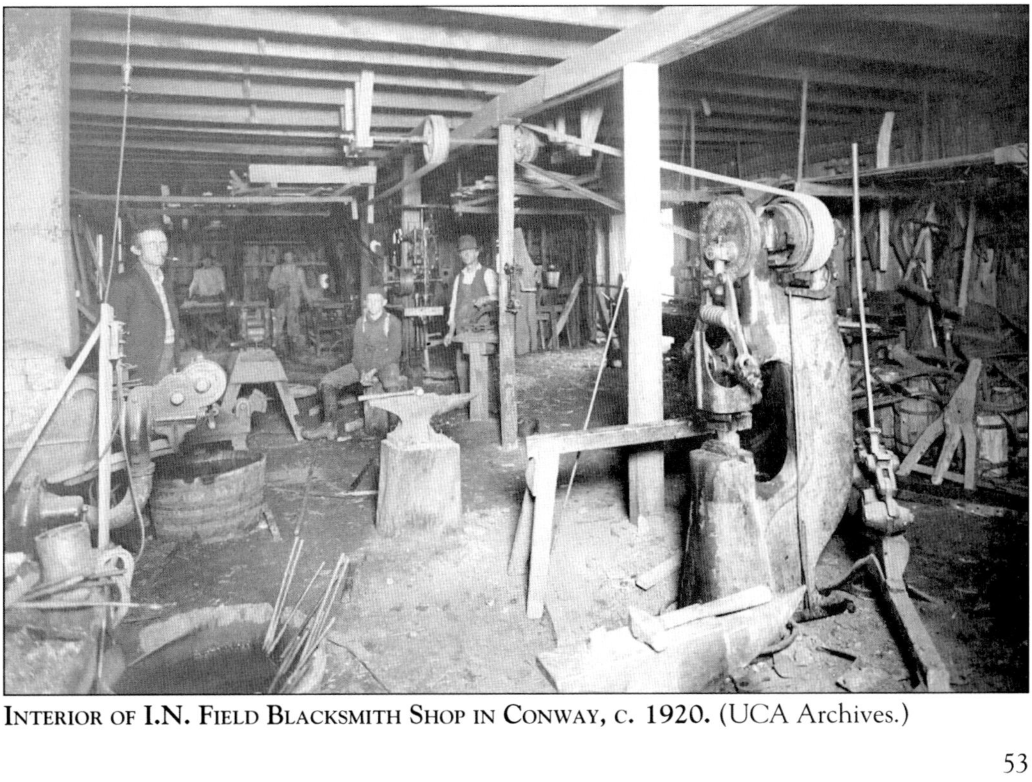

Interior of I.N. Field Blacksmith Shop in Conway, c. 1920. (UCA Archives.)

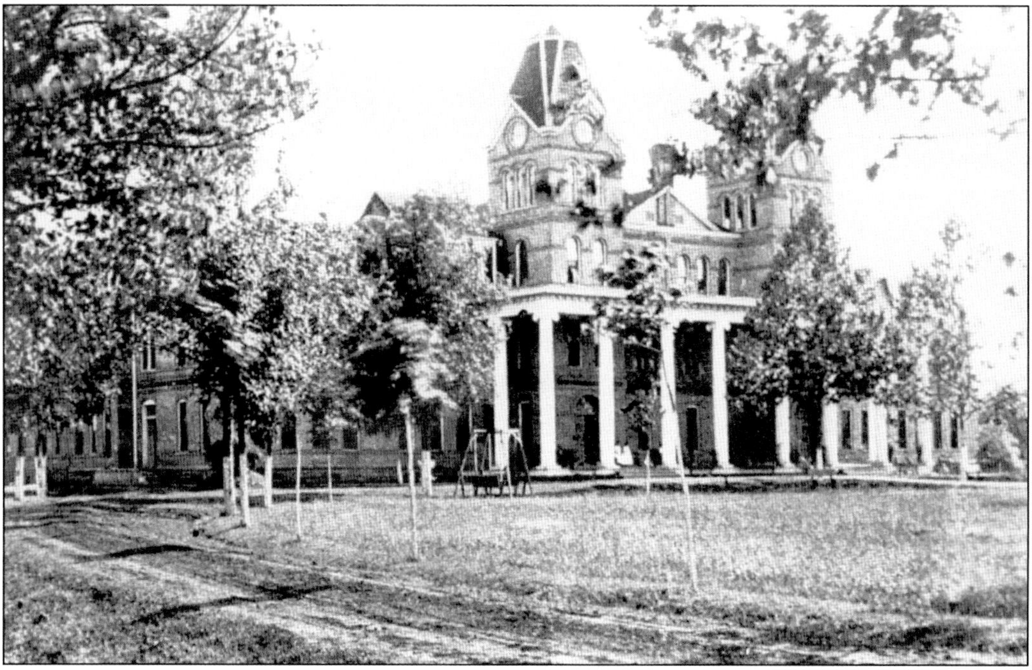

OLD MAIN AT CENTRAL BAPTIST COLLEGE FOR WOMEN IN CONWAY, C. 1914. (UCA Archives.)

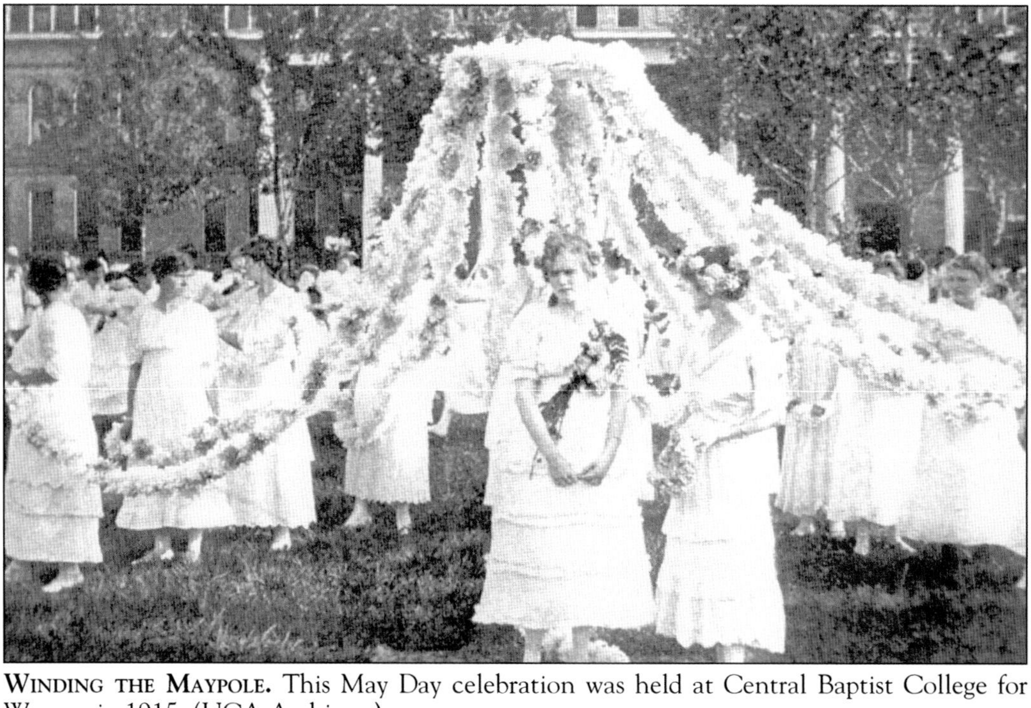

WINDING THE MAYPOLE. This May Day celebration was held at Central Baptist College for Women in 1915. (UCA Archives.)

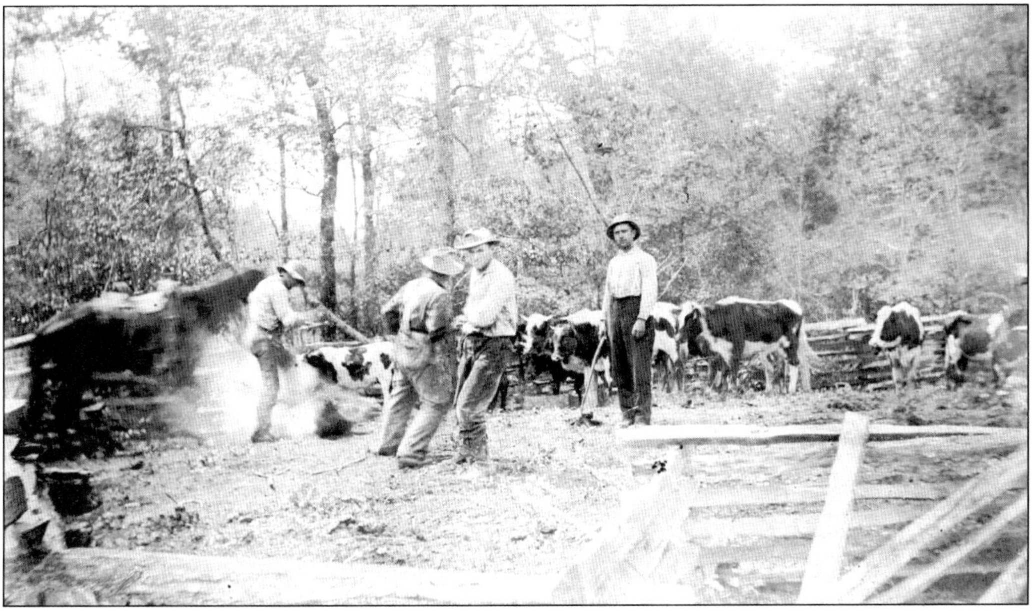

Branding Cattle at the Sherice Ranch on Bull Creek in Eastern Faulkner County. In this summer 1908 photograph, Clarence Sherice is the third man from the left. (UCA Archives.)

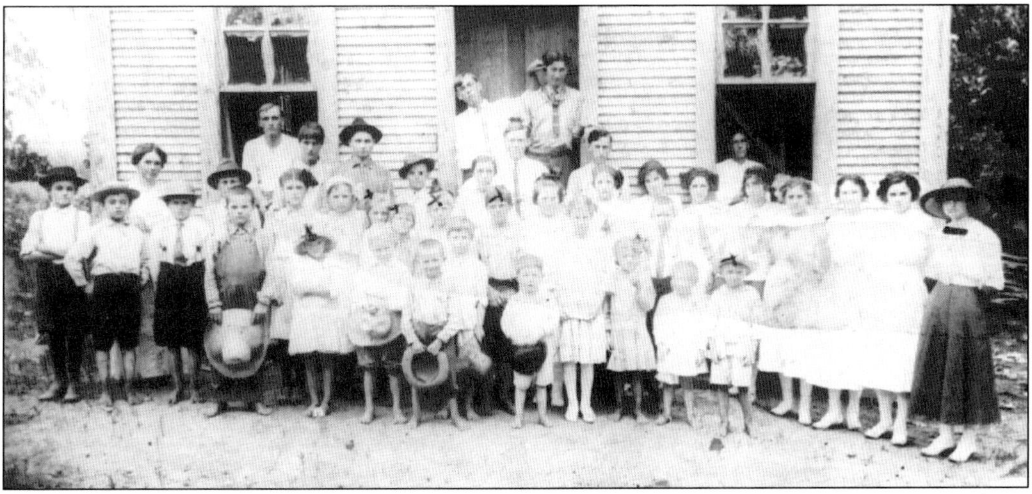

Pickles Gap School, Faulkner County, 1913. Notice that most of the younger students are barefoot and one boy in the doorway is pulling the other's ear. Seen here, from left to right, are as follows: (front rows) Mrs. Lula Moore (teacher), Roy Day (in window), John Reese, Ed Day, Willie Dunn, Jabie Hopkins, Namon Selkens (in door), Earl Reynolds, and William Keller; (second row) Nell Ash, Essie Manning, Ora Day, Josephine Stevens, Floy Stevens, Emsley Stevens, Cary Denton, Adele Blackwell, Elsie Love, Lillian Keller, Grace Jameson, Ruby Reynolds, Cora Blackwell, Bird Ash, and Gertrude Blackwell; (third row) Carol Dunn, Floyd Davis, Jimmie Moore, Cecil Hay, Dell Stevens, Carl Southerland, George Southerland, Lester Southerland, George Davis, Corene Southerland, Erma Lee Davis, Mabel Davis, and Harry Stevens. (UCA Archives.)

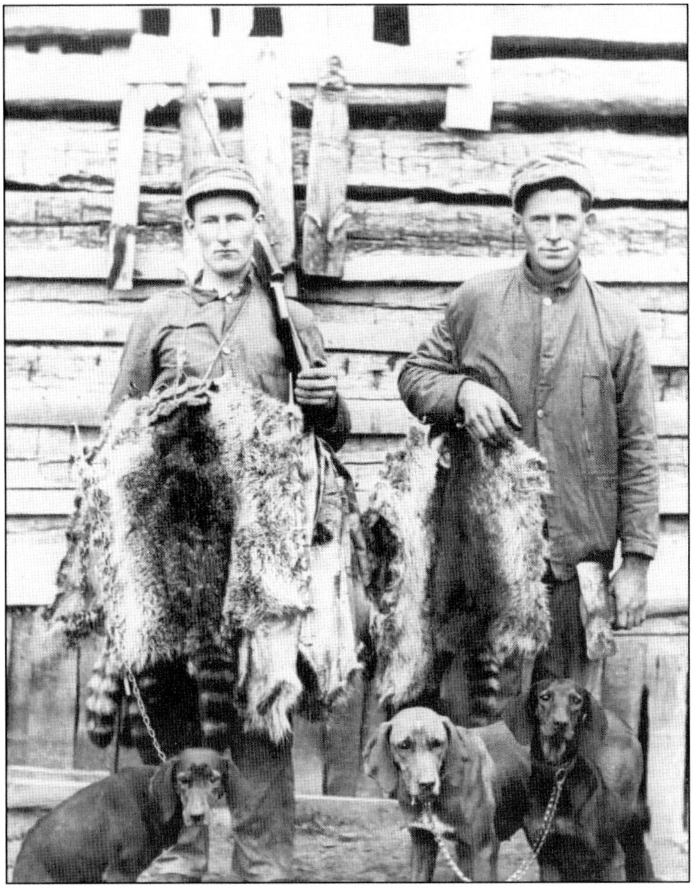

COON HUNT IN FAULKNER COUNTY IN THE EARLY 1920s. L.L. Earnhart (left) and Brad Hogan have more than two dozen pelts. Conway resident Joe Mosby, an official with the Arkansas Game and Fish Commission, said hunters typically used dogs to tree a raccoon and then would shoot the coon out of the tree. If the raccoon lodged in a branch as it fell, the hunter would chop down the tree to recover the animal. This explains why Hogan has a double-bitted axe in his hand. While coon hunting has pretty much disappeared in Faulkner County, it remains popular elsewhere in Arkansas. The photograph was taken by Ben Earnhart. (UCA Archives.)

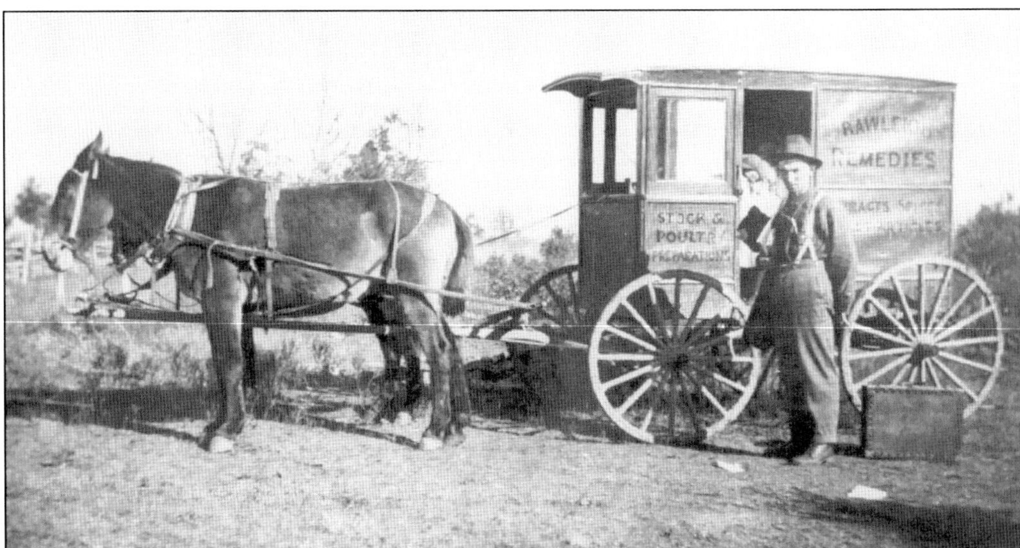

MARVIN E. THOMAS WITH THE RAWLEIGH REMEDIES WAGON IN CONWAY, C. 1920. Thomas ran the service from 1918 until 1922, selling abstracts, spices, toiletries, and general remedies, as well as stock and poultry preparations. (UCA Archives.)

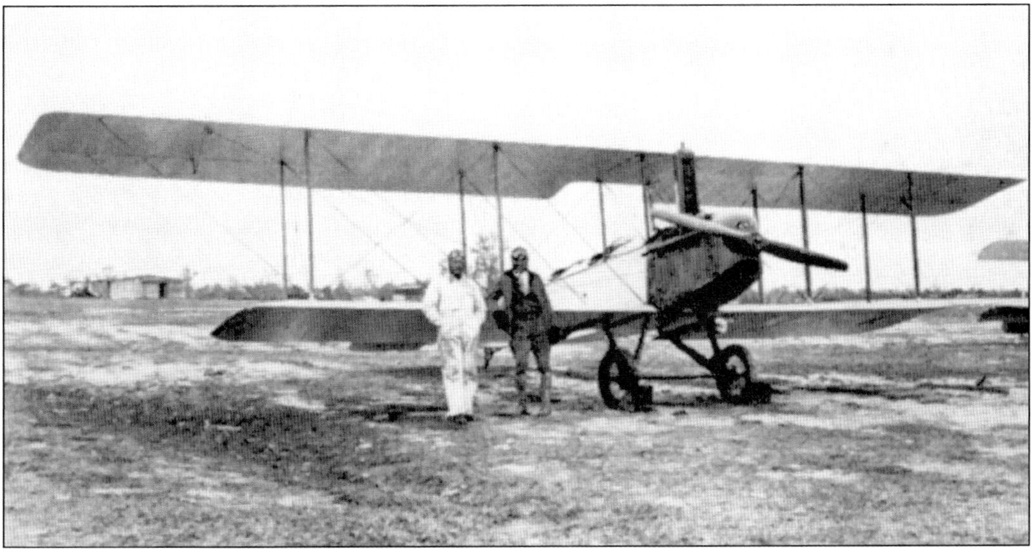

"BUCK" CARTER AND BILL BERRY WITH BIPLANE. This image was photographed on November 11, 1927, in Faulkner County. (UCA Archives.)

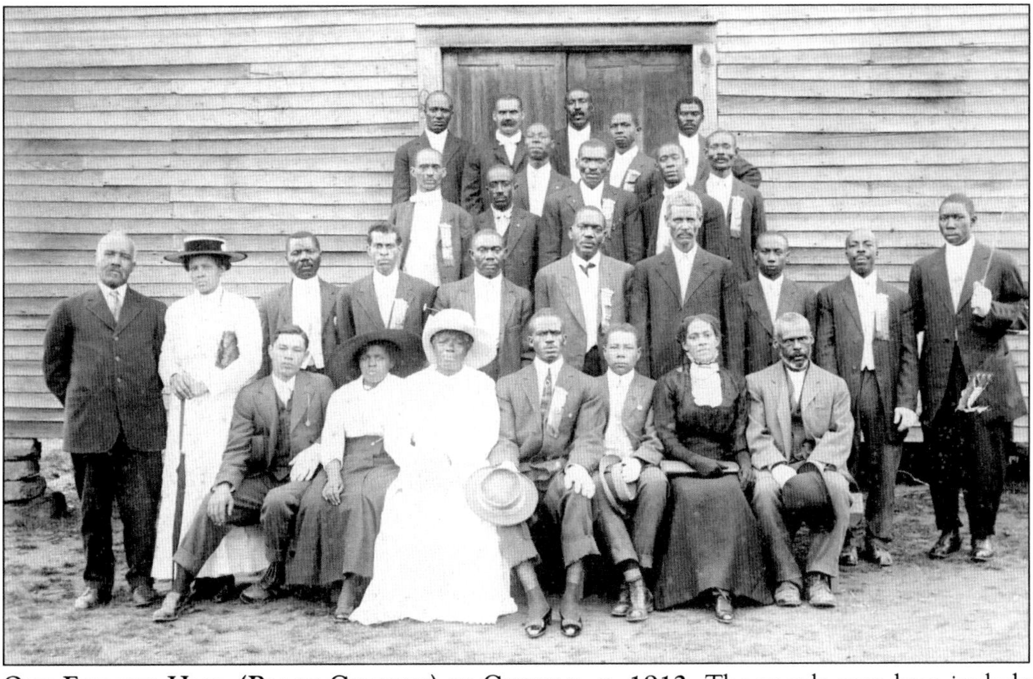

ODD FELLOWS HALL (BLACK CHAPTER) IN CONWAY, C. 1912. The people seen here include Dr. A.C. Mattison, Alex Jones, Columbus Blair, Sam Perry, Ben Stewart, Sherman De Vass, Marshall Burton, Claude Eads, ? Crenshaw, Jim Thompson, Jim Jones, Albert Zynamon, John Dorman, and Willie Spann. (UCA Archives.)

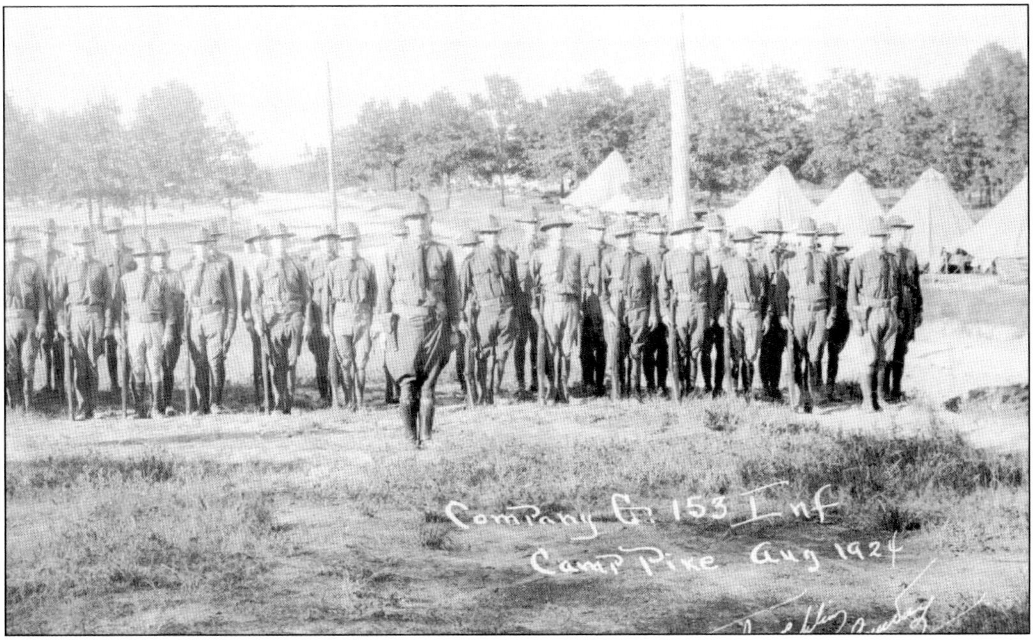

TROOP PORTRAIT, COMPANY G, 153D INFANTRY, AT CAMP PIKE. The right half of a 7-by-18-inch original photograph was taken with a banquet camera in August 1924. UCA Archives.)

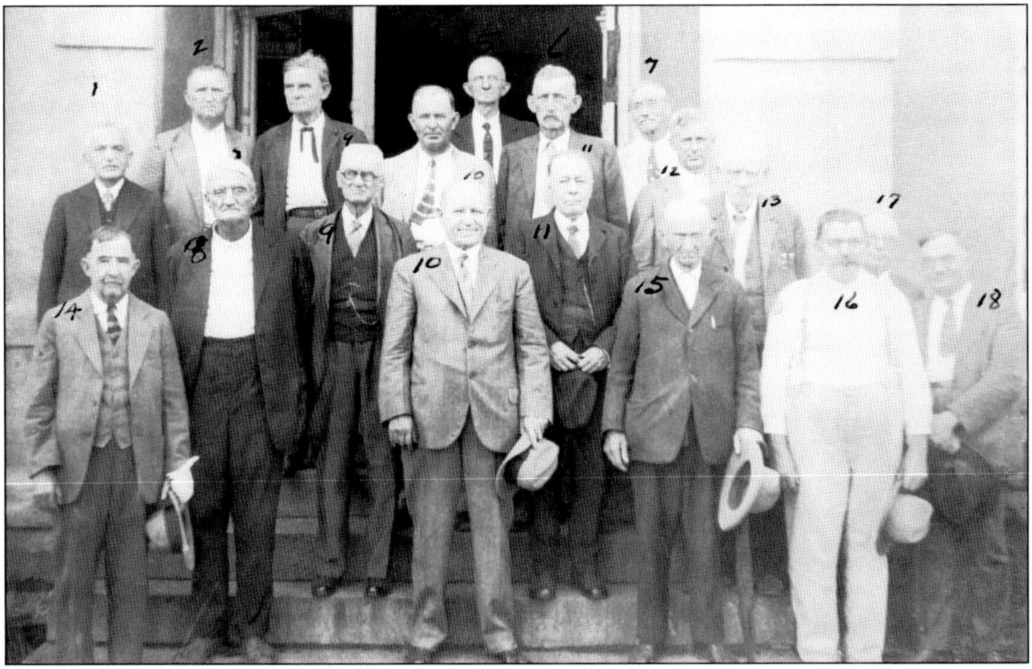

OLD SETTLERS ASSOCIATION IN CONWAY, C. 1928. Pictured are Jo Frauenthal (1), J.D. Mode (2), I.M. Campbell (3), A.M. Ledbetter (4), Ben L. Griffin (5), Tom Flippin (6), W.T. Wilson (7), R.B. McCulloch (8), Dr. G.S. Brown (9), George W. Donaghey (10), J.H. Hartje (11), W.D. Cole (12), Minor Wallace (13), J.D. Collier (14), P.H. Prince (15), W.J. Snow (16), H.B. Ingram (17), and Rev. Alex McPherson (18). (UCA Archives.)

Three

A Time of Change

The year before the Hiegel Lumber Company provided the Arkansas State Teachers College with a new library, a young welder named Dave Ward returned home to Conway from the Oklahoma oil fields to marry Bertha Cazort and open a blacksmithy and welding shop at 900 Hairston Street. Carl Brady, who owned a local trucking company, asked Ward to build a bus on a truck frame in the summer of 1933. The project turned out very well, so Ward borrowed $50 to buy pencils with his name on them. Ward frequently got up before dawn to ride a bus down one road or another to the state line, giving out the pencils.

"People were riding around in death traps in those days," Ward once observed, "and I knew my buses were better." Ward built his first all-steel bus body in 1936 and soon building buses had eclipsed his other work. He discontinued his welding business to devote full time to the Ward Bus Company, which moved into a new building on Harkrider Street in 1939. The expanding business moved to a 200-acre site at the intersections of Highways 286 and 65 in 1953. Ward eventually employed one out of every four factory workers in Faulkner County, and the Ward Bus Company became the largest bus factory west of the Mississippi River. A personable, down-to-earth man known for his hard work and sense of humor, Dave Ward actively gave back to his neighbors as a member of state and local boards and commissions. He turned the business over to his sons Charles and Steve in the mid-1970s. The Ward family eventually sold the company, which is now the American Transportation Corporation (AmTran). Development of the Ward Bus Company heralded the growth of manufacturing as an important component of the county's economy. Much of that industrial development, however, took place in the revitalized economy following World War II. In 1932, as folks struggled through the depths of the Great Depression, Faulkner County only had five industrial plants: Conway Compress Company, Conway Cotton Oil Company, Faulkner Dairy Company, George Reeves Mattress Company, and Nona Lee Dress Company. Dave Ward wouldn't build his first bus for another year, and war clouds wouldn't kick start the moribund national economy until a new decade had dawned.

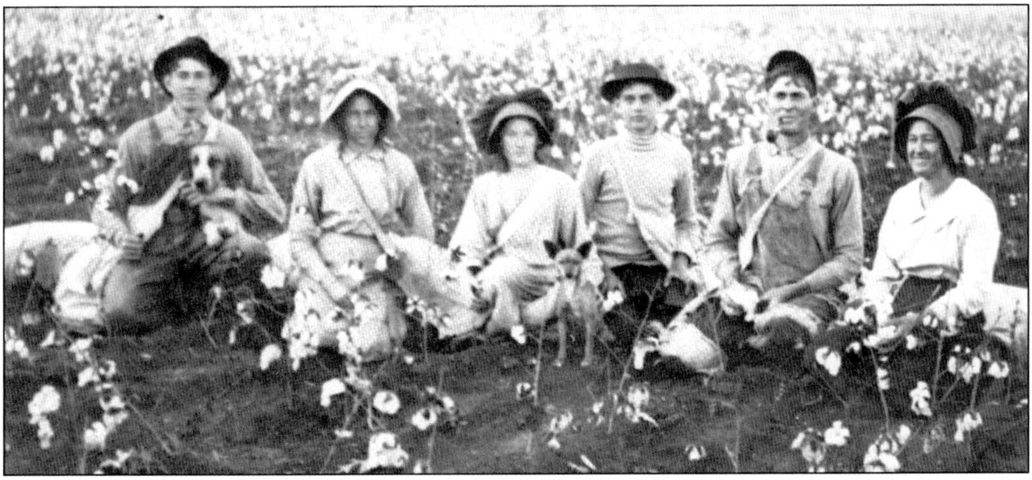

The Frazier Family Picking Cotton in Cypress Valley in 1935. (UCA Archives.)

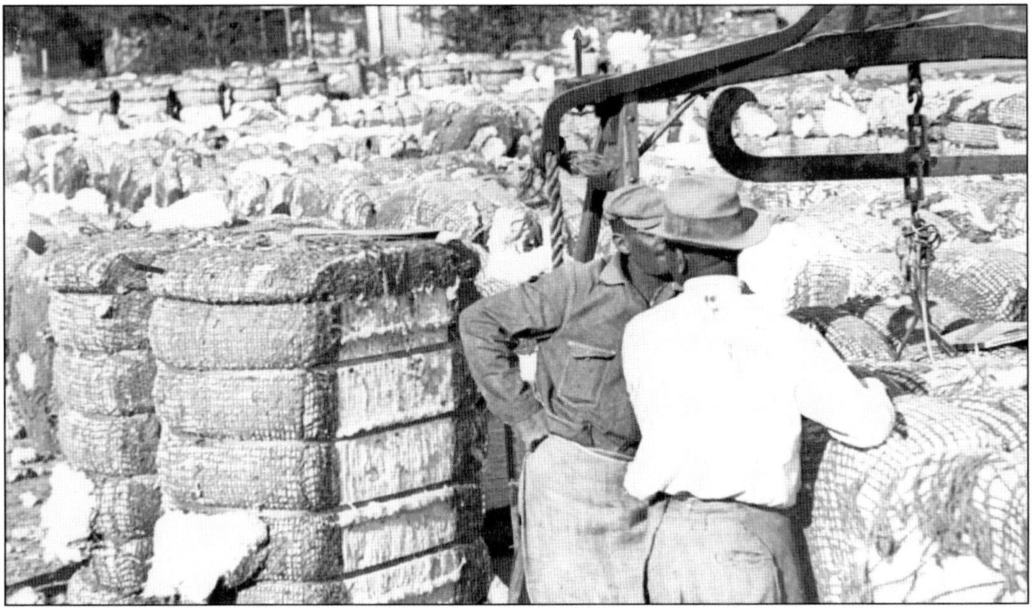

COTTON YARD IN CONWAY, C. 1930. In 1931, the county produced about 39,000 bales of cotton. Production dropped to less than 200 bales in 1976, four years after the last gin went out of business in Faulkner County. Since production averaged 3/4 bale per acre, this meant that only 250 acres of cotton remained in production within the county during 1976. (UCA Archives.)

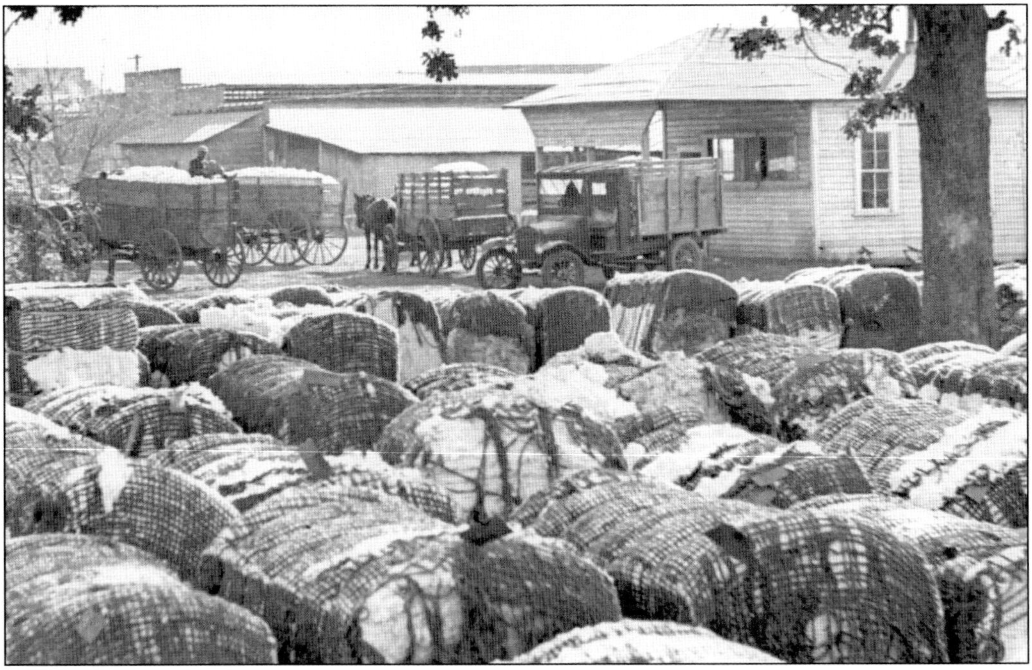

COTTON YARD IN CONWAY, C. 1930. While Faulkner County had 21 cotton gins in 1931, the last gin closed following the 1972 season after processing 925 bales during a single season. The last gin lost money that year, since it needed to process 1,000 bales just to break even. (UCA Archives.)

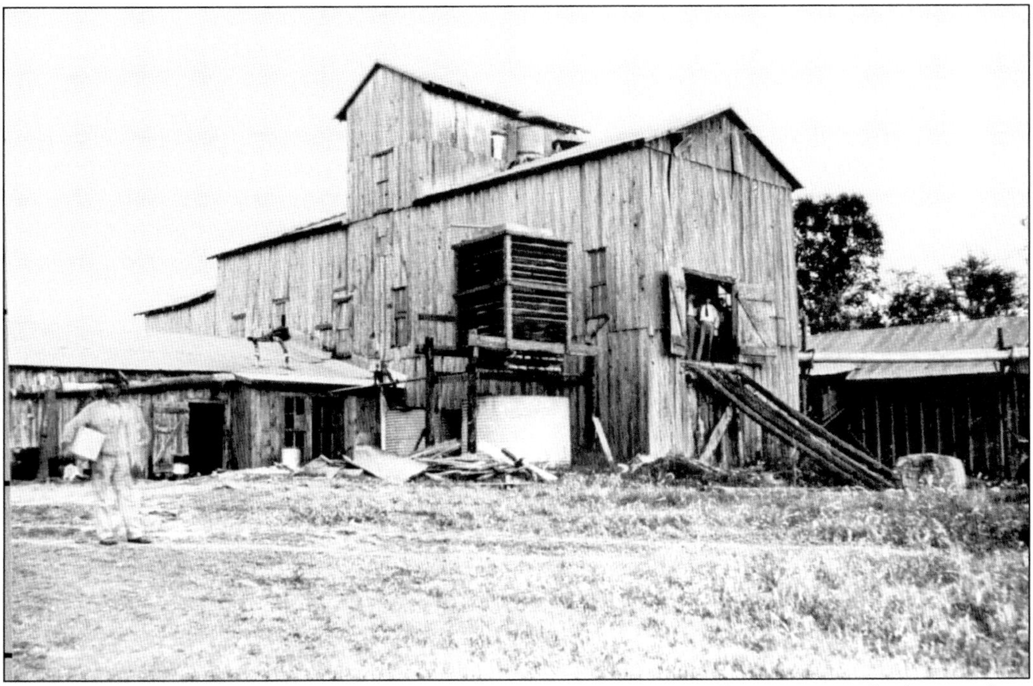

COTTON GIN AT LITTLE PLANTATION NEAR LOLLIE, C. 1930. Faulkner County had more than 20 gins at one time. (UCA Archives.)

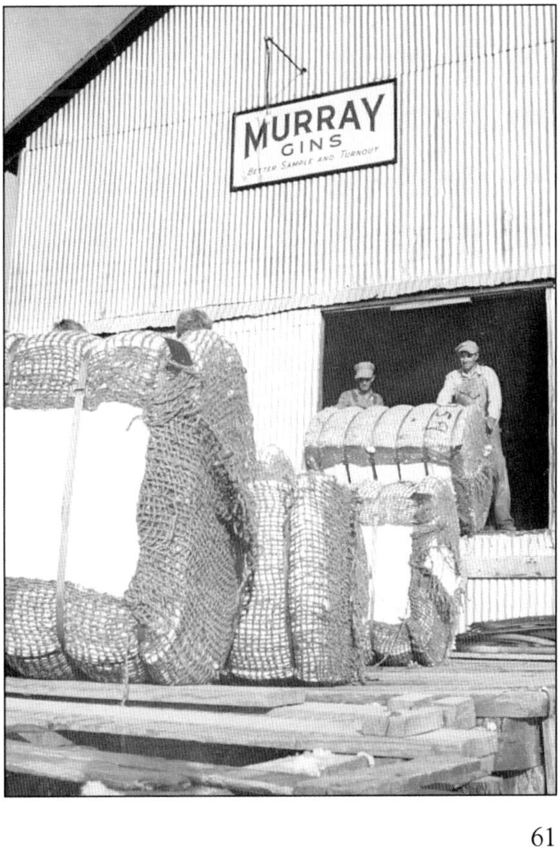

THE ENDERLIN AND SAITER GIN IN CONWAY, C. 1930. (UCA Archives.)

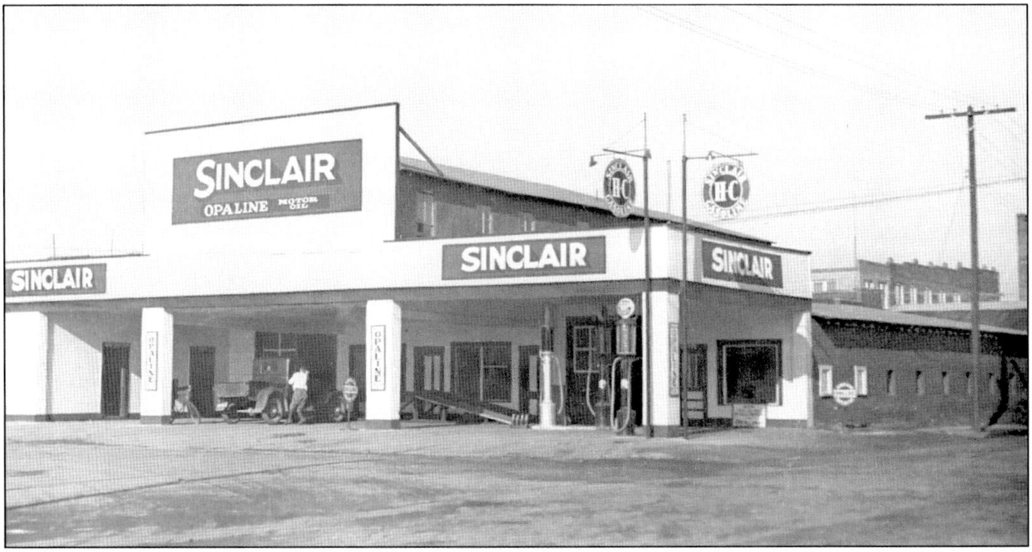

SINCLAIR GAS STATION IN CONWAY, C. 1935. The station was built on the front of the old Springer Wagon Yard, which was built *c.* 1918 at the corner of Spring and Chestnut Streets in Conway. Back when Conway had fewer than 3,000 residents, the town supported at least a dozen wagon yards, which provided shelter for farmers and their teams when hauling crops to market or coming to town for supplies. (UCA Archives.)

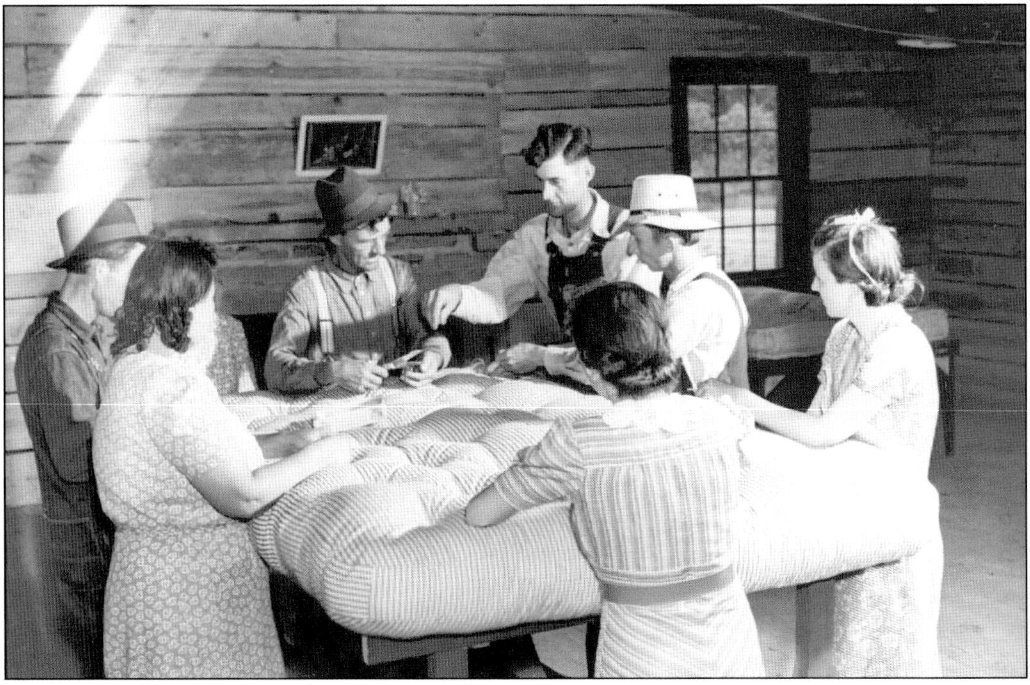

FARMERS AND WIVES TUFTING A MATTRESS IN CENTERVILLE, C. 1940. (Arkansas History Commission.)

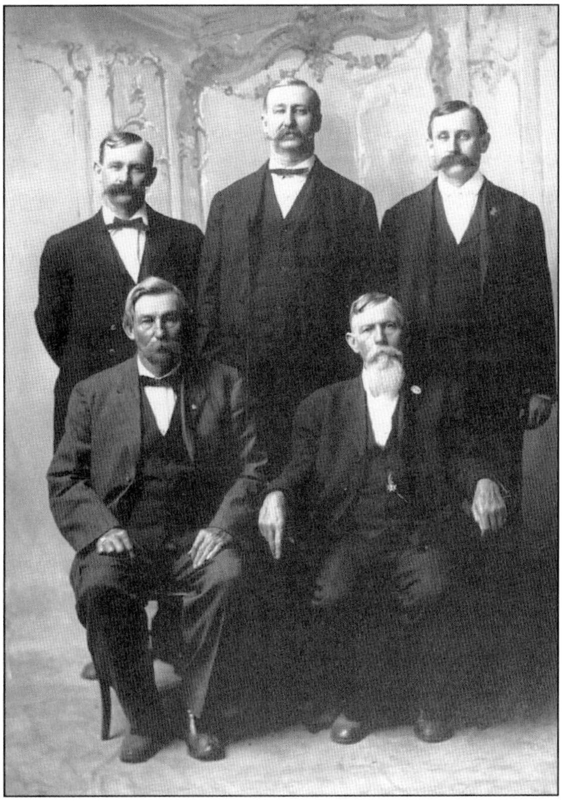

DR. GEORGE DOUGLAS DICKERSON AND SONS OF CONWAY, C. 1930. Seen here, from left to right are as follows: (seated) Dr. Prentiss Dickerson and Dr. George Douglas; (back row) Rod Cephas Dickerson, Arthur Gill Dickerson, and William Haskell Dickerson. Dr. George Douglas Dickerson was born August 5, 1859, and died January 23, 1914. (UCA Archives.)

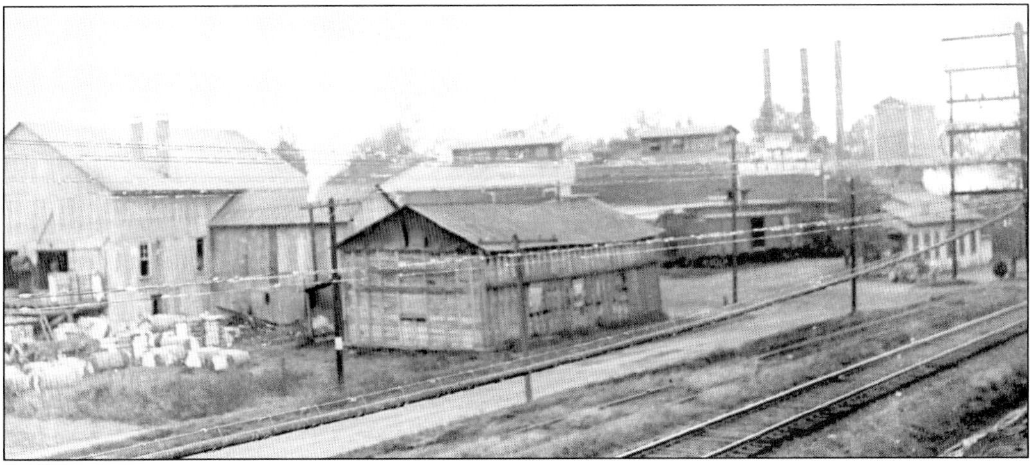

COTTON OIL MILL ON MILL STREET IN CONWAY, C. 1930. The building at the far left is the Bob Adams Gin, which was rebuilt after the original gin burned in 1937. Robert Fulton Adams worked as a teacher and farmer as a young man; he later ran several cotton gins and worked for the county sheriff and collector's office during the "off seasons." (UCA Archives.)

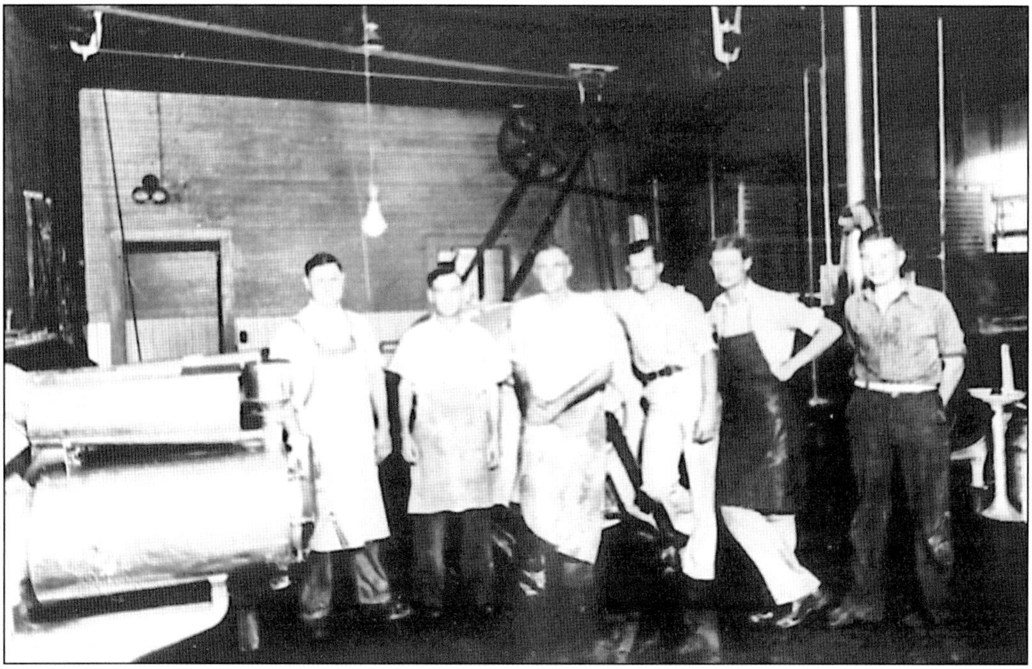

Faulkner Dairy Company Personnel. Shown here is an ice cream machine on the left, a brine tank on the right, and a pasteurizer in the right background. The people seen here, from left to right, are B.H. Hawk, Rector White, R.L. Wilson, Robert Wilson, "Rip" Gooch, and Russell Johnson. (UCA Archives.)

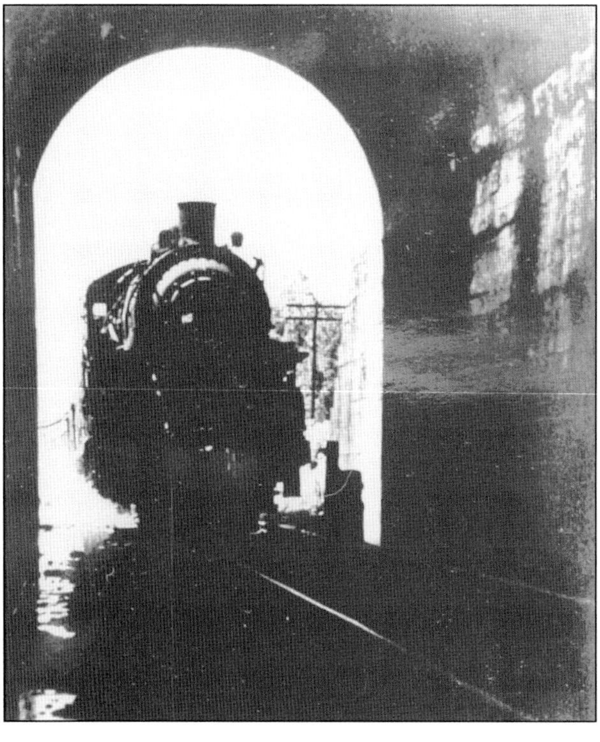

The Locomotive *Southerner*. Photographed by R.B. Clark during the summer of 1931, the *Southerner* can be seen entering the tunnel, just before its stop in Conway. Clark used a tripod-mounted camera, which was tripped by a remote-control cable, while Clark remained outside of the tunnel. (UCA Archives.)

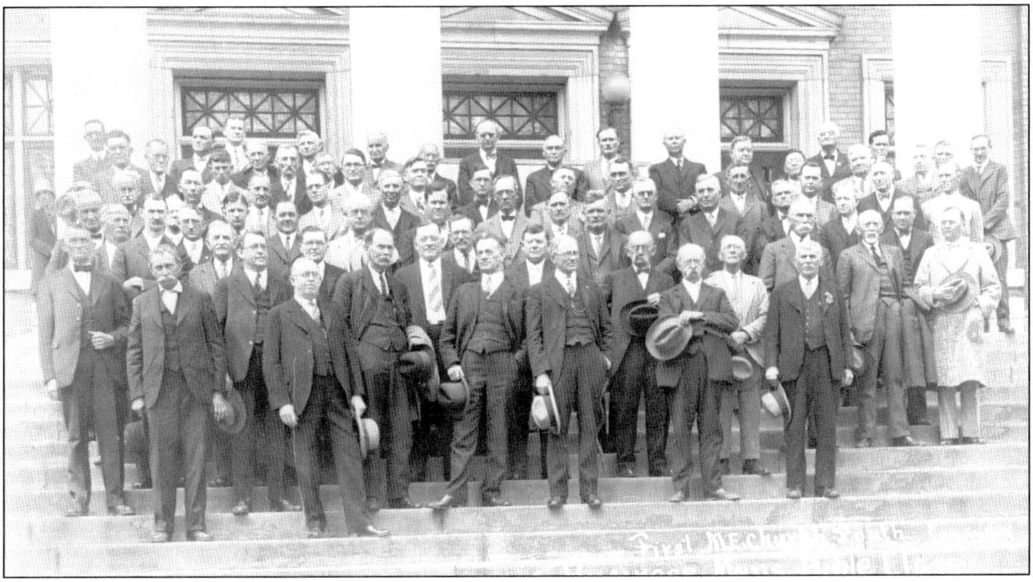

Methodist Businessmen's Bible Class in Conway, First M.E. Church South, Date Unknown. This group includes president C.A. Holland, instructor C.C. Denney, and secretary J.W. James. (UCA Archives.)

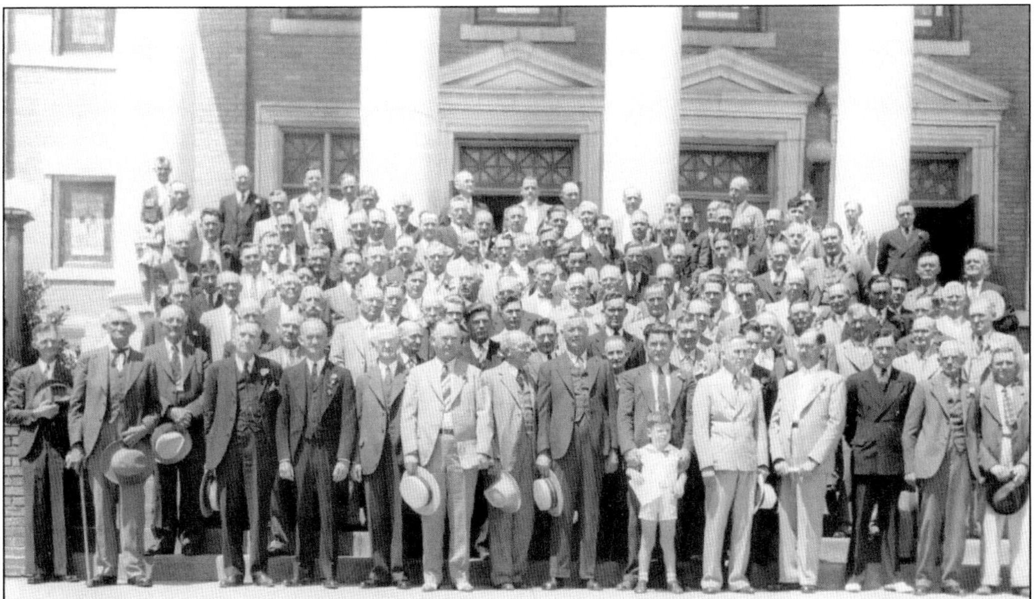

Methodist Businessmen's Bible Class in Conway, c. 1935. (UCA Archives.)

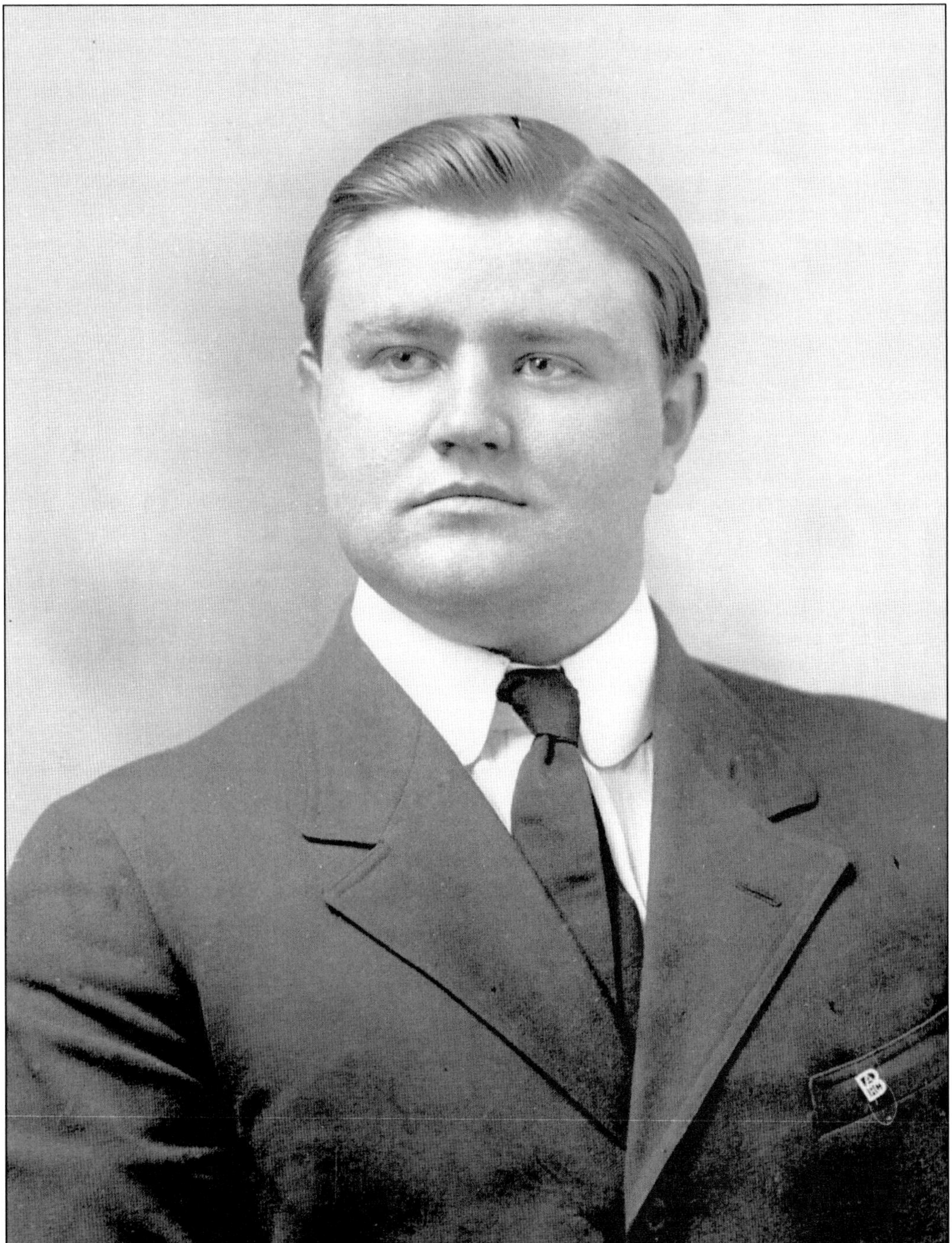

BEVERLY PAUL CLAYTON, 1895–1961. Clayton is shown here as a senior at Hendrix College, *c.* 1914. His parents, William B. and Carrie J. Clayton, were pioneer residents of Faulkner County. He earned a bachelor's degree from Hendrix College and a master's in history from the University of Chicago. He taught at the old Central College in Conway for several years until serving with the army during WW I. Paul then joined Mode & Clayton Wholesale Grocery and eventually became manager. (UCA Archives.)

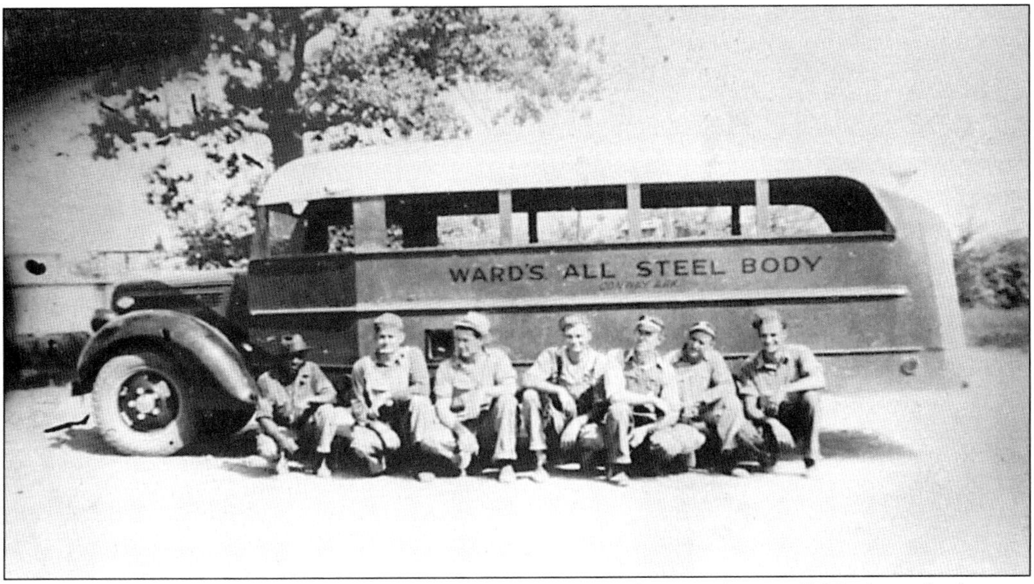

Ward Bus Body Shop and Crew, c. 1936. Dave Ward opened a small blacksmith shop in the fall of 1933 on Hairston Street. He sold his first bus to the Hermitage School District at Warren. In 1936, he made his first all-steel bus and discontinued all other types of blacksmith work. In 1939, he built the structure subsequently occupied by Baldwin Piano Company on Harkrider Street. This photograph was probably taken in 1936 and may show the first all-steel bus. Most of Ward's photographs and momentos of those early days were destroyed when the Ward home burned in December 1950. This snapshot barely escaped, as shown by the charred corner. Dave Ward is third from the left. (UCA Archives.)

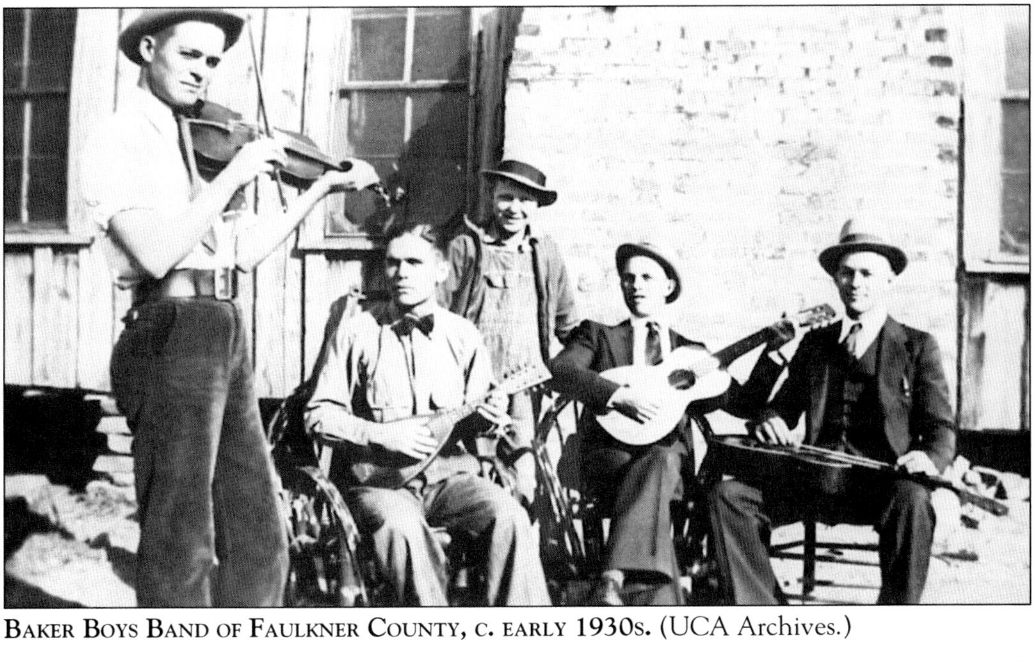

Baker Boys Band of Faulkner County, c. early 1930s. (UCA Archives.)

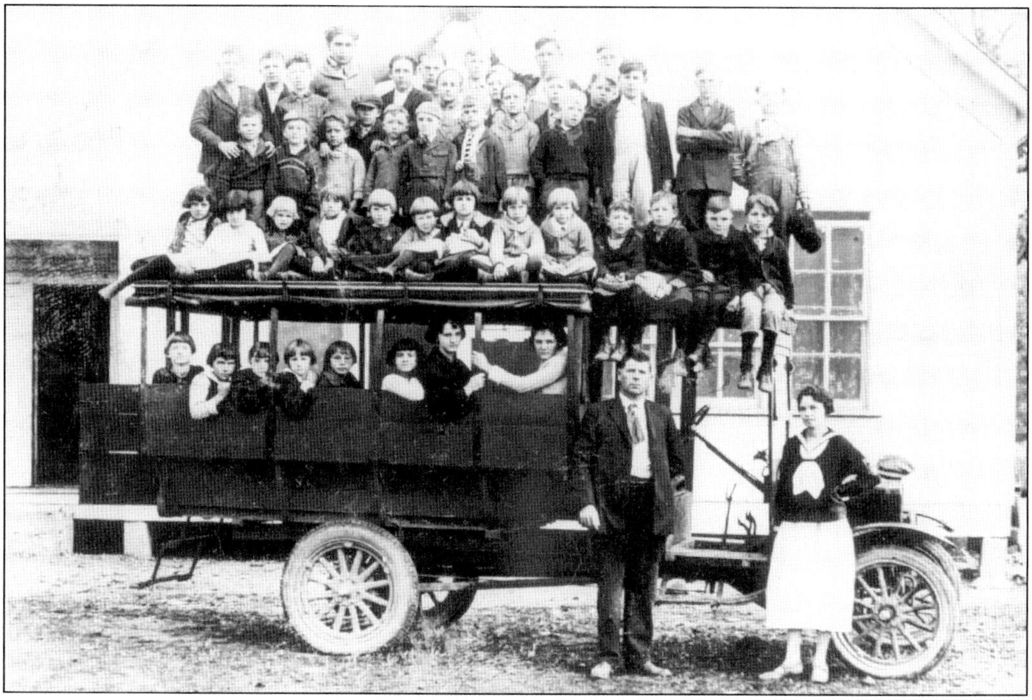

The First School Bus in Hempstead County. The converted Model-T Ford is open for the driver and has no sides for the riders. When the bus went uphill, the kids sometimes had to get off and push. It was anemic and unsafe buses such as this that Dave Ward wanted to replace with robust, steel-bodied buses of his design. This photograph was taken at Piney Grove. (Southwest Arkansas Regional Archives.)

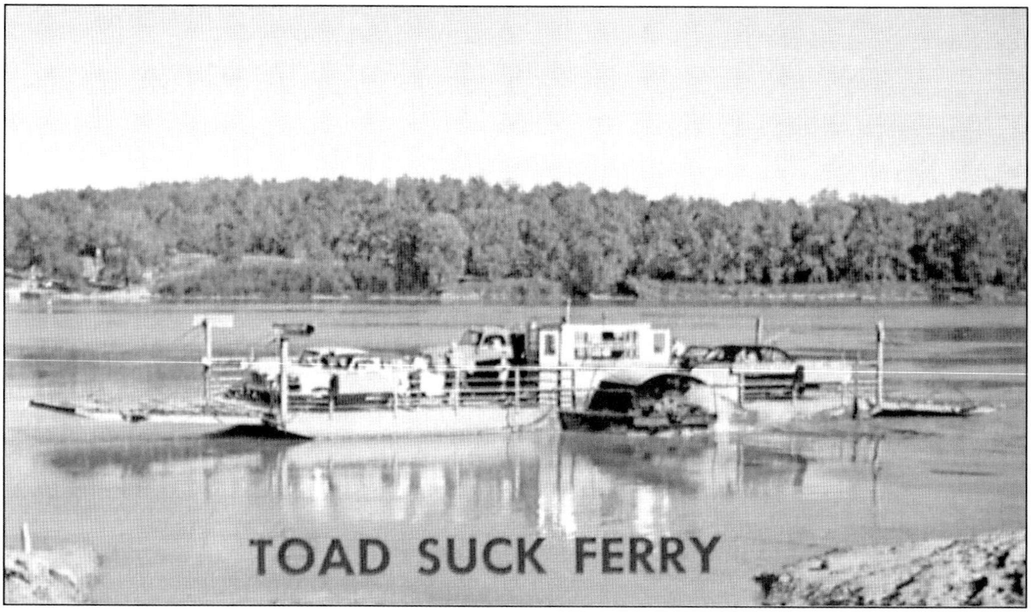

Toad Suck Ferry. The ferry provided service where Arkansas Highway 60 crossed the Arkansas River, about 6 miles west of Conway. The ferry was first established about the time of the Civil War. (UCA Archives.)

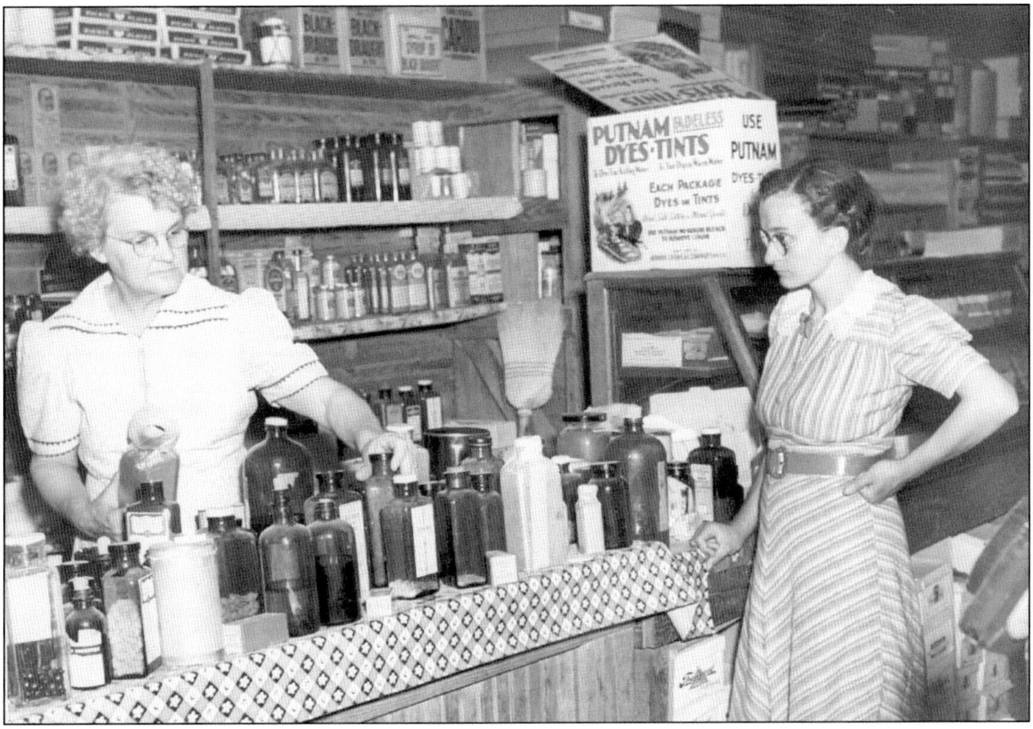

A Faulkner County Doctor's Office. Medicine is being sold in this May 1940 photograph. (Arkansas History Commission.)

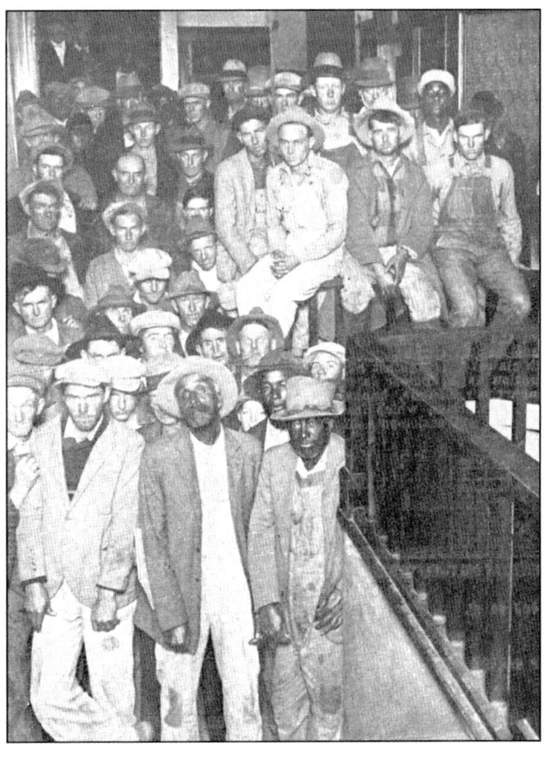

Farmers Seeking "Farm Relief" at the Red Cross in Conway During the Great Depression. While these farmers were devastated by drought and in need of bread, the Federal Farm Board was appealing to farmers in other parts of the country to actually produce less wheat. While there was a surplus of wheat in Kansas, people were going hungry in Faulkner County. (Arkansas History Commission.)

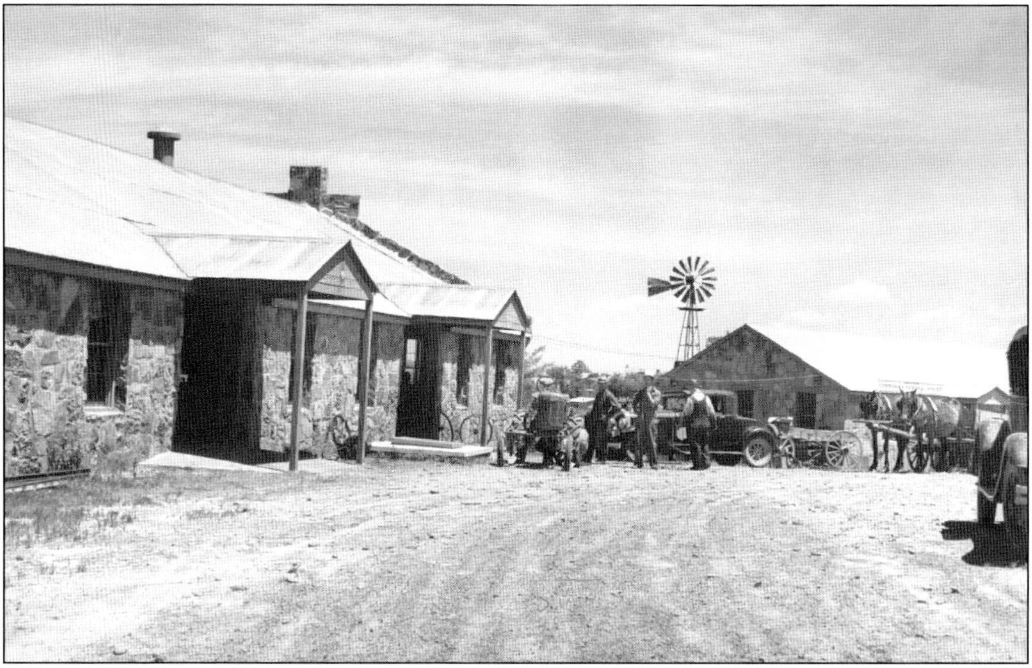

Farmers Bringing Equipment to Centerville for Repair. The Community Service Center is the building on the right by the windmill. (Arkansas History Commission.)

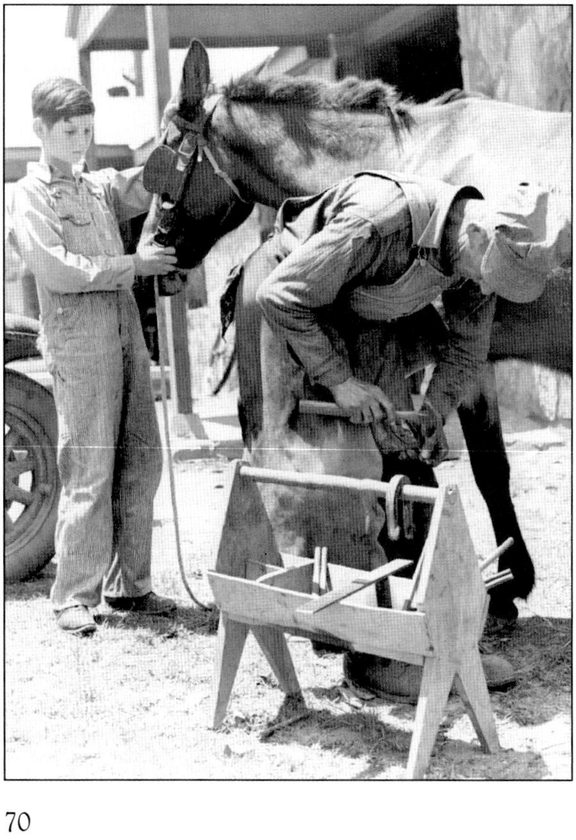

Shoeing a Mule at the Blacksmithy in Centerville, c. 1940. (Arkansas History Commission.)

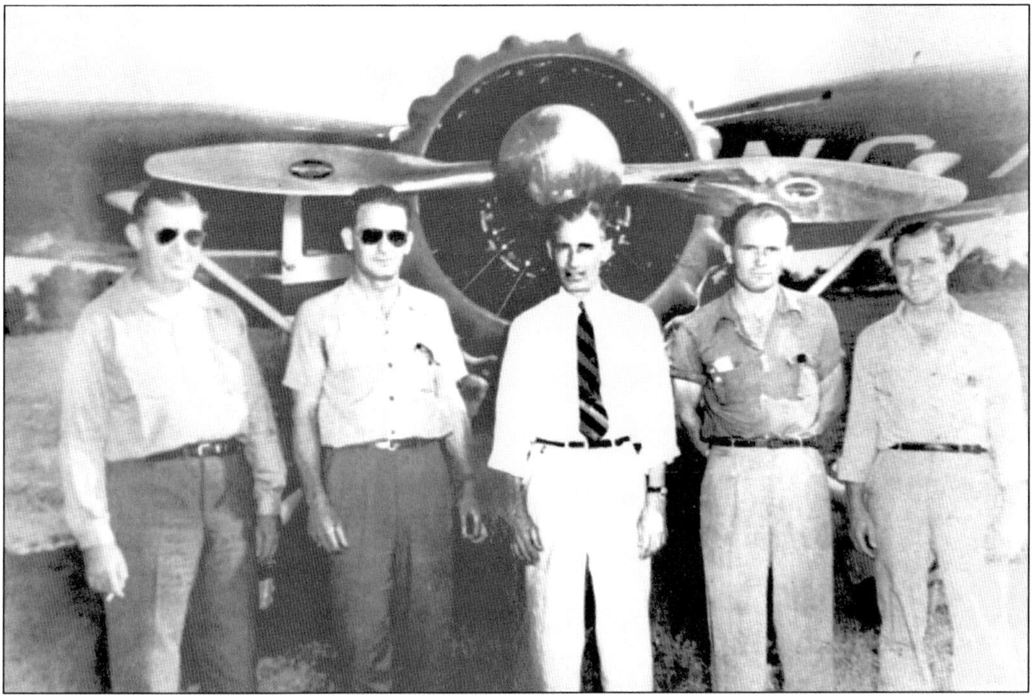

Aviation Training in Conway, c. 1940. Seen here, from left to right, are William M. Berry, Buck Carter, S. Theodore Smith, Dennis Cantrell, and Kenneth Starnes. Berry and Smith established a partnership to purchase Conway's first airplane, a small American Eagle biplane that was manufactured in Little Rock. Cantrell and Starnes were key figures in the War Department's Civil Pilot Training Program in Conway during WW II. Carter was the private pilot of Col. T.H. Barton and the flight instructor who trained Berry in 1924. (UCA Archives.)

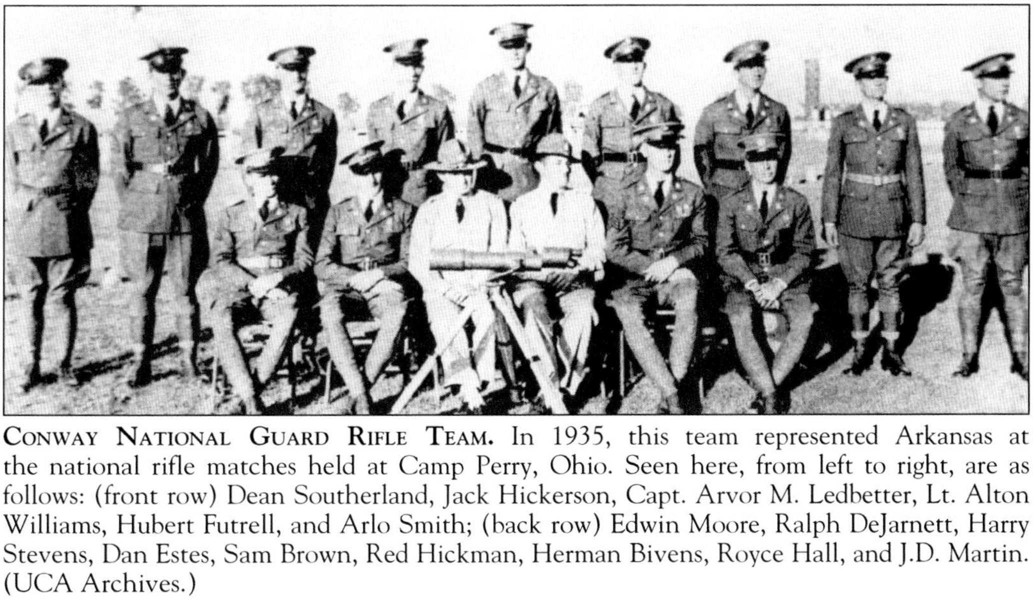

Conway National Guard Rifle Team. In 1935, this team represented Arkansas at the national rifle matches held at Camp Perry, Ohio. Seen here, from left to right, are as follows: (front row) Dean Southerland, Jack Hickerson, Capt. Arvor M. Ledbetter, Lt. Alton Williams, Hubert Futrell, and Arlo Smith; (back row) Edwin Moore, Ralph DeJarnett, Harry Stevens, Dan Estes, Sam Brown, Red Hickman, Herman Bivens, Royce Hall, and J.D. Martin. (UCA Archives.)

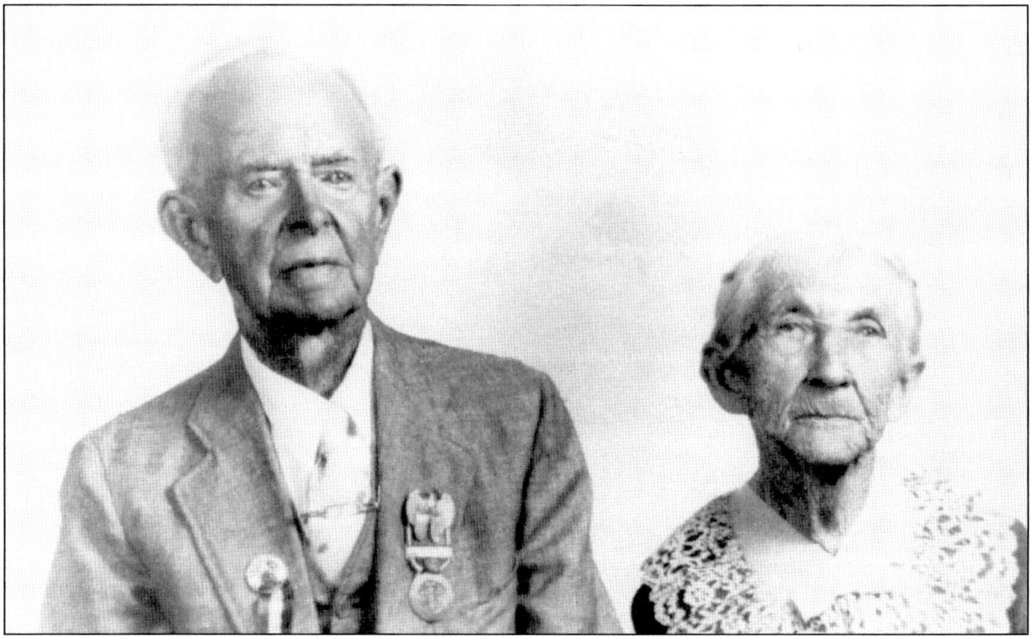

EARLY SETTLERS OF ENOLA, GEORGE WASHINGTON AND ADALINE DALTON, C. 1937. George came to the area with his parents in 1851; he joined the Union army at the age of 15. He returned to Enola after the war, working as a farmer, teacher, ordained minister, and writer. His medals were earned for service during the Civil War. (UCA Archives.)

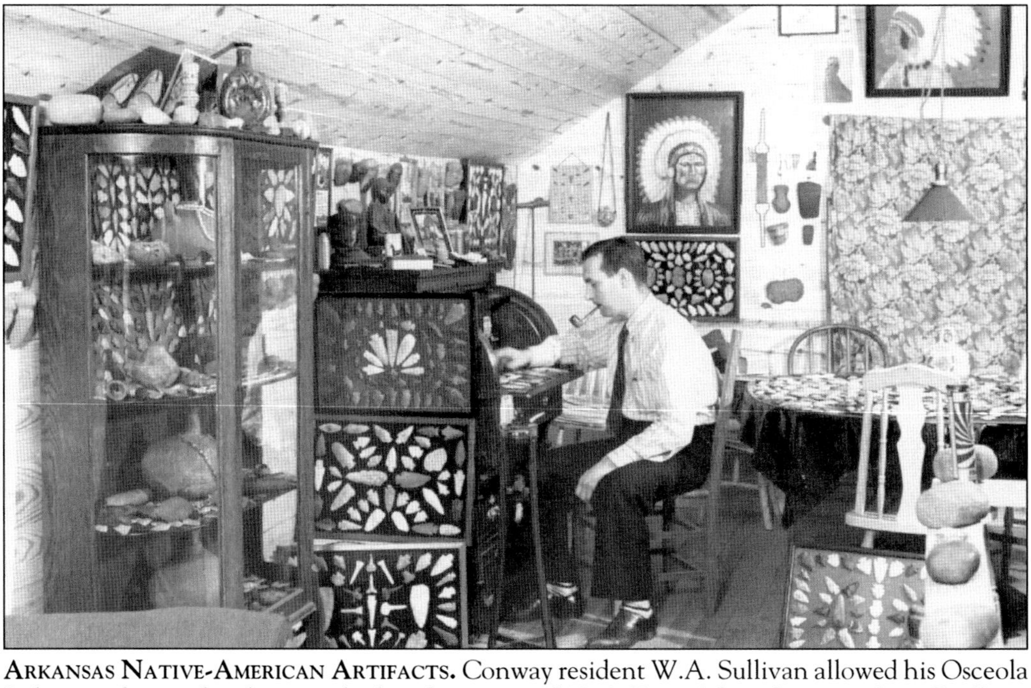

ARKANSAS NATIVE-AMERICAN ARTIFACTS. Conway resident W.A. Sullivan allowed his Osceola Indian artifacts to be photographed in the spring of 1940. Few of the relics were from Faulkner County. (UCA Archives.)

Hendrix College Presidents. Presidents seen here, from left to right,are Stonewall Anderson (1902–1910), Alexander C. Miller (1887–1902), and John Hugh Reynolds (1913–1945). (UCA Archives.)

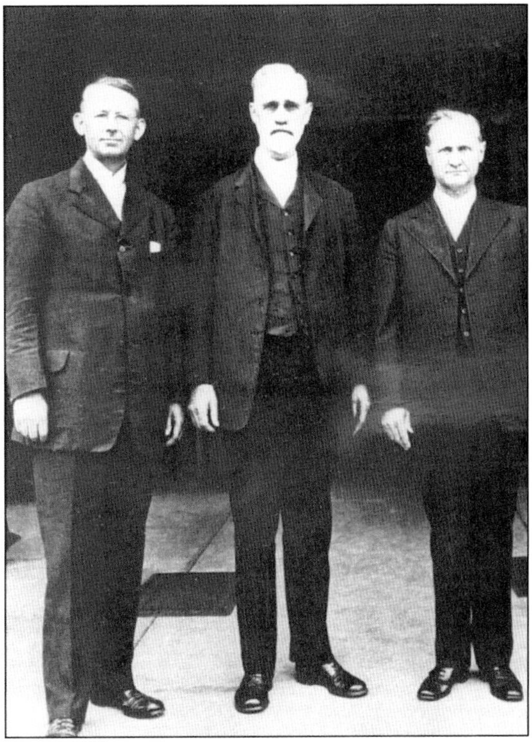

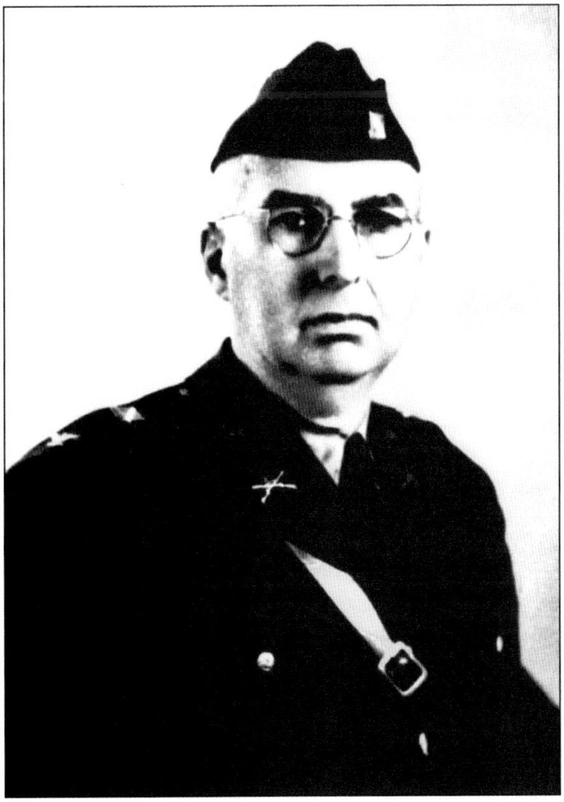

Col. Heber Lowry McAllister, President of Arkansas State Teachers College, c. 1940. (UCA Archives.)

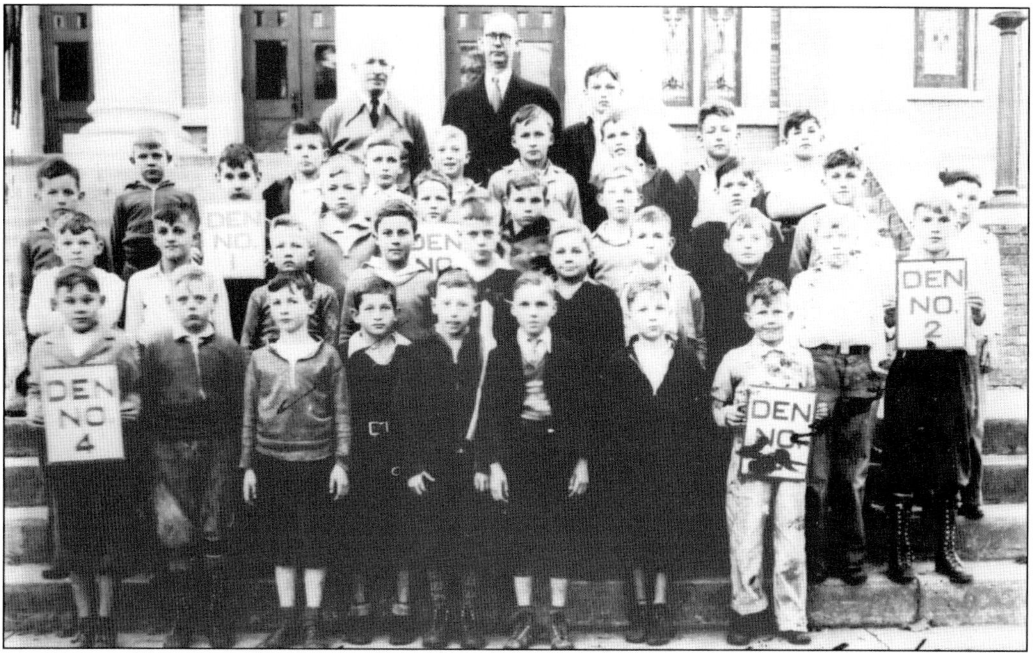

CUB SCOUT DEN NO. 4 IN FRONT OF METHODIST CHURCH IN CONWAY. Scoutmasters T.M. Boyd and G.Y. Short can be seen in this 1935 photograph. Scouting has been a part of life in Faulkner County since 1919. (UCA Archives.)

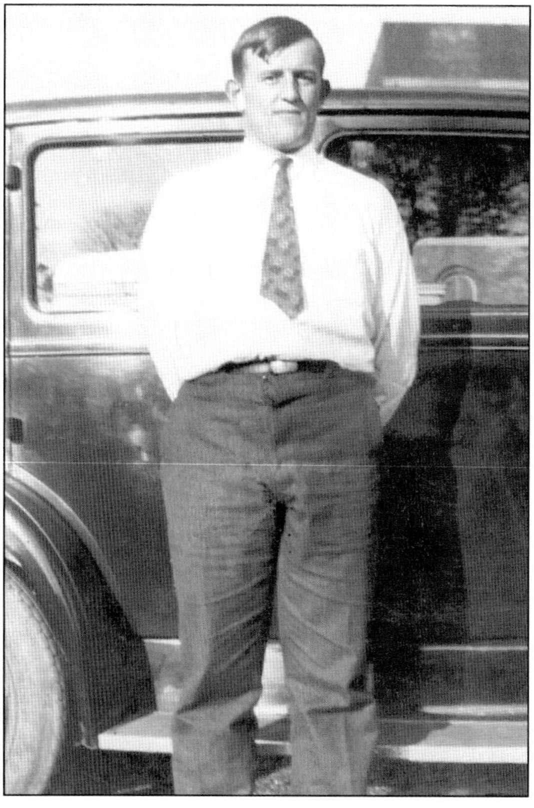

AMOS HOLTER OF CONWAY, C. 1930. (UCA Archives.)

Four

Faulkner County Goes to War

Even as women filled men's jobs in the defense industry during WW II, the military services found they needed women to fill non-combat positions to free up men for the fight. Congress established the Women's Army Auxiliary Corps (WAAC) and authorized opening seven training camps in Texas, Kentucky, and Arkansas. The Arkansas State Teachers College (ASTC) in Conway became one of those camps.

The college faced the challenge of supporting the students already at ASTC, while accommodating 600 WAACs, who would be stationed in Conway. This required a considerable renovation project, such as turning the gymnasium into classrooms, enlarging the dining hall, and providing quarters for the army personnel. WAAC Branch No. 3 opened for business on February 10, 1943. The WAACs ranged in age from 21 to 45; many were already college graduates. WAAC training at ASTC provided the necessary clerical, administrative, military protocol, and stenographic skills to handle the mountain of paperwork needed to keep the army running efficiently. A few WAACs even participated in a mock airborne assault of the airfield at Stuttgart by paratroopers and glider troops. After six weeks of training, the first five classes of WAACs were posted to active duty. Thereafter, the training was lengthened to eight weeks.

The program was such a success that the U.S. War Department requested 600,000 more WAACs, and President Roosevelt elevated the women's status by eliminating the word "Auxiliary" from the organization's name in July 1943.

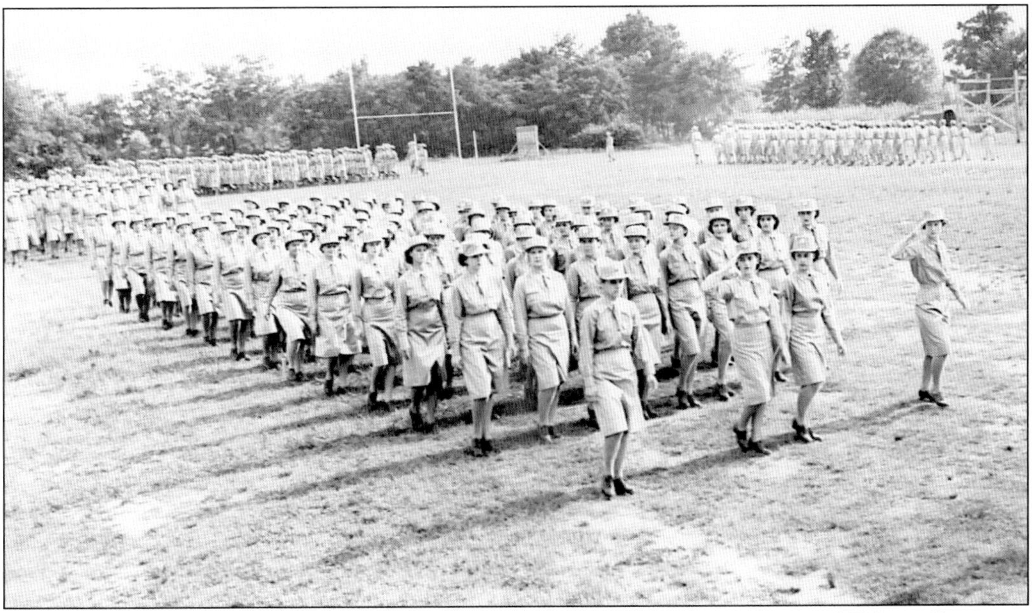

Retreat Parade of Company A Class 4, WAAC Branch No. 3 at ASTC in Conway, May 14, 1943. (UCA Archives.)

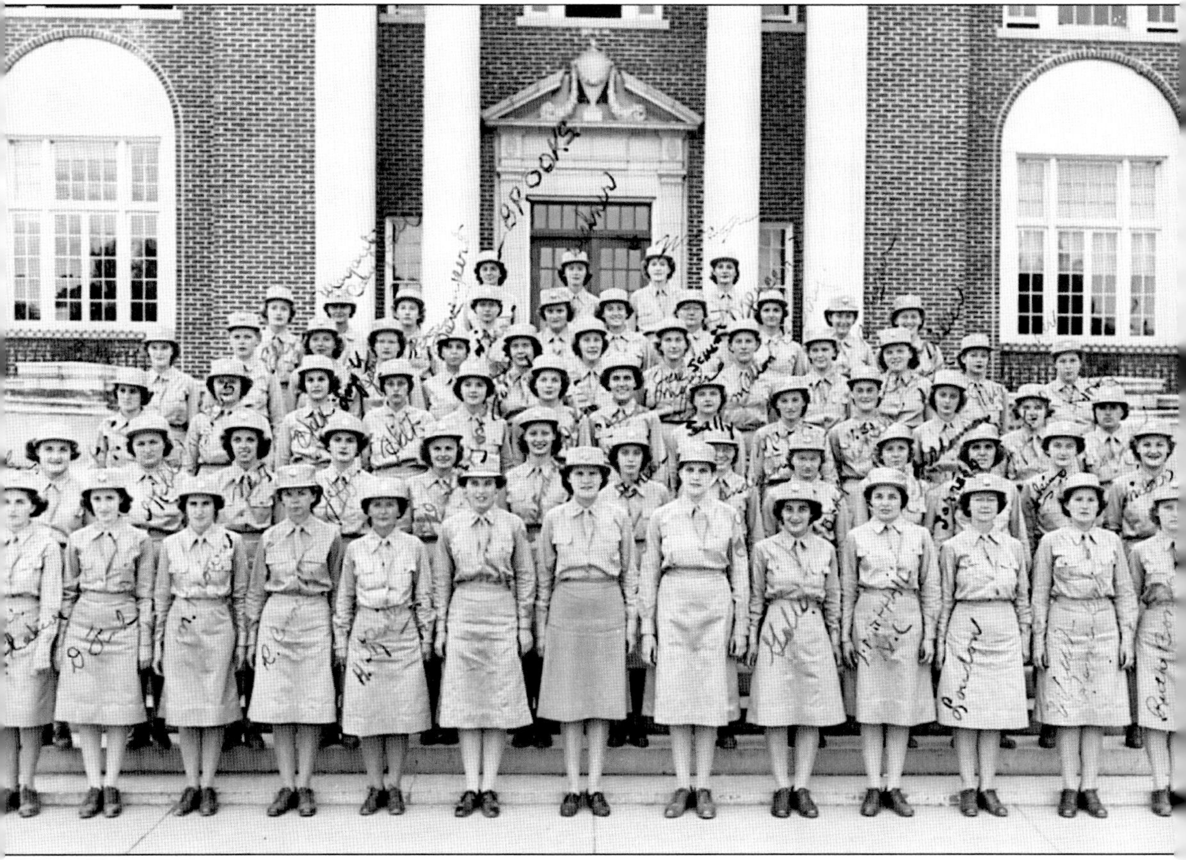

CONWAY WAAC CLASS 6 IN FRONT OF MAIN HALL, JULY 16, 1943. Seen here, from left to right, are as follows: (first row) Private Flahive, Private Fink, Private Brown, Private Connell, Private O'Reilly, Lieutenant Harper, Lieutenant Berger, Staff Sergeant Evans, Private Gallo, Private McPhail, Private Loudon, Private Wills, and Private Boney; (second row) Privates Spedden, Kibler, Nutt, Jeffry, Drew, Woodwell, Erwil, Anderson, Black, Cheek, Johnson, Jenkins, and Miller (Jones); (third row) Privates Newman, Baker, Holt, Hilt, Gosney, Duke, Kinder, Sweatland, Marston, Shumaker, Shannon, Hutsko, and Shoemaker; (fourth row) Privates Muir, Murry, Lazar, Jowers, Davenport, G. Wilson, Lepp, Meyers, Allan, Moore, Buell, Nunamaker, and King; (fifth row) Privates Eden, Campbell, Rogers, M. Wilson, Wythe, Fine, Hines (Schenk), Perry, Rodman, and R. Miller; (sixth row) Privates Brooks, Weshner, Morgan, and Mercer. (UCA Archives.)

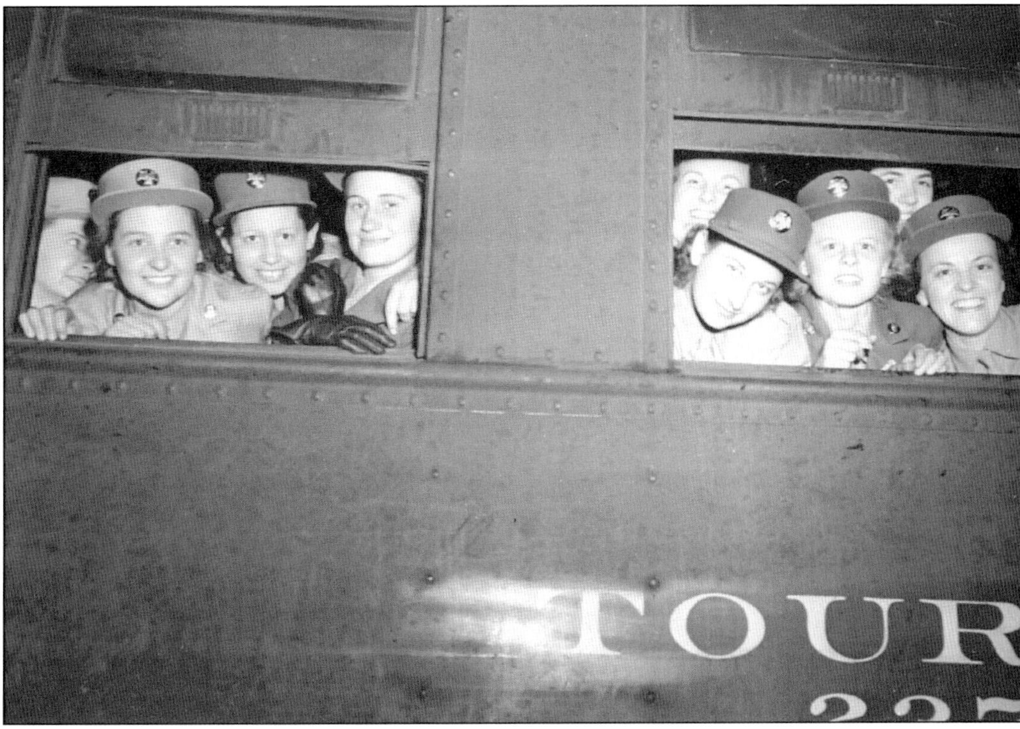

WAAC Trainees Arriving in Conway from Georgia, April 9, 1943. These women would become WAAC Class No. 4. (UCA Archives.)

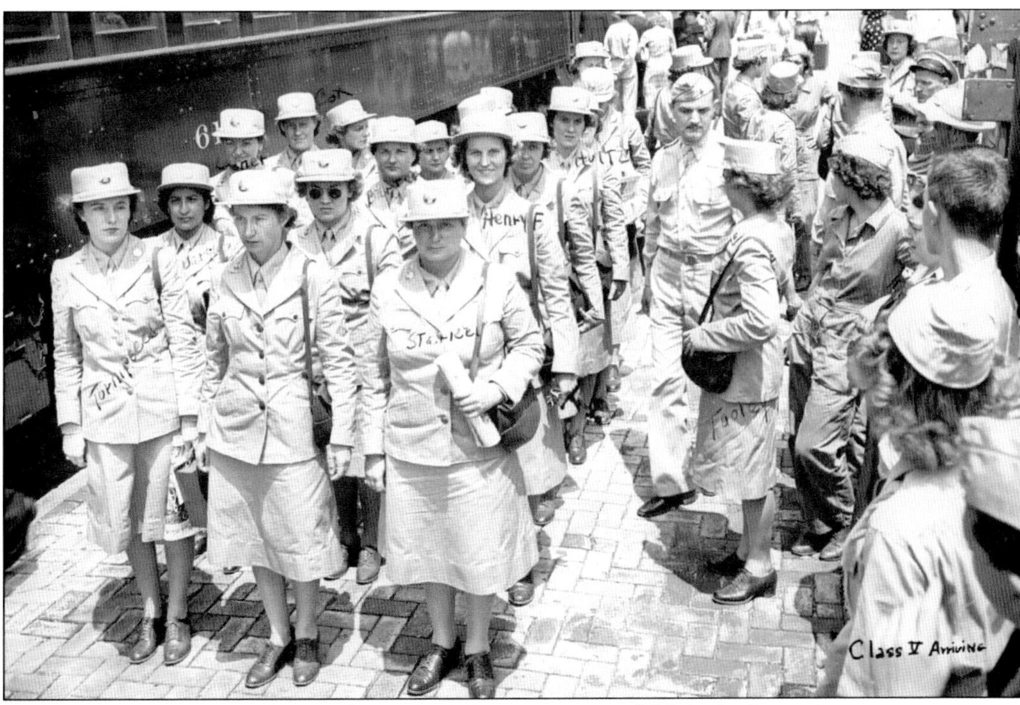

WAAC Class 5 Arriving in Conway, May 27, 1943. (UCA Archives.)

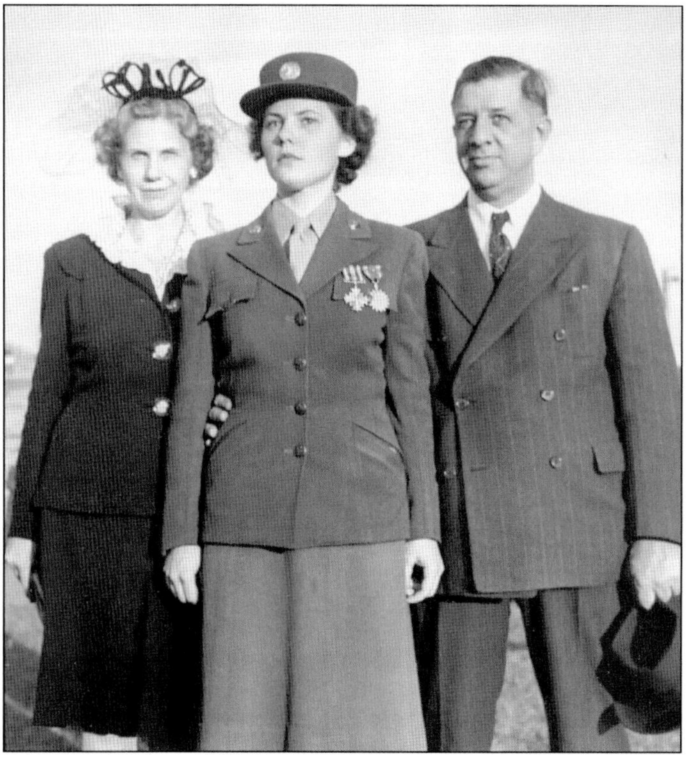

Private in the WAAC, Mrs. Earl Kent. Kent stands with the parents of her husband, who became missing in action during WW II. (UCA Archives.)

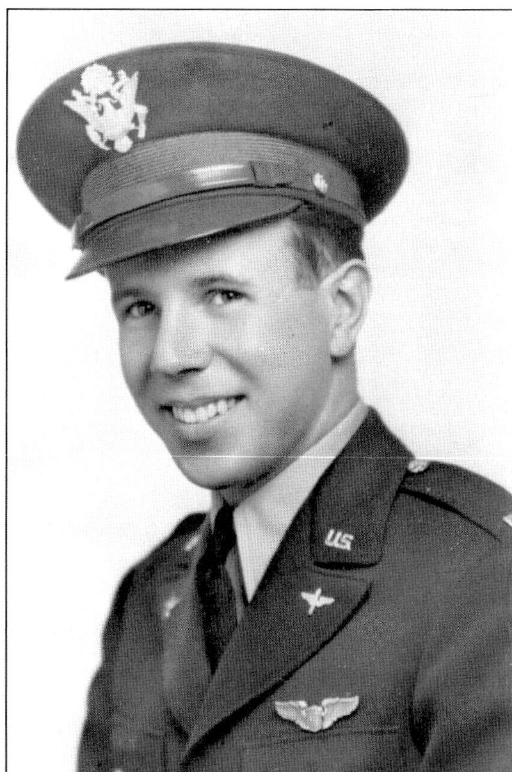

Lt. Earl C. Kent. Kent married a WAAC being trained in Conway; he was later reported missing in action. (UCA Archives.)

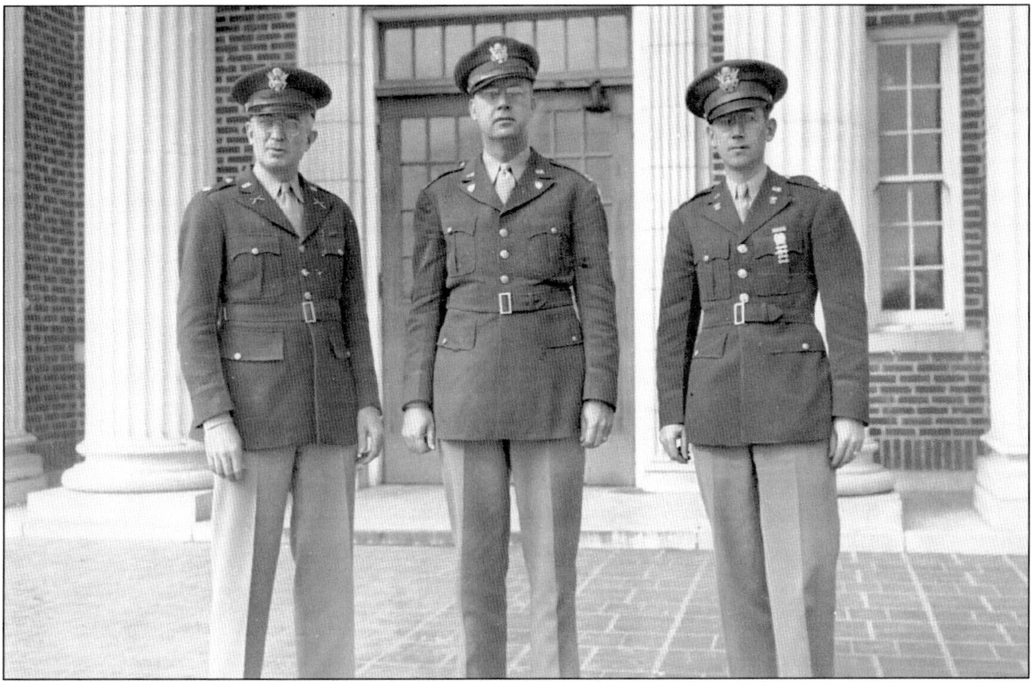

WAAC COMMANDING OFFICER, LT. COL. WILLIARD H. CRAWFORD. Conway's Branch No. 3 supported 19 male staff officers for program administration and 20 instructors, most of whom were female WAAC officers. Capt. Louis W. Jackson was director of training, and Capt. Raymond Brooks was the adjutant. (UCA Archives.)

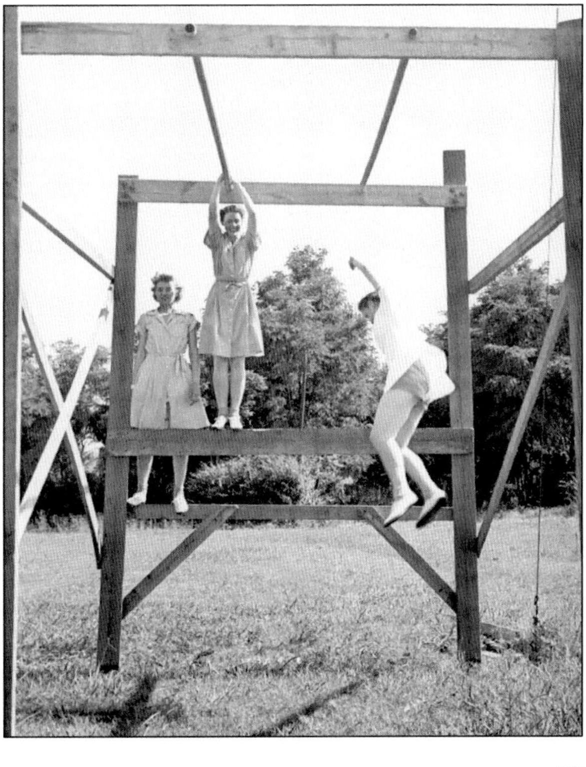

WOMEN UNDERGOING PHYSICAL TRAINING AT WAAC BRANCH NO. 3 IN CONWAY. (UCA Archives.)

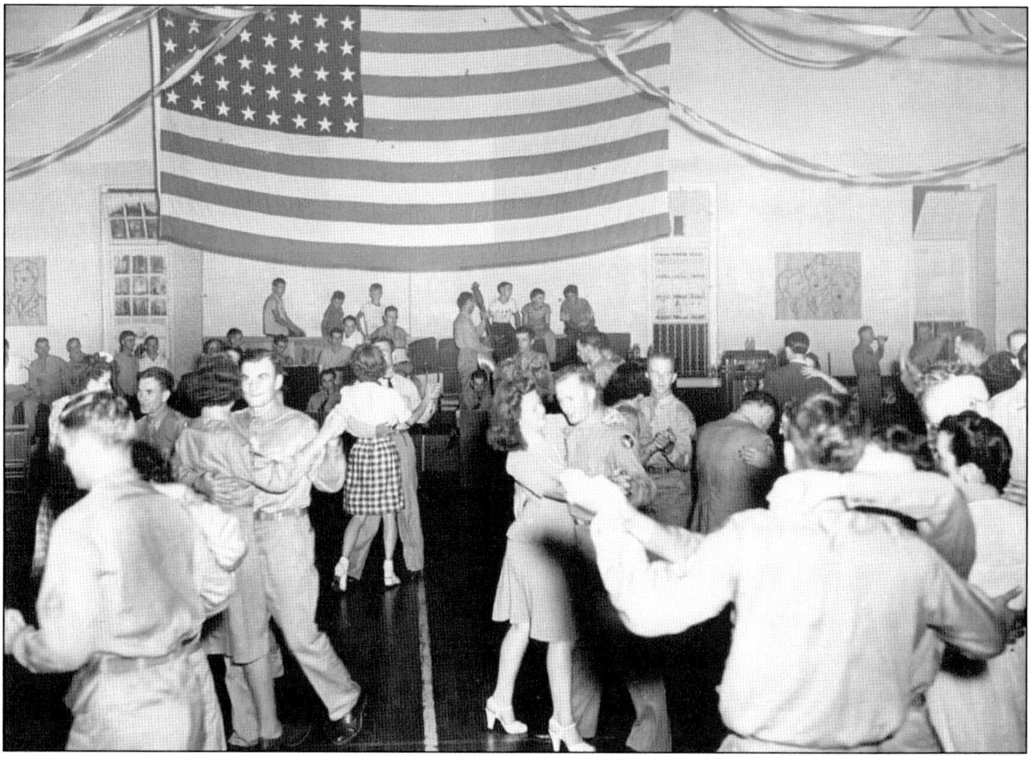

USO DANCE IN CONWAY DURING WW II. (UCA Archives.)

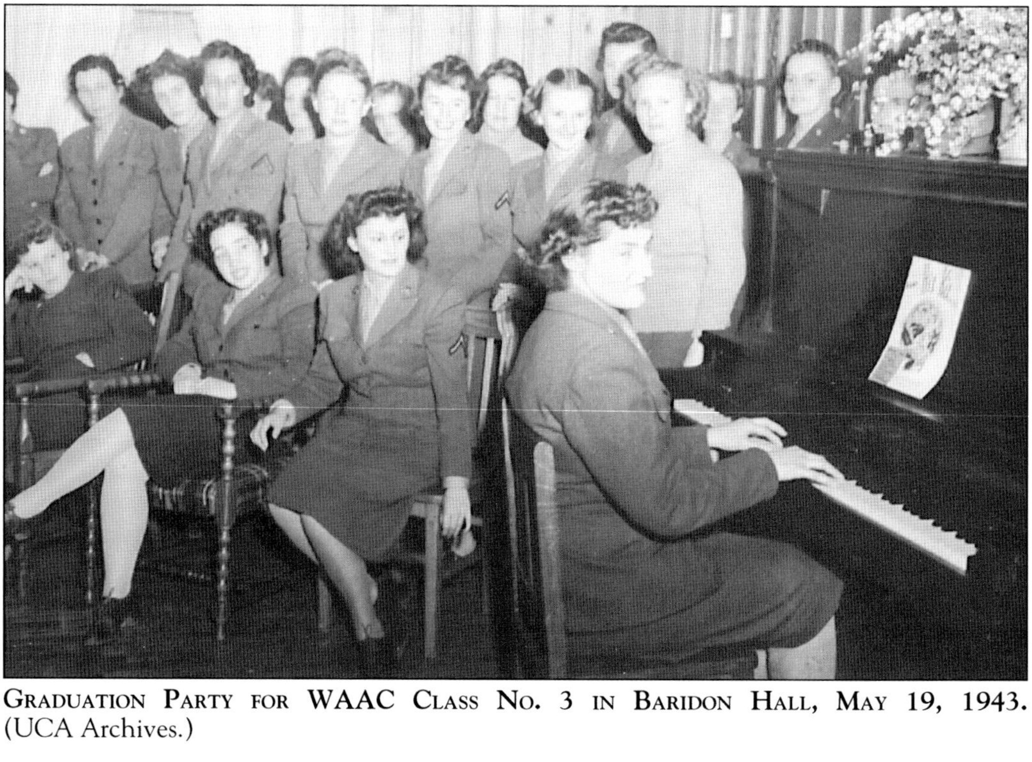

GRADUATION PARTY FOR WAAC CLASS NO. 3 IN BARIDON HALL, MAY 19, 1943. (UCA Archives.)

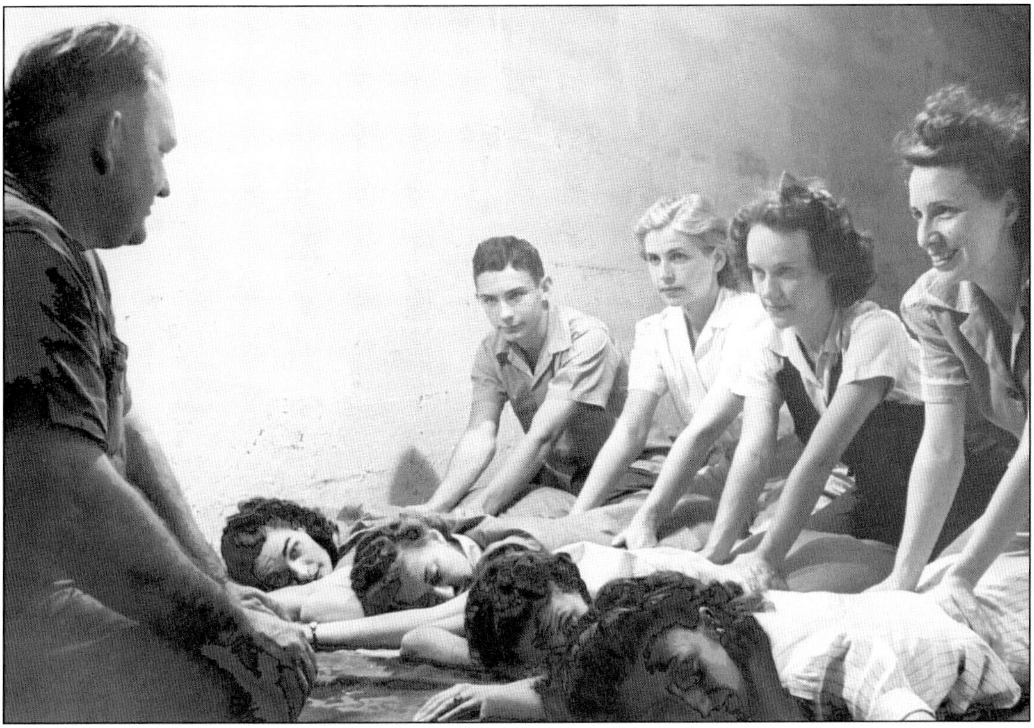

First Aid Class in Conway during WW II. Kelsey Parker (left) is the instructor. Janice Rhode is the farthest one lying down. Shown kneeling, from left to right, are Bob Atkinson, Mrs. Percy Goyne, and Sara Morehead. (UCA Archives.)

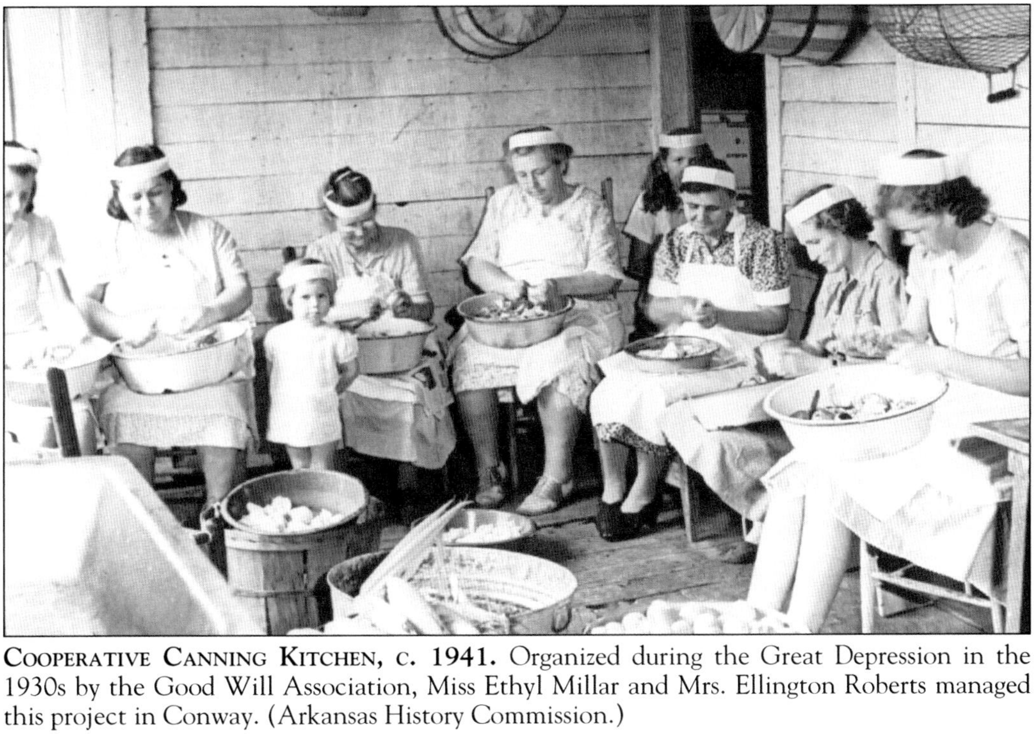

Cooperative Canning Kitchen, c. 1941. Organized during the Great Depression in the 1930s by the Good Will Association, Miss Ethyl Millar and Mrs. Ellington Roberts managed this project in Conway. (Arkansas History Commission.)

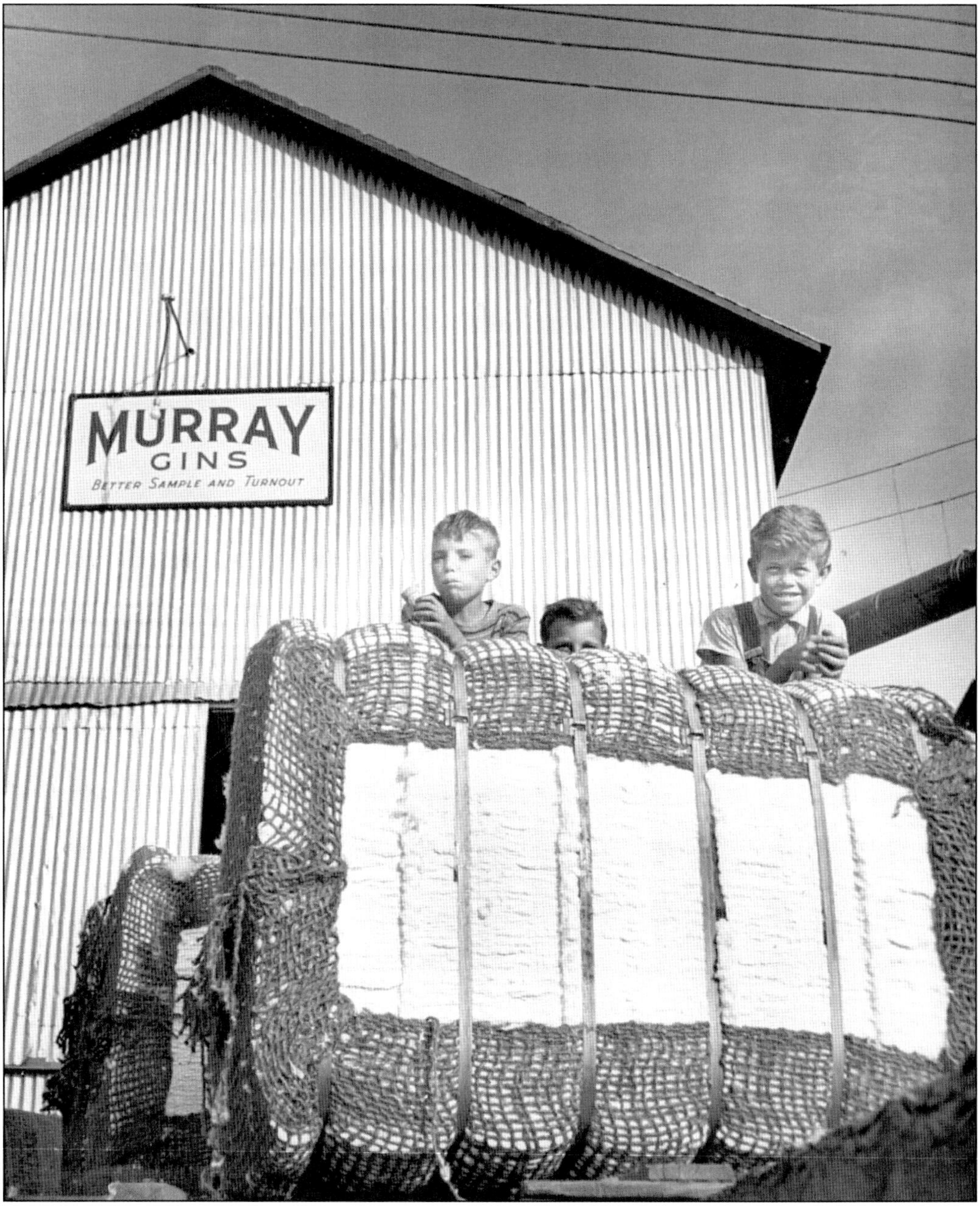

Life Goes On. Although WACs were being trained for war elsewhere in town, boys were still being boys at the Enderlin and Saiter Gin in Conway. Murray Gin is the brand of the equipment. Joseph Saiter is on the far right. (UCA Archives.)

Five

THE FABULOUS FORTIES AND FIFTIES

The success of WACs trained in Faulkner County, combined with the yeoman service provided by women working in factories during the war, helped change the role and expectations of women in American society. The GI Bill, which provided educational grants to war veterans, revolutionized higher education in Faulkner County as well as the rest of the country. The bill enabled unprecedented numbers of people to seek a college education. Furthermore, the bill enabled people from a diverse cross section of American society to participate in the college experience. The resulting democratization of higher education would contribute significantly to the evolution of American culture.

While ASTC and Hendrix prospered thanks to the many veterans taking advantage of the GI Bill, the Central Baptist College for Women began to founder and closed its doors in 1947. About this time, the new Arkansas Missionary Baptist Association (now called the Baptist Missionary Association of Arkansas) purchased the vacant 11-acre campus in Conway and opened for business in 1952. The school expanded by 10 acres, broadened its curriculum, and changed its name to Central Baptist College in 1962.

The people of Faulkner County had survived the Great Depression, nurtured three colleges through difficult times, and helped win a world war. Yet even as a revitalized economy stimulated growing optimism in a brighter future, a new threat emerged to darken the horizon. The two superpowers that emerged from the ashes of war began an ideological battle for supremacy on the world stage. Walter Lippmann popularized the term *Cold War* for this intense rivalry between the United States and the Soviet Union, a rivalry that would see the Faulkner County become the base for intercontinental ballistic missiles armed with nuclear warheads.

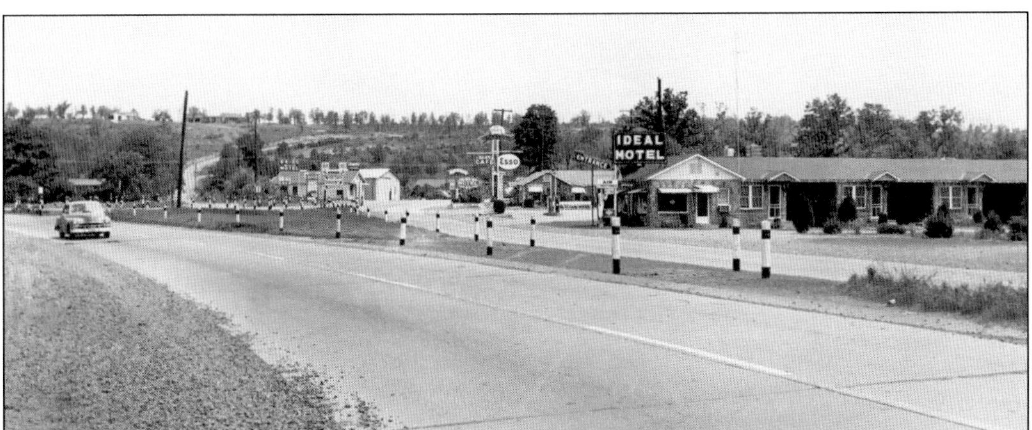

JUNCTION OF HIGHWAYS 64 AND 65 IN CONWAY, C. JULY 1955. (Arkansas History Commission.)

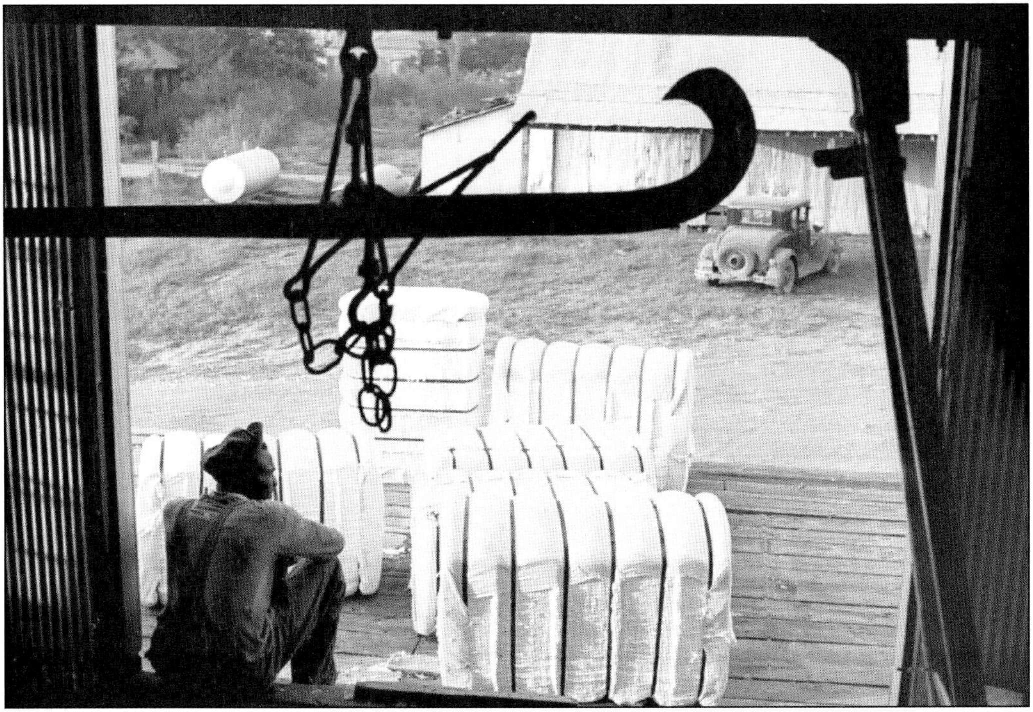

Otis Moore Gin in Conway, c. 1945. Paul Faris photographed this image. (UCA Archives.)

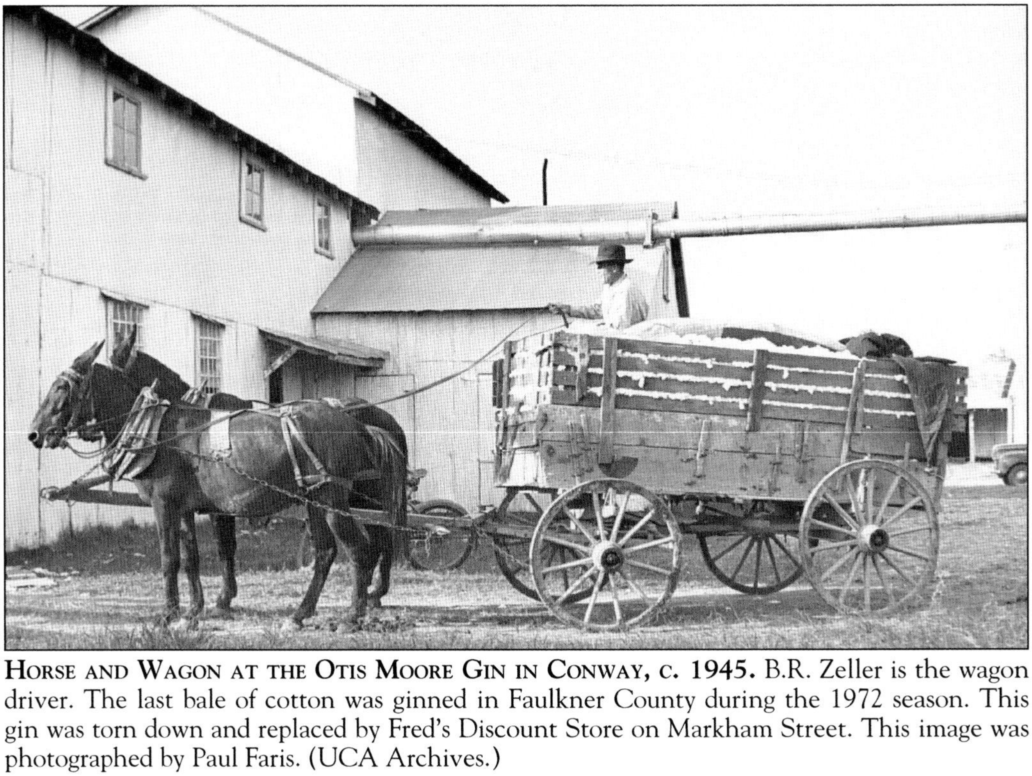

Horse and Wagon at the Otis Moore Gin in Conway, c. 1945. B.R. Zeller is the wagon driver. The last bale of cotton was ginned in Faulkner County during the 1972 season. This gin was torn down and replaced by Fred's Discount Store on Markham Street. This image was photographed by Paul Faris. (UCA Archives.)

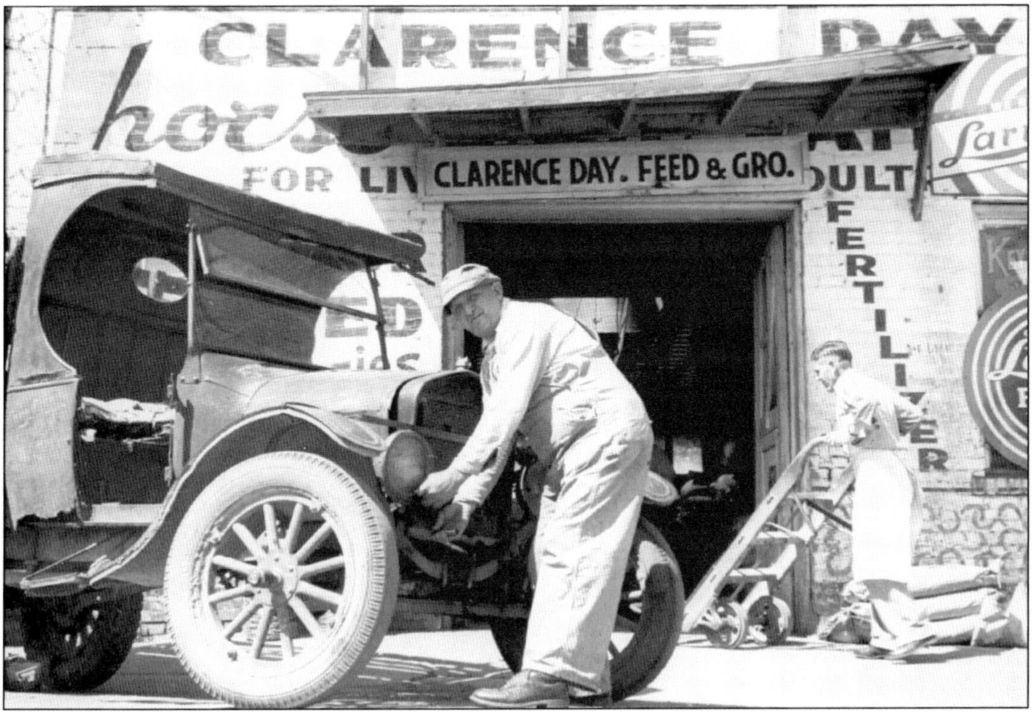

MODEL-T FORD TRUCK. Fred Fields with his Model-T Ford truck was a familiar sight in Conway. He promised to haul anything "that ain't nailed down, with a smile and a whistle." This photograph was taken in front of Clarence Day Feed & Grocery in 1949. (UCA Archives.)

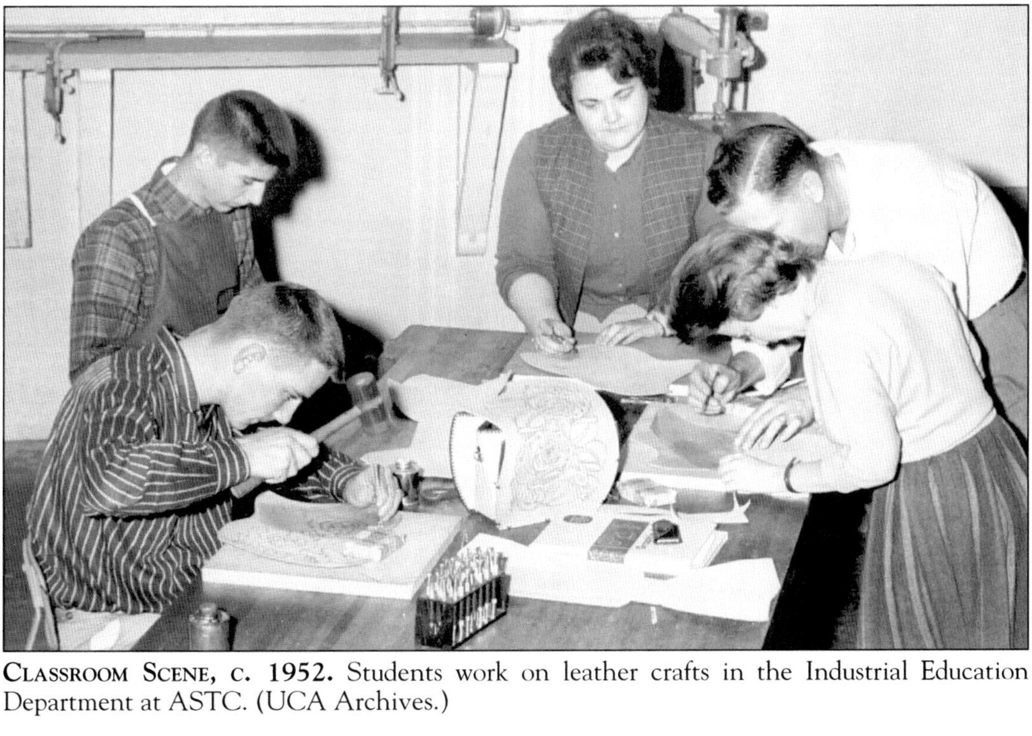

CLASSROOM SCENE, C. 1952. Students work on leather crafts in the Industrial Education Department at ASTC. (UCA Archives.)

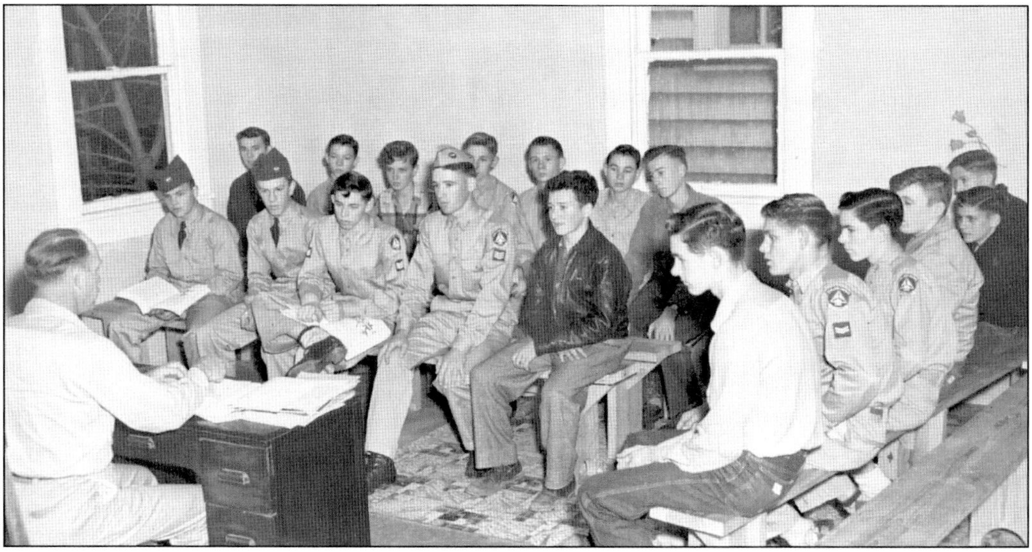

Civil Air Patrol in Conway, c. 1950. (UCA Archives.)

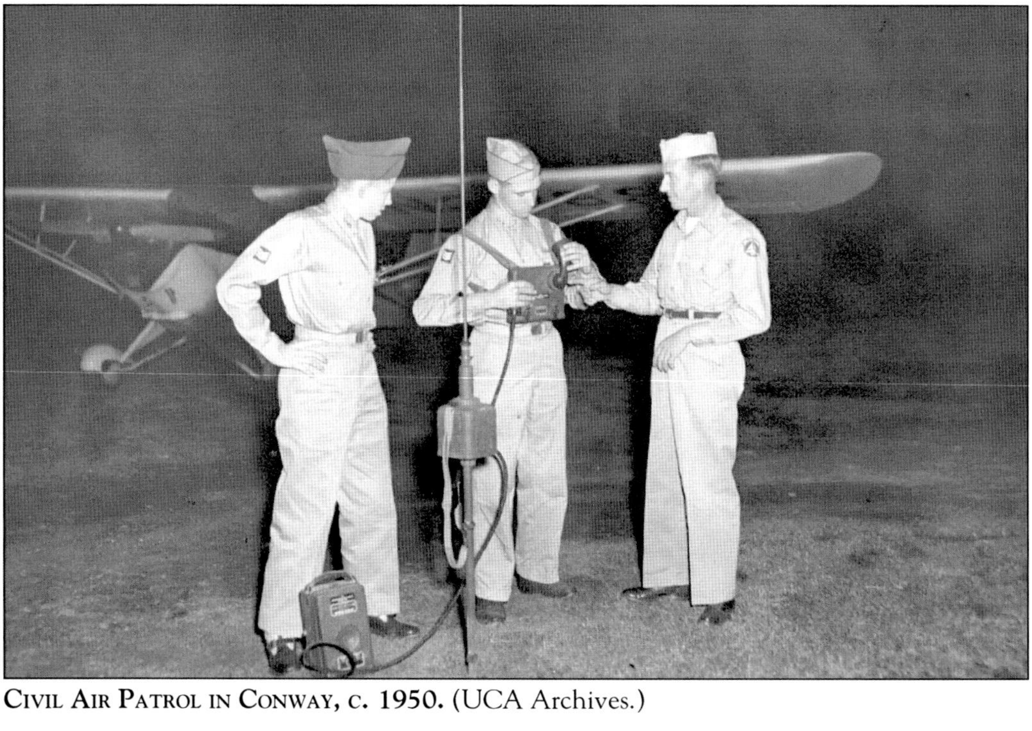

Civil Air Patrol in Conway, c. 1950. (UCA Archives.)

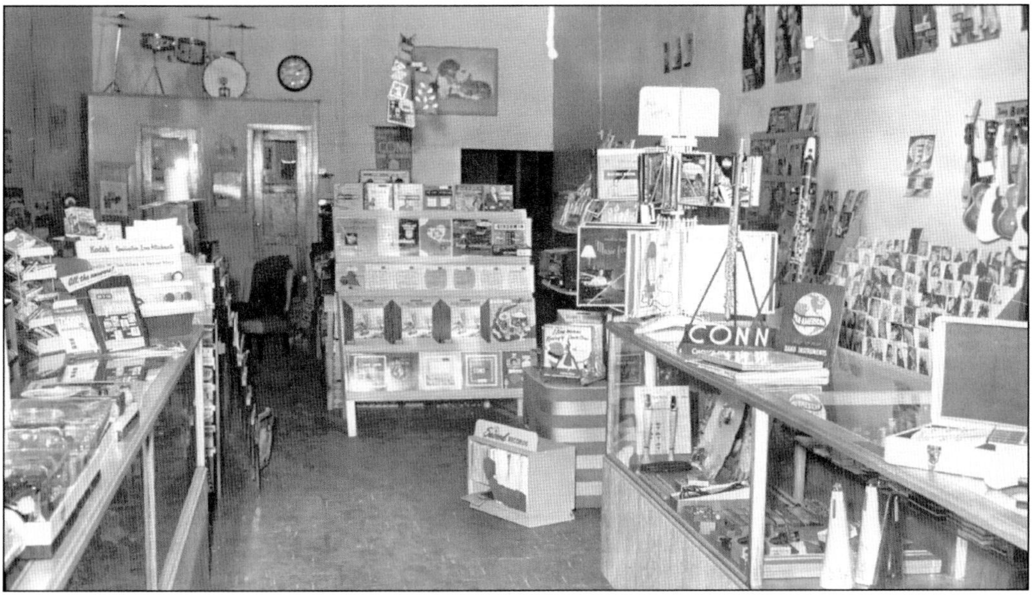

Interior of Olsen's Music & Photo Center at 806 Front Street in Conway, c. 1955. Established in 1947 by Jasper M. "Jap" Olsen, the store moved to Prince Street in 1999 as Olsen's Photo. A gracious and charming gentleman, Jap Olsen continues to provide service to the community after more than a half century. (UCA Archives.)

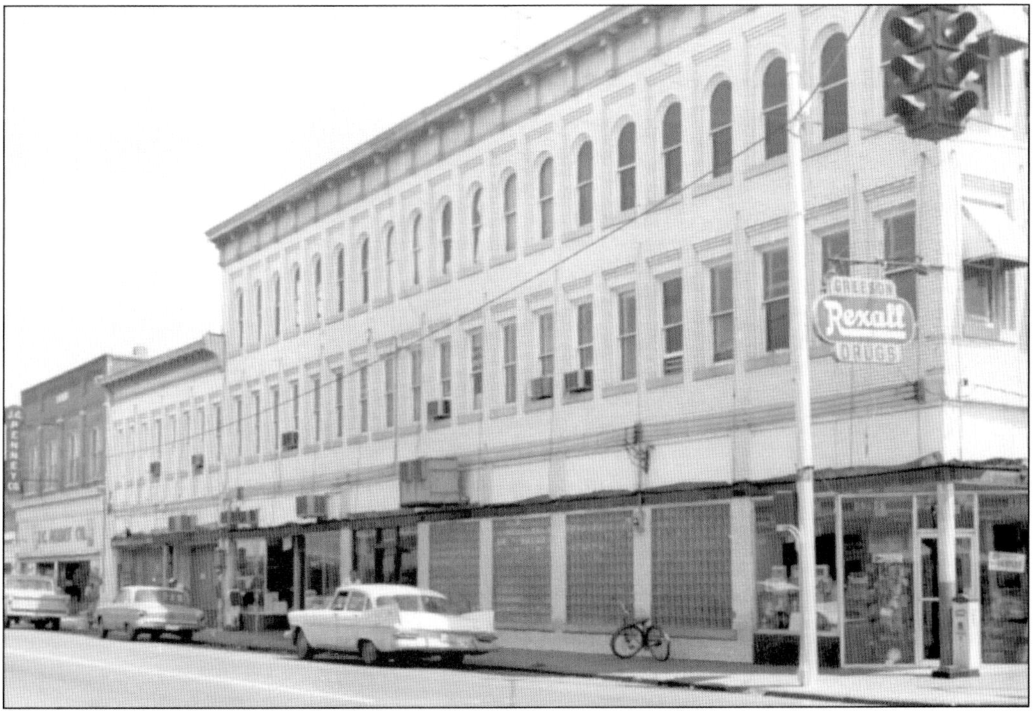

Greeson's Drug Store on Front Street in Downtown Conway, Looking East, c. 1965. Long a landmark in Conway, Royce Wilkins took over the store in 1924. Mrs. Wilkins continued to run the place when Royce died in 1941. Greeson's finally went out of business in 1966. (UCA Archives.)

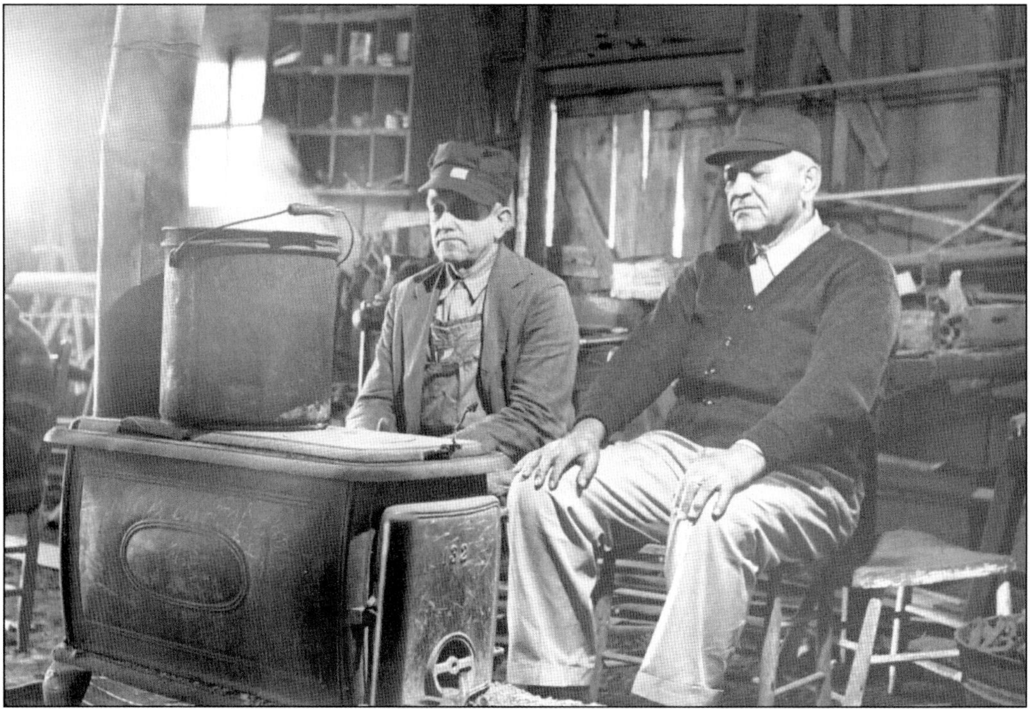

WILL MATTISON BLACKSMITH SHOP AT MARKHAM AND MILL STREETS IN CONWAY. Paul Faris photographed Will Mattison (right) and a helper, *c.* 1955. (UCA Archives.)

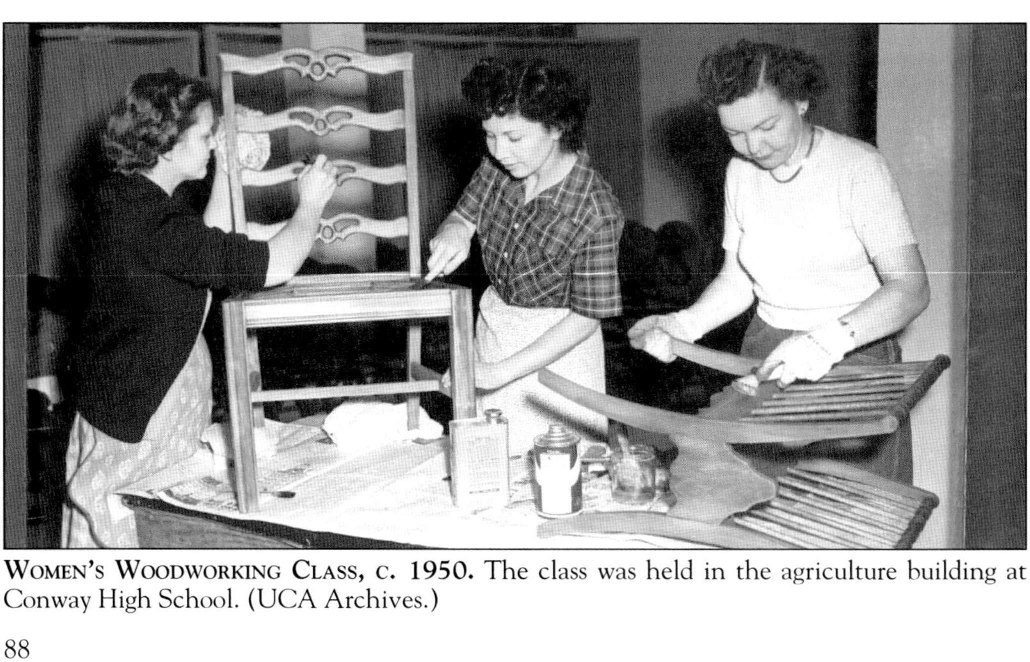

WOMEN'S WOODWORKING CLASS, C. 1950. The class was held in the agriculture building at Conway High School. (UCA Archives.)

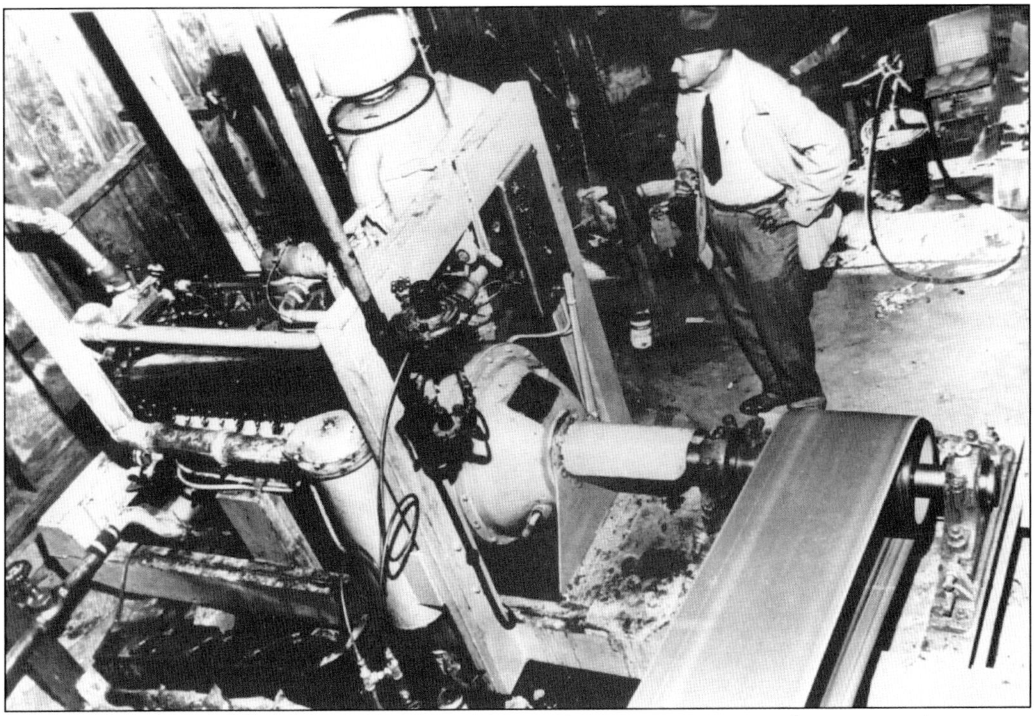

LITTLE PLANTATION AT LOLLIE, c. 1950. An airplane engine was used to power the cotton gin at this time. John Elijah Little purchased 3,200 acres in 1887 and built one of the largest and most successful plantations in Arkansas. He named the area Lollie in honor of his new bride, Lollie Trundle Little, who died about a year after giving birth to a daughter in 1892. (UCA Archives.)

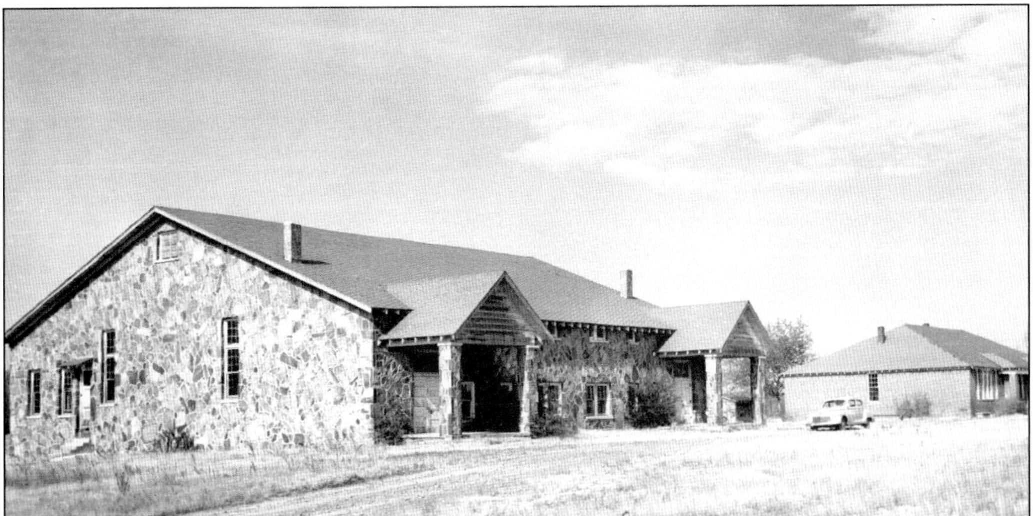

HOLLAND SCHOOLHOUSE AND GYMNASIUM IN 1954. These buildings reflect the typical masonry construction used by the Works Progress Administration (WPA), which sponsored a great deal of construction throughout the rural United States during the Great Depression of the 1930s. (UCA Archives.)

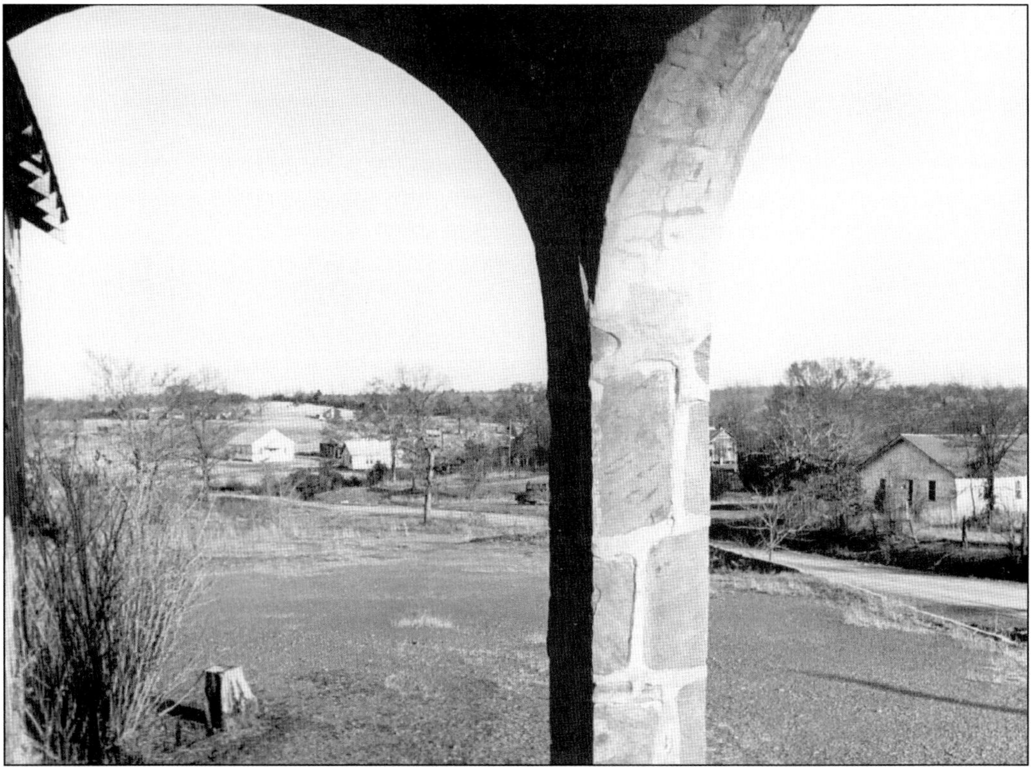

Countryside at Copperas Springs near Guy, c. 1950. (UCA Archives.)

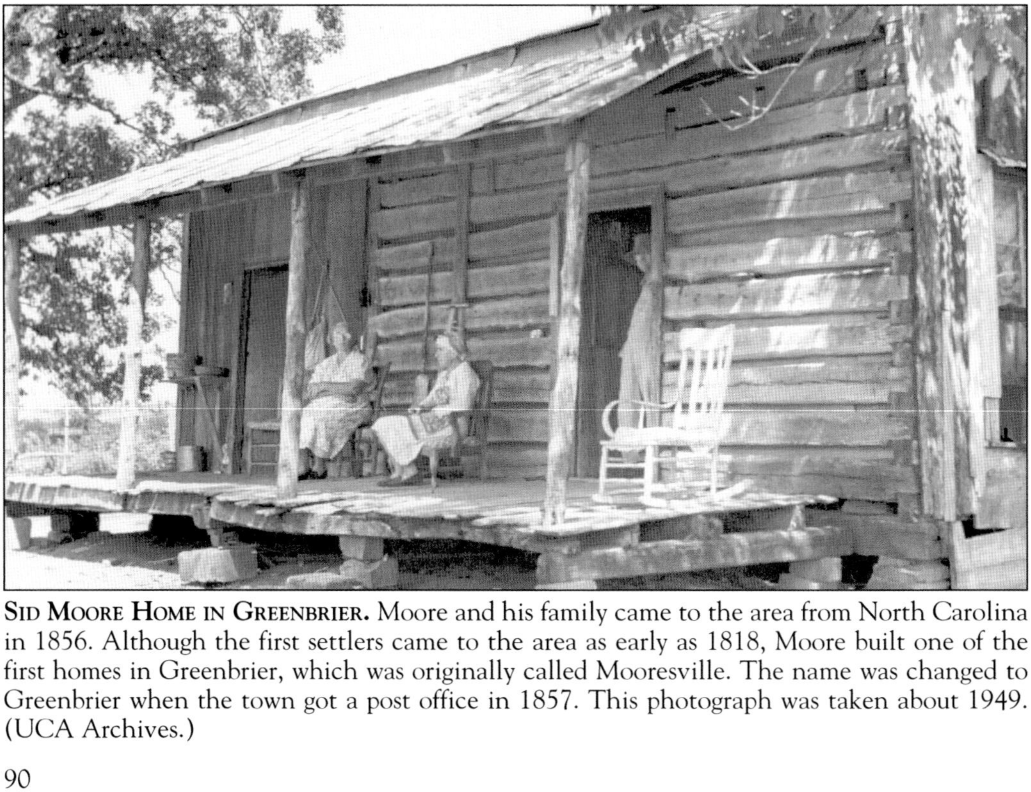

Sid Moore Home in Greenbrier. Moore and his family came to the area from North Carolina in 1856. Although the first settlers came to the area as early as 1818, Moore built one of the first homes in Greenbrier, which was originally called Mooresville. The name was changed to Greenbrier when the town got a post office in 1857. This photograph was taken about 1949. (UCA Archives.)

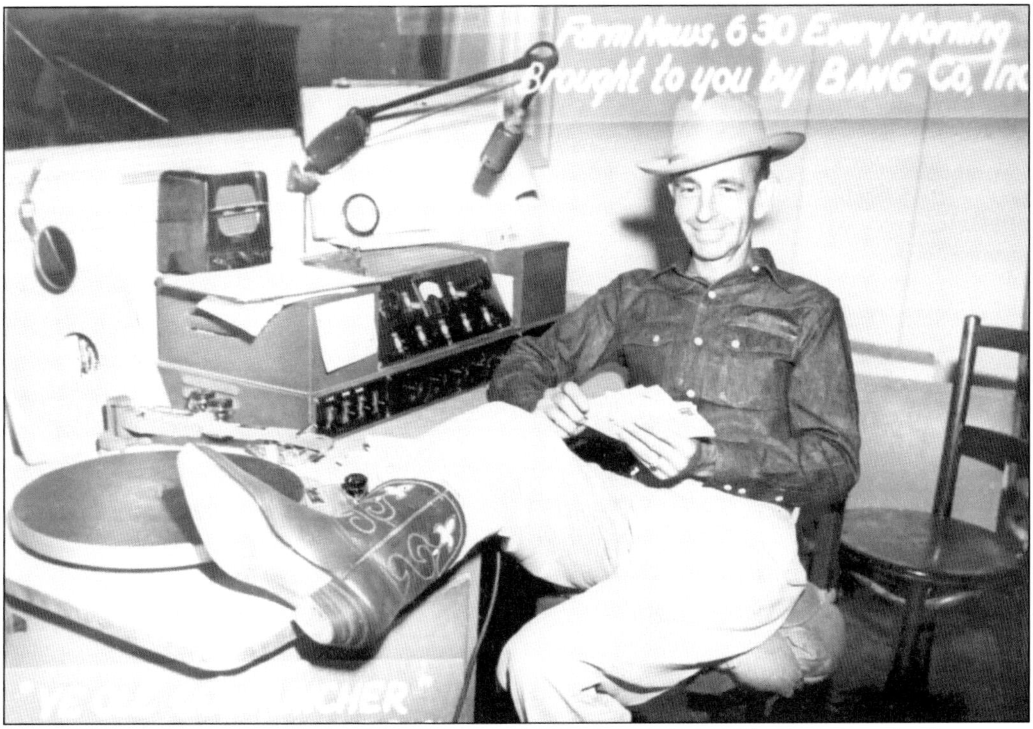

Herman Stermer, c. 1951. Stermer was chief engineer and "Ye Ole Cow Puncher" at radio station KCON in Conway. At the time the photograph was taken, James Clayton was general manager of the station. KCON continued operations until it was donated to the University of Central Arkansas in the spring of 1998. (UCA Archives.)

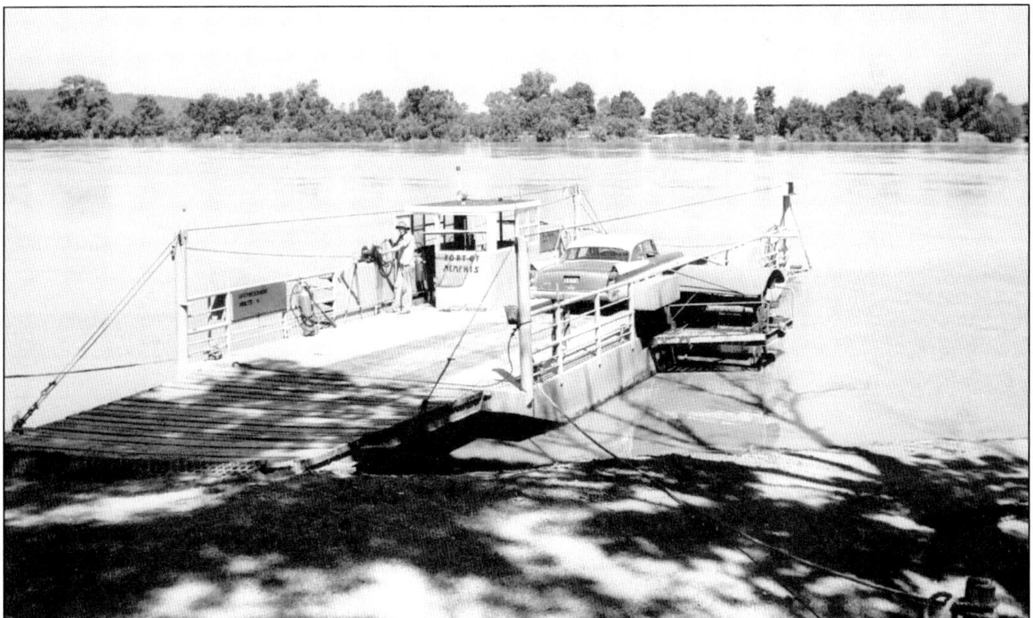

Toad Suck Ferry Across the Arkansas River, just West of Conway, c. 1960. This photograph was taken before the construction of the bridge, lock, and dam. (UCA Archives.)

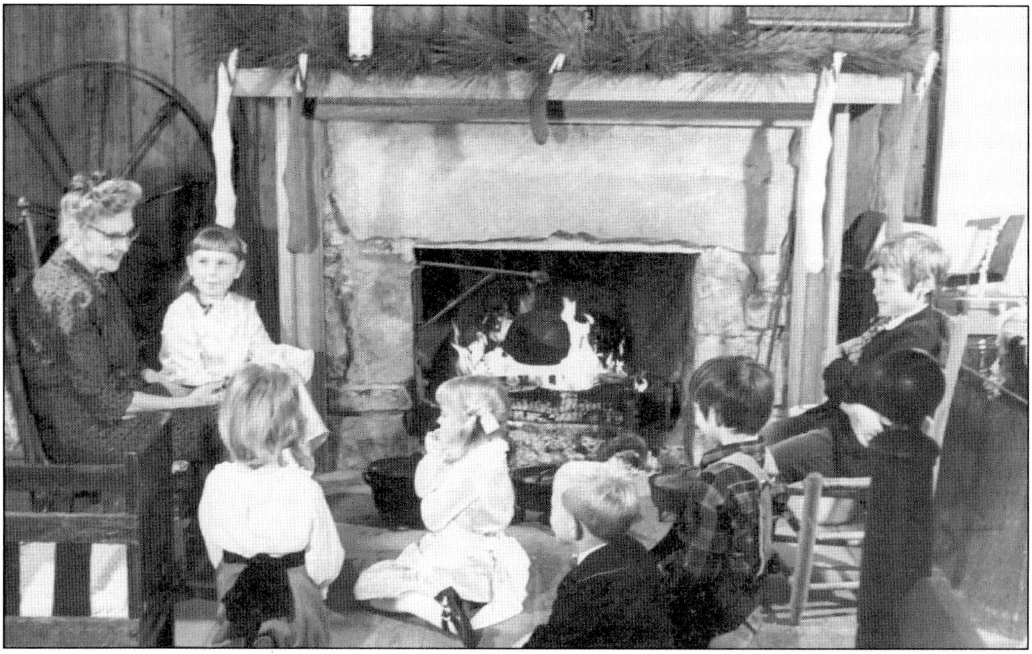

MRS. MABEL SHERIN AND CHILDREN AT THE FIREPLACE IN FAULKNER COUNTY'S "GREATHOUSE," CHRISTMASTIME 1950. The log cabin restoration is located on Courthouse Lawn. (UCA Archives.)

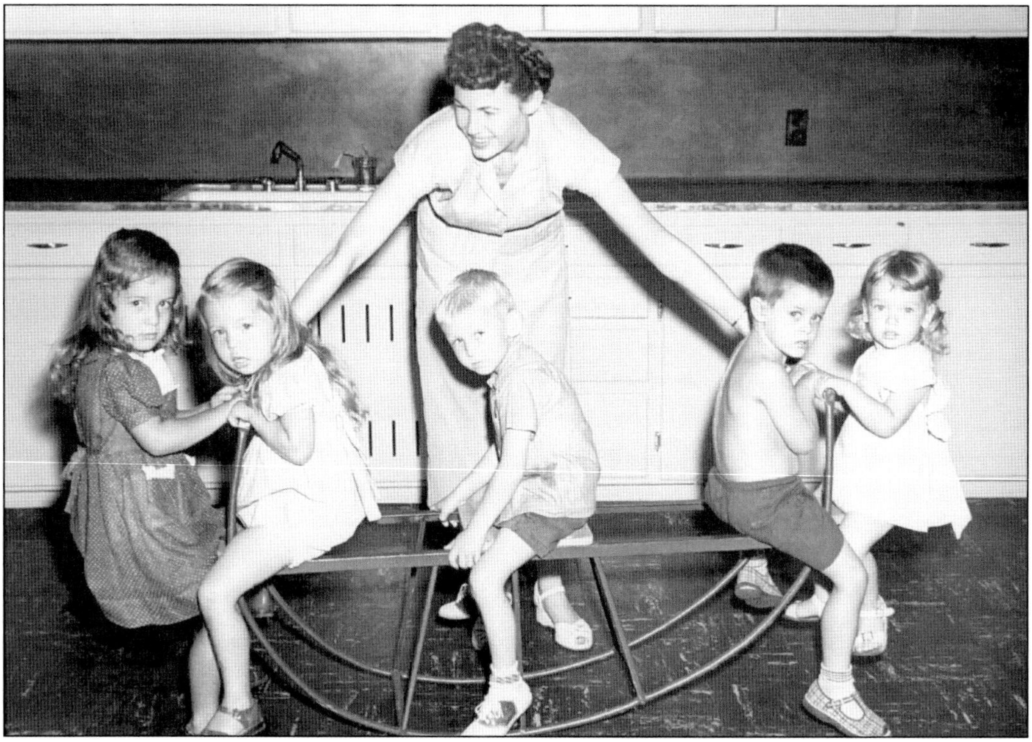

STUDENTS PLAYING TEETER-TOTTER AT IRBY ELEMENTARY SCHOOL, C. 1951. (UCA Archives.)

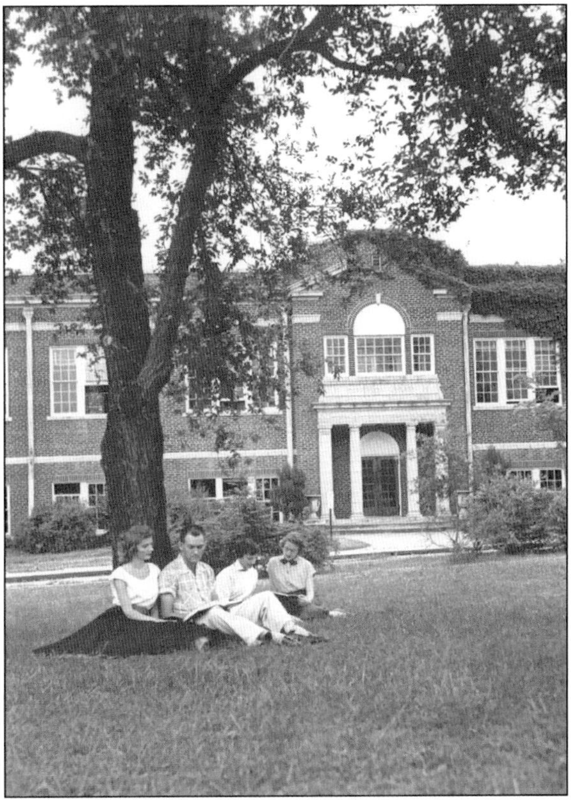

Students in front of the Torreyson Library on the ASTC Campus, c. 1955. Sitting, from left to right, are Gwen Grey of Paris, Clitus Ivey of Newport, Etha Jane McCubbin of Paris, and Nell Harpole of Jacksonville. Enrollment at the Arkansas State Teachers College skyrocketed thanks to the influx of WW II veterans whose education was financed by the GI Bill. The bill made a college education available to a vast population of people who would not otherwise have been able to afford college. (UCA Archives.)

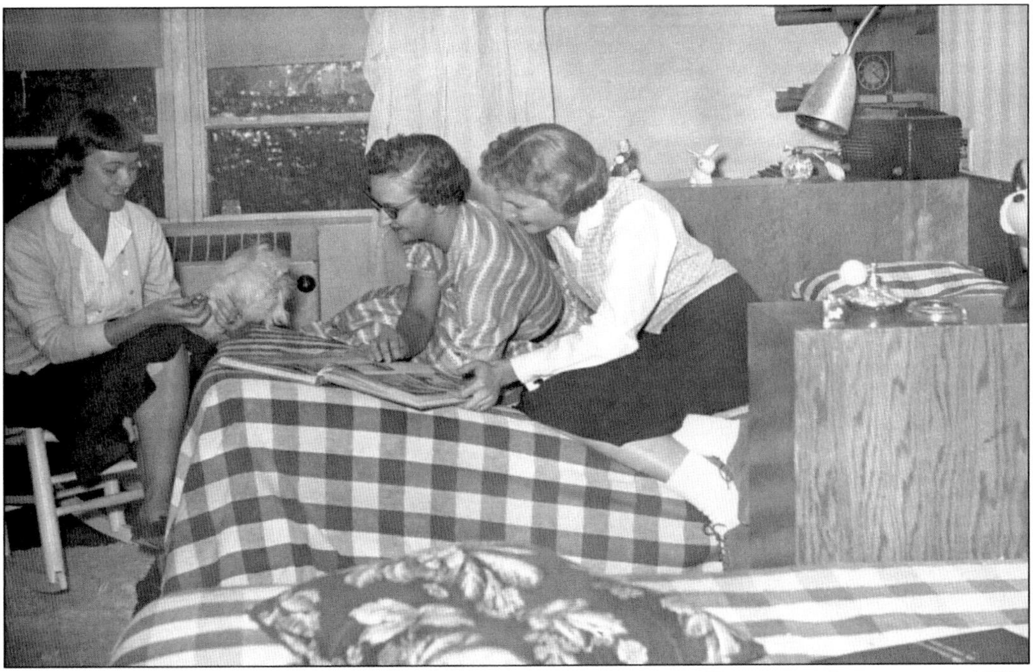

Three Students in a Dorm Room at the Arkansas State Teachers College, c. 1953. They are looking through the *Scroll*, which is the campus yearbook. (UCA Archives.)

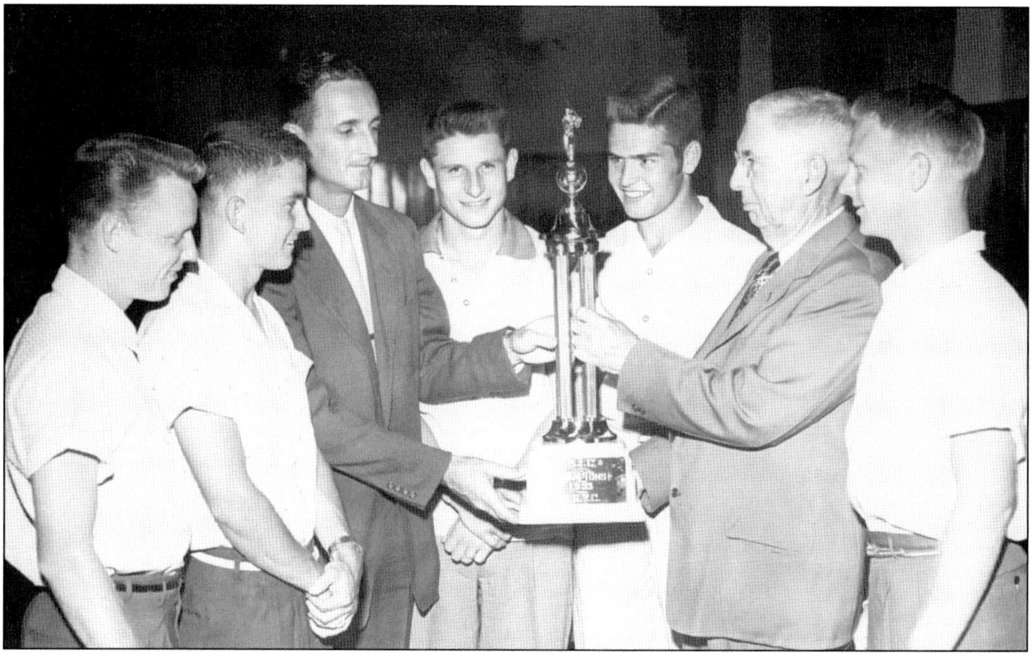

Coach Paul Coleman and Members of the ASTC Baseball Team, c. 1955. They are receiving the Arkansas Intercollegiate Conference (AIC) Championship Trophy. (UCA Archives.)

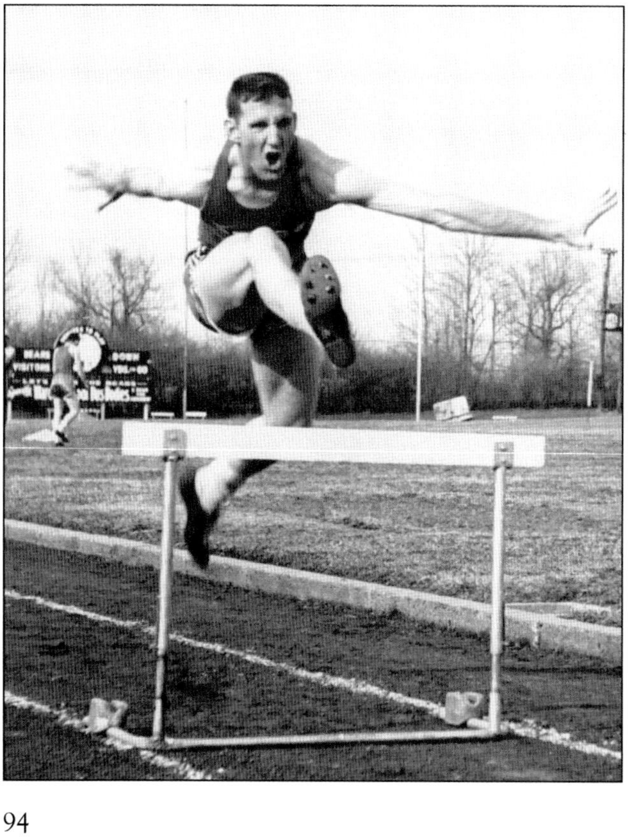

Frank Dicus. He ran the low hurdles for ASTC's track team in 1959. (UCA Archives.)

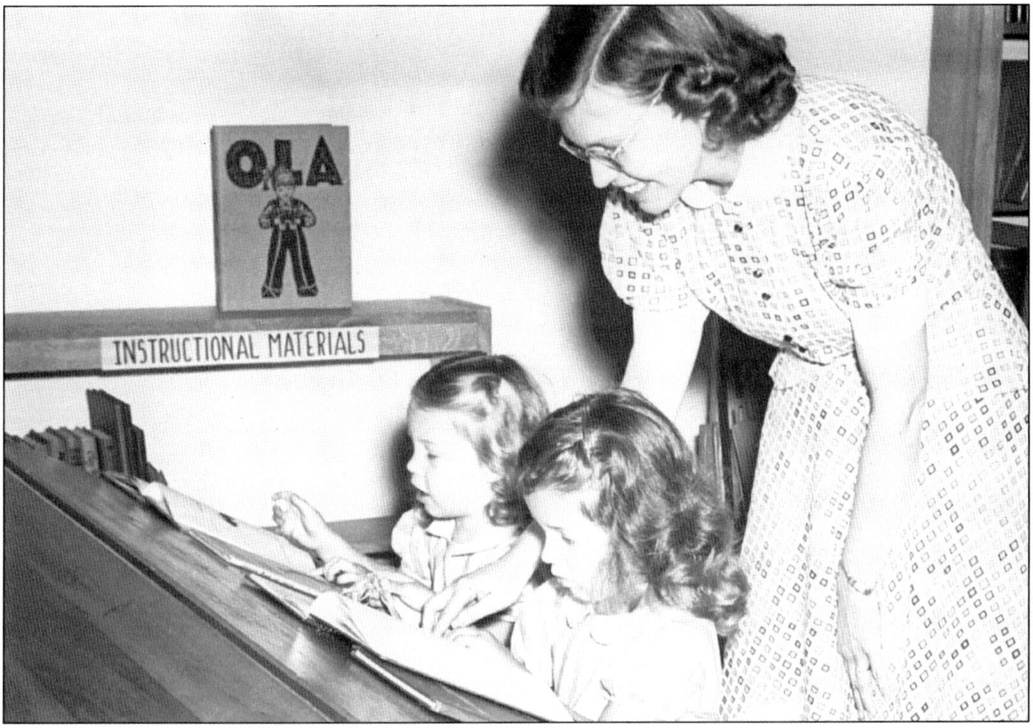

FUTURE TEACHER. A student teacher helps two young girls with their reading at Irby Elementary on the ASTC campus in 1951. (UCA Archives.)

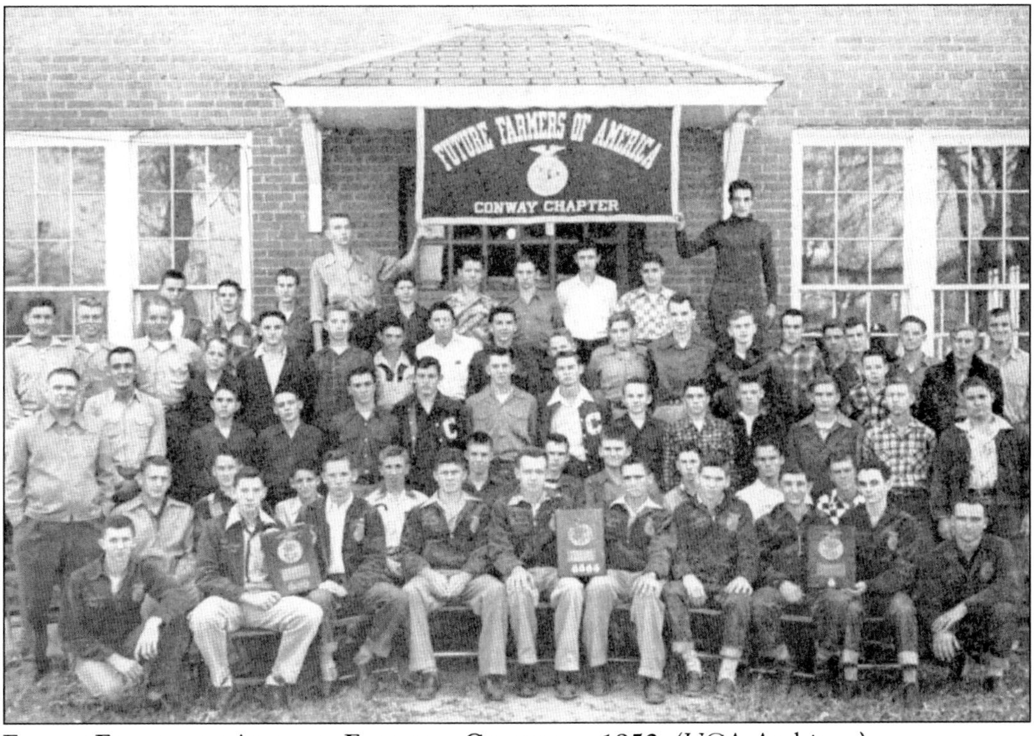

FUTURE FARMERS OF AMERICA, FAULKNER COUNTY, C. 1952. (UCA Archives.)

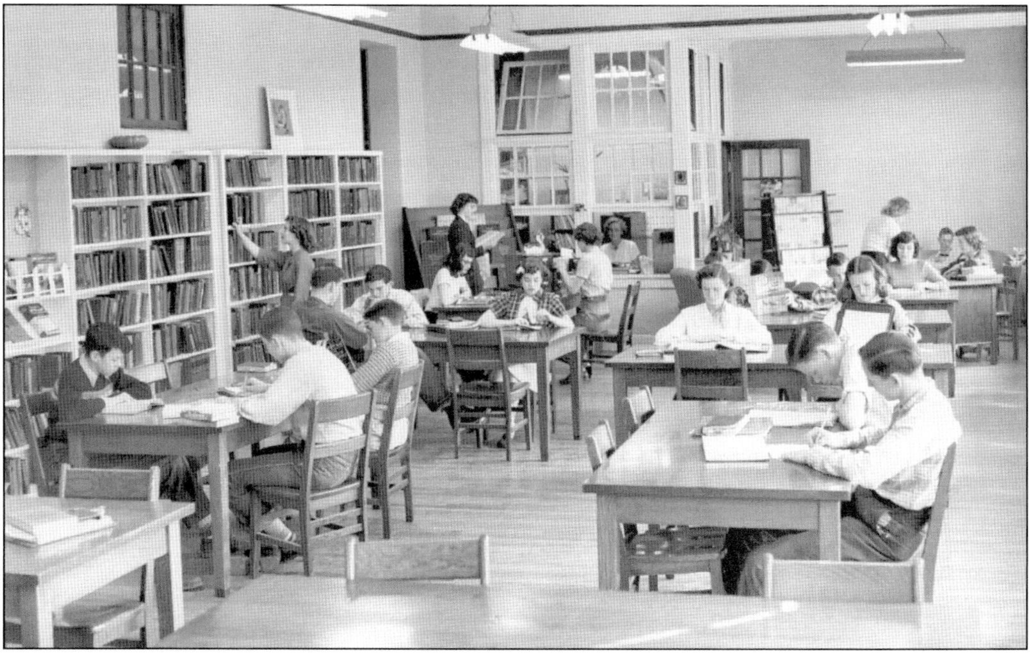

Conway High School Library, c. 1949 or 1950. Sam Fausett photographed this image. (UCA Archives.)

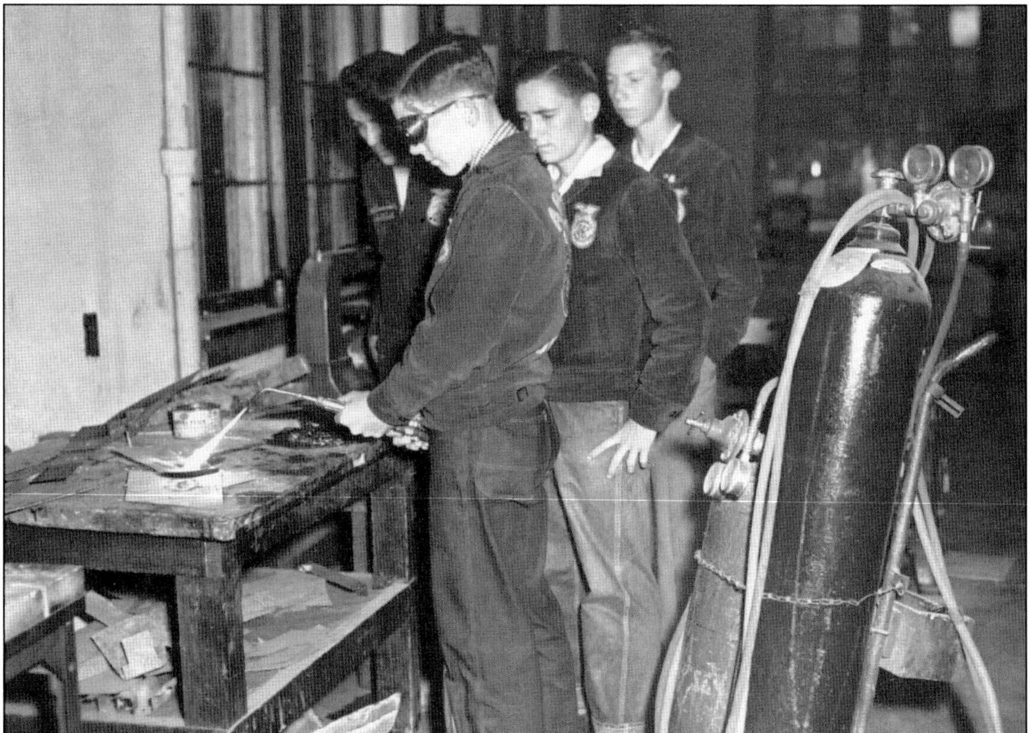

Industrial Arts Class in the Agriculture Building at Conway High School, c. 1950. (UCA Archives.)

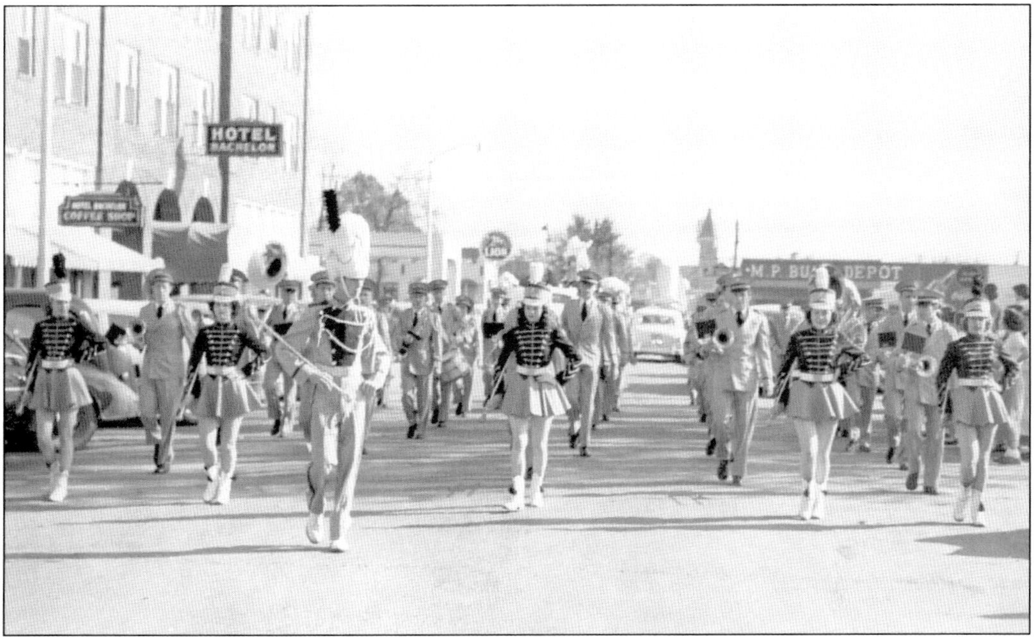

CONWAY HIGH SCHOOL MARCHING BAND, C. 1950. (UCA Archives.)

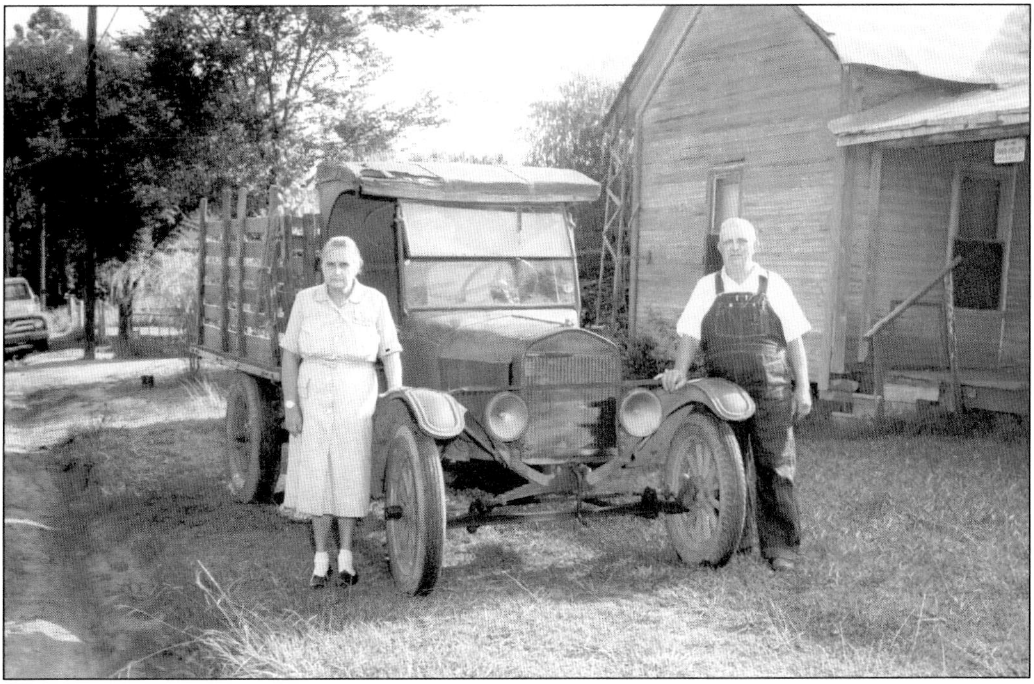

MR. AND MRS. FRED FIELDS, C. 1950. Robert B. Clark photographed them at their Spencer Street home in Conway. (UCA Archives.)

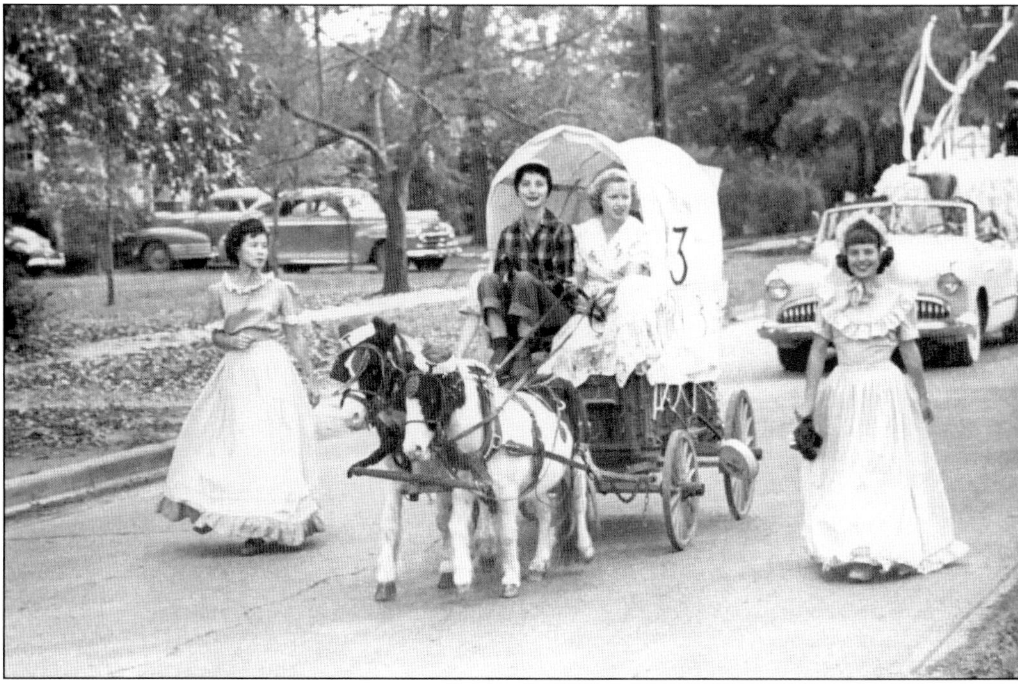

ASTC Homecoming Parade in Conway, c. 1950. Miniature horses pull a covered wagon in this view. (UCA Archives.)

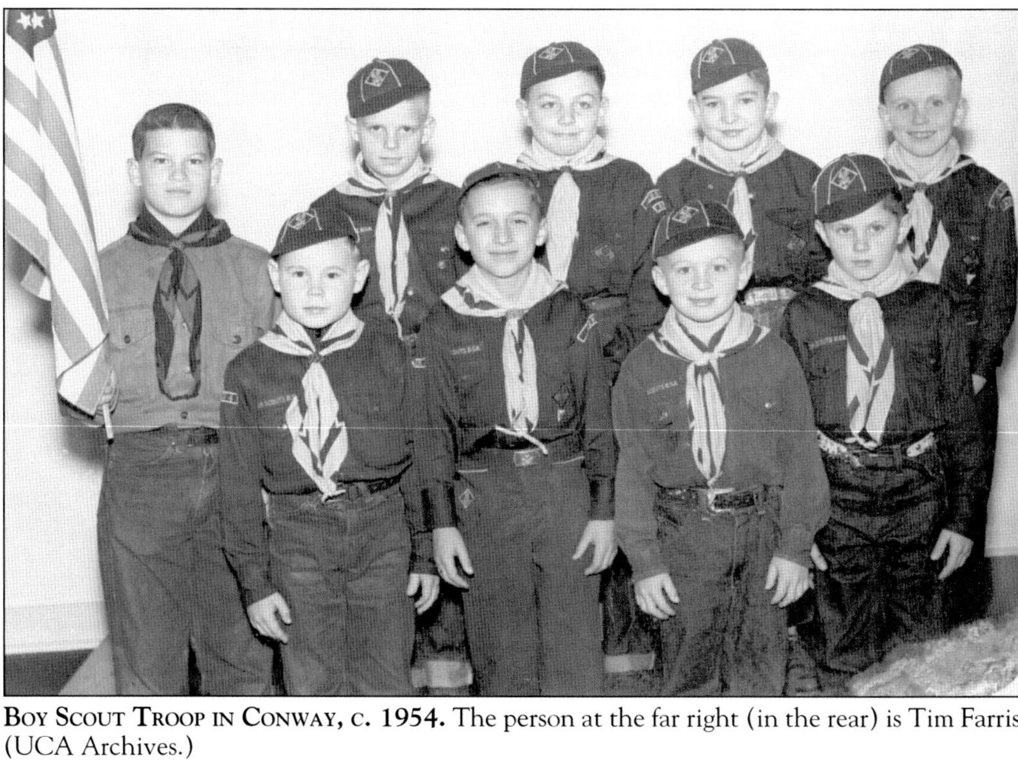

Boy Scout Troop in Conway, c. 1954. The person at the far right (in the rear) is Tim Farris. (UCA Archives.)

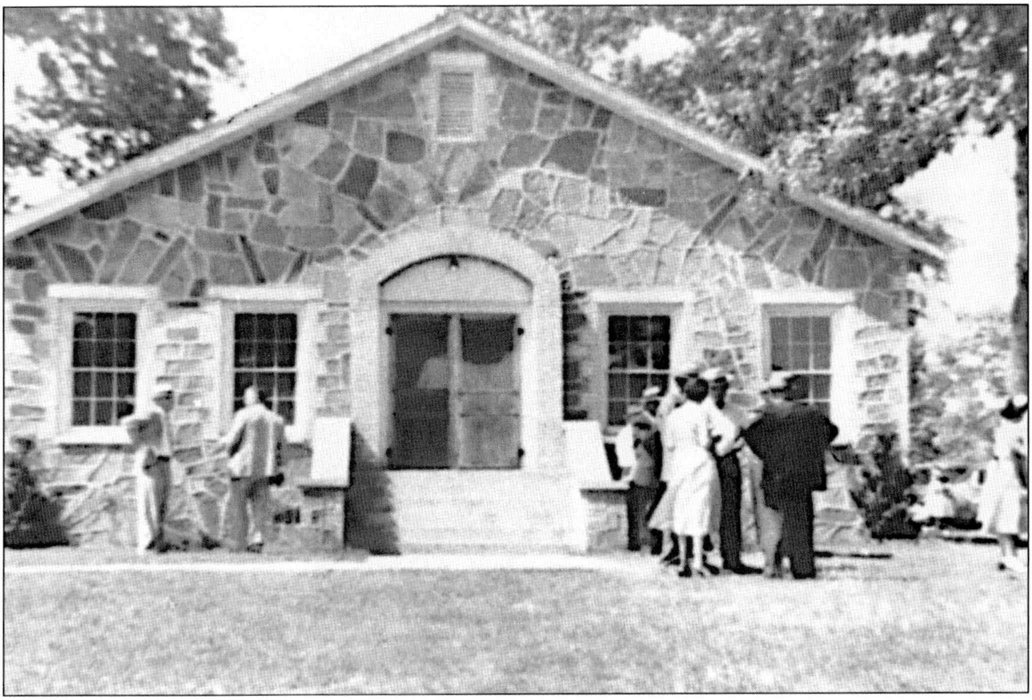

METHODIST CHURCH IN CENTERVILLE. The town was established on a plateau that was part of the stage coach route between Little Rock and Batesville. The first settler of the area was Dr. O.J. Owen. While repairing a broken wagon wheel, his family decided they liked the place, so they stayed. (UCA Archives.)

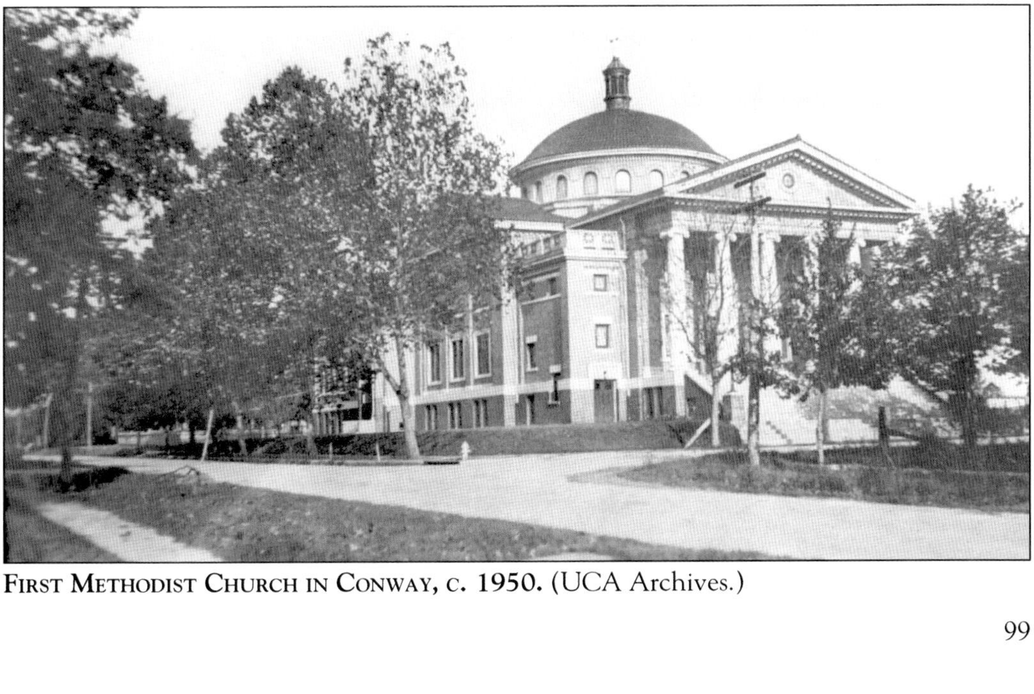

FIRST METHODIST CHURCH IN CONWAY, C. 1950. (UCA Archives.)

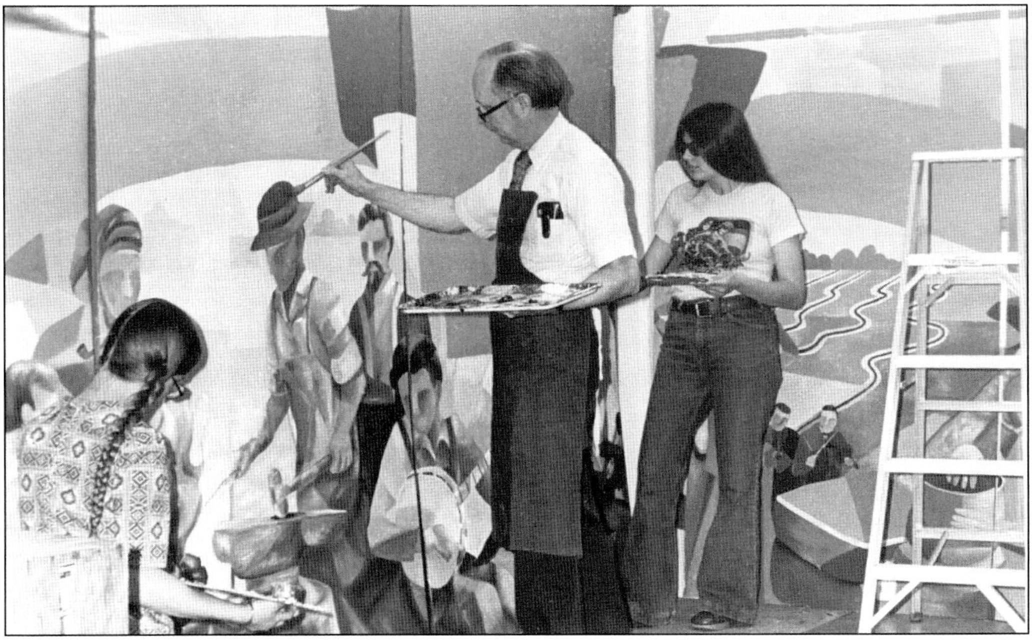

JUDY FRIEDEL, DR. JERRY POOLE, AND SUSAN BAUER. These three are painting a mural at the University of Central Arkansas in this 1977 image. (UCA Archives.)

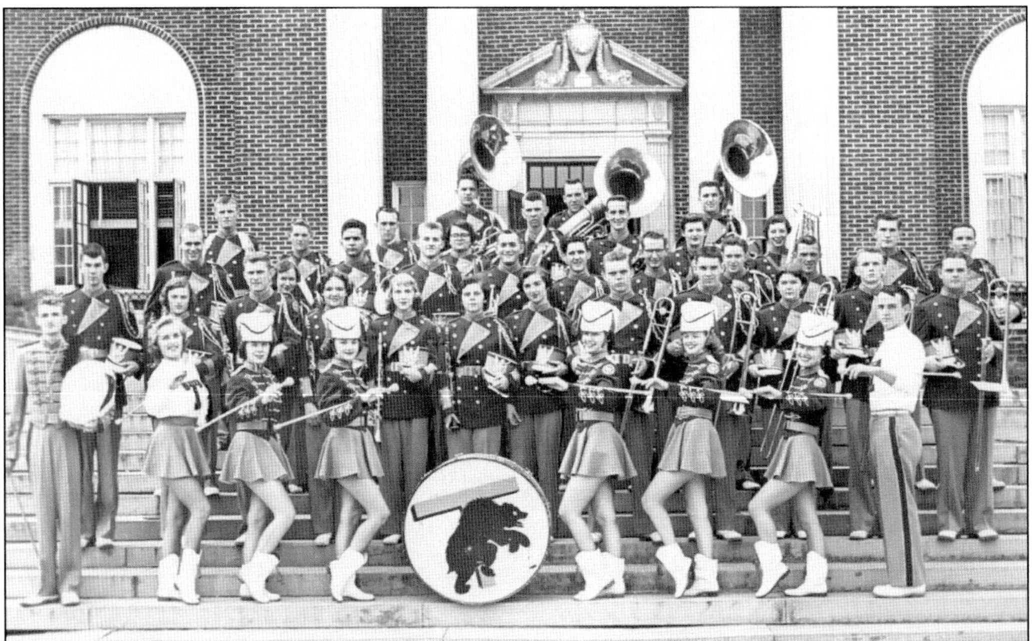

ASTC MARCHING BAND ON THE STEPS OF OLD MAIN IN 1957. Jim MacBridges (at far left) was the drum major. (UCA Archives.)

Presidential Hospitality. Guy "Mutt" Jones played host to President Harry S. Truman in 1950. (UCA Archives.)

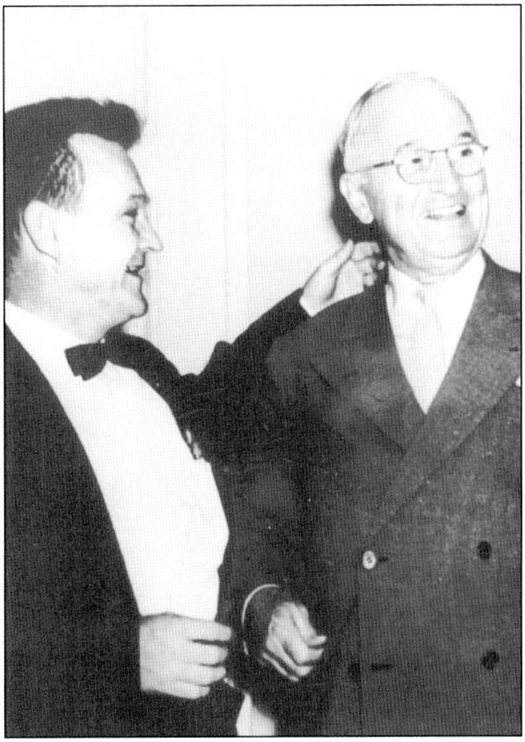

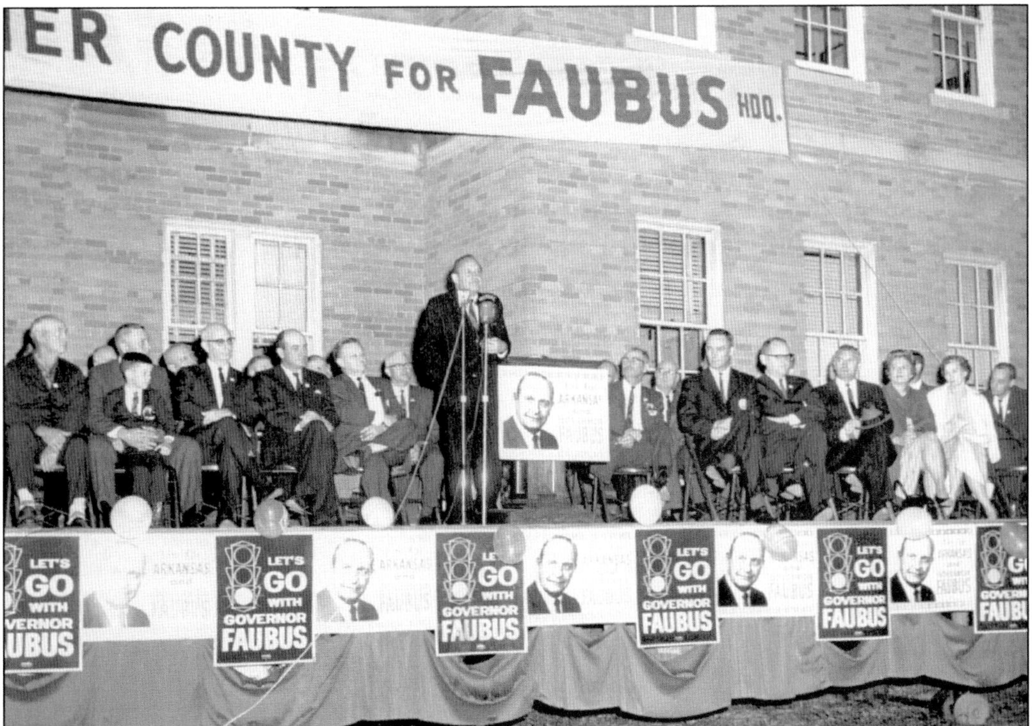

Political Rally for Governor Faubus on the Steps of the Faulkner County Courthouse in Conway, c. 1958. (UCA Archives.)

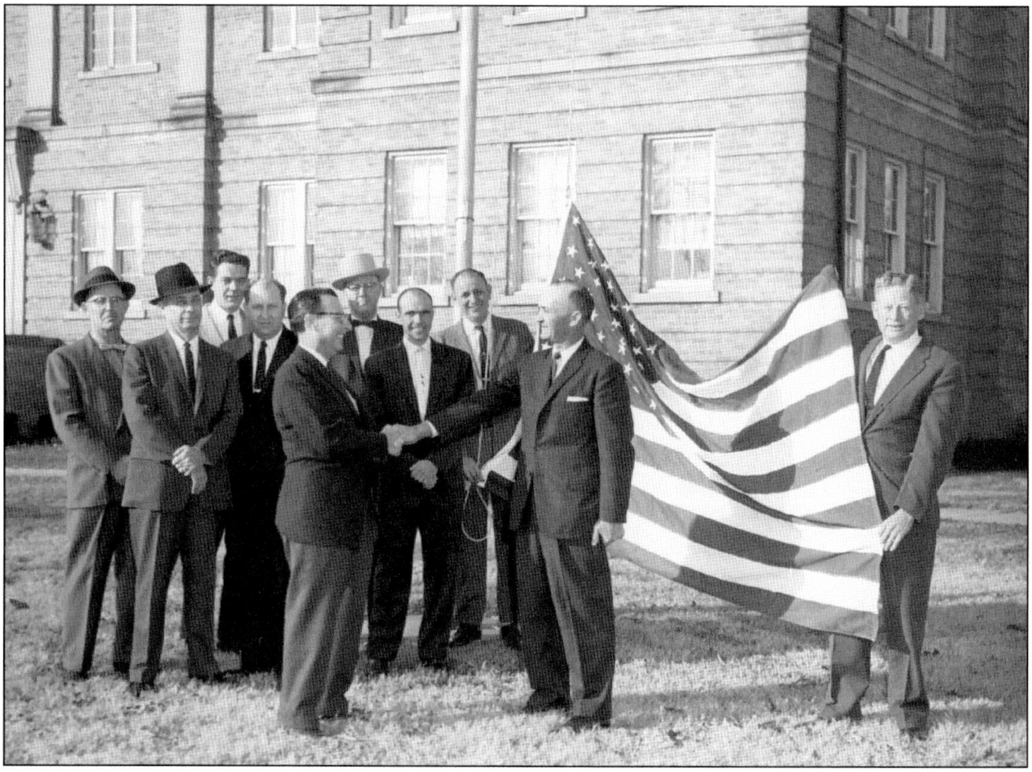

Flag Dedication at Courthouse Cemetery in 1961. Shown here, from left to right, are Jack Ward, Joe Castleberry, Wendele Bryan, and Bill Purtle. The flag presenters, from left to right, are J.W. Yoeman, E.A. "Calf" Dickens, Jerrell Coker, Woodrow Husten. Judge Tom D. Reedy is receiving the flag; Hiram Gillian is holding the flag. (UCA Archives.)

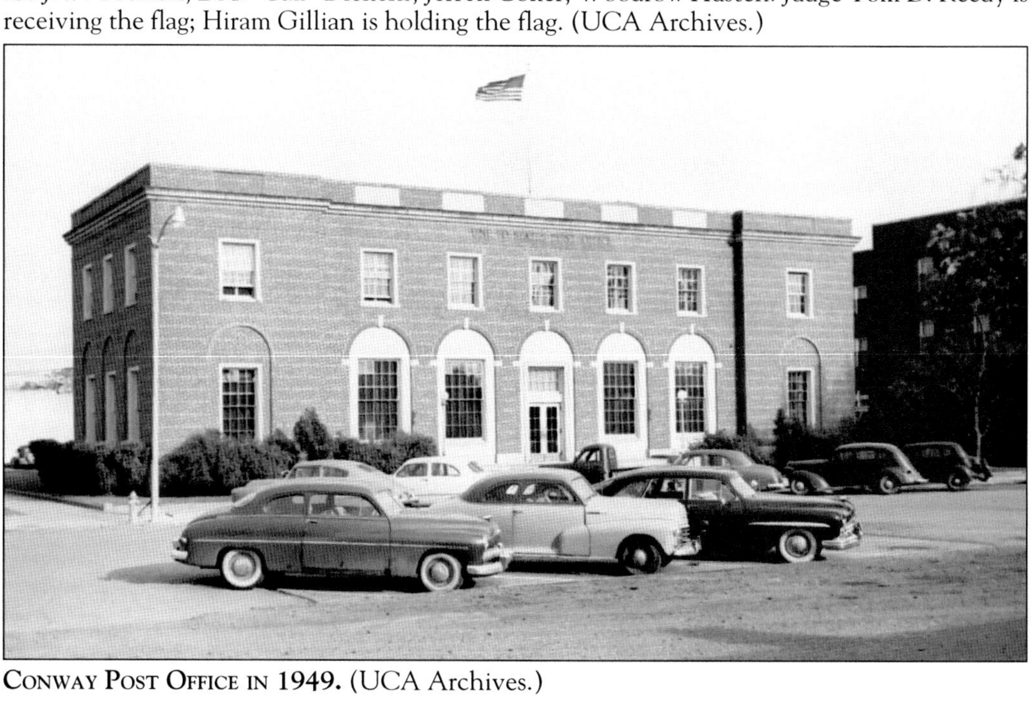

Conway Post Office in 1949. (UCA Archives.)

Six

WINNING THE PEACE

The years after WW II have been kind to Faulkner County, which has seen substantial economic growth fueled by the development of industry and higher education. Much of this prosperity has also been fueled by Conway's increasingly important role as a bedroom community for Little Rock. This, in turn, has stimulated the service sector of the county's economy. However, winning the peace after WW II was not always without peril, thanks to the Cold War. One of the most sobering effects of the Cold War on local residents was the deployment of missiles with nuclear warheads in central Arkansas. This made central Arkansas a priority target for Soviet ICBMs. When the Cold War thawed, the U.S. Air Force gratefully decommissioned the missile silos, and Faulkner County lost its trouble-prone neighbors.

Conway's colleges proved to be much better neighbors. In the late 1940s and early 1950s, ASTC began to change its mission from training teachers to providing degrees in the sciences and liberal arts. After changing its name to the University of Central Arkansas (UCA) in 1975, the school embarked on a long-term program to upgrade its faculty and recruit more high-school students. The program really started succeeding in the late 1980s. Enrollment at UCA increased from 6,698 in 1988 to 9,567 in 1993, a growth of 43% in just five years.

Meanwhile, Hendrix College achieved national prominence as an outstanding liberal arts school. Various national college guides have ranked Hendrix as one of the 300 best liberal arts colleges in the county (in terms of both quality and affordability), and one of the 300 toughest schools (in terms of competitive admission requirements). About 1,000 students attend Hendrix, which is the only nationally ranked liberal arts college in the state. Conway Baptist College also grew during this period, expanding its curriculum and adding 10 acres to the campus on German Lane. Its focus evolved and broadened, so the name was changed to Central Baptist College in 1962. Enrollment grew to about 275 students.

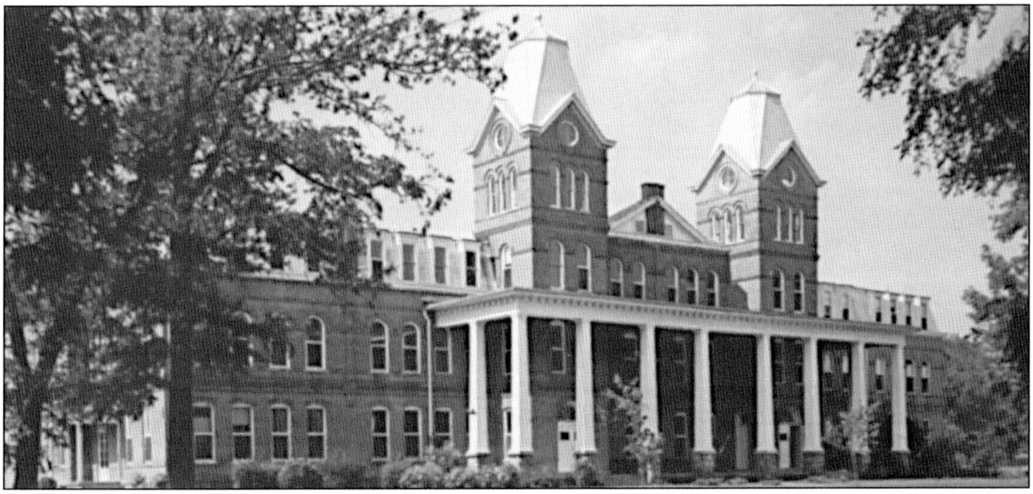

CENTRAL BAPTIST COLLEGE IN CONWAY. The card was postmarked January 8, 1963. (Arkansas History Commission.)

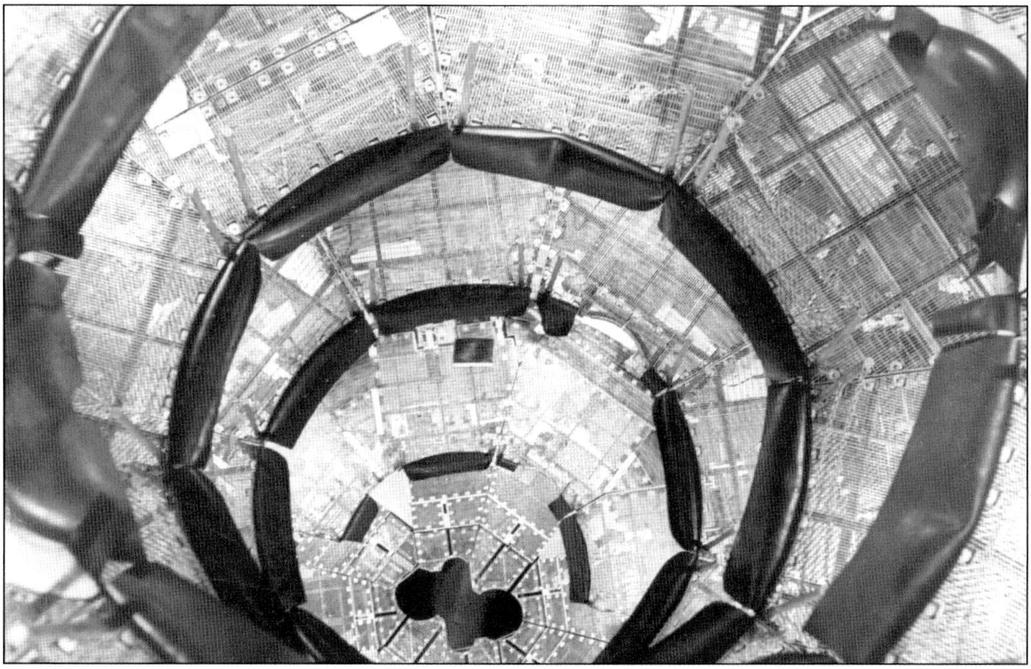

INTERIOR OF TITAN II MISSILE SILO, C. 1960. (UCA Archives.)

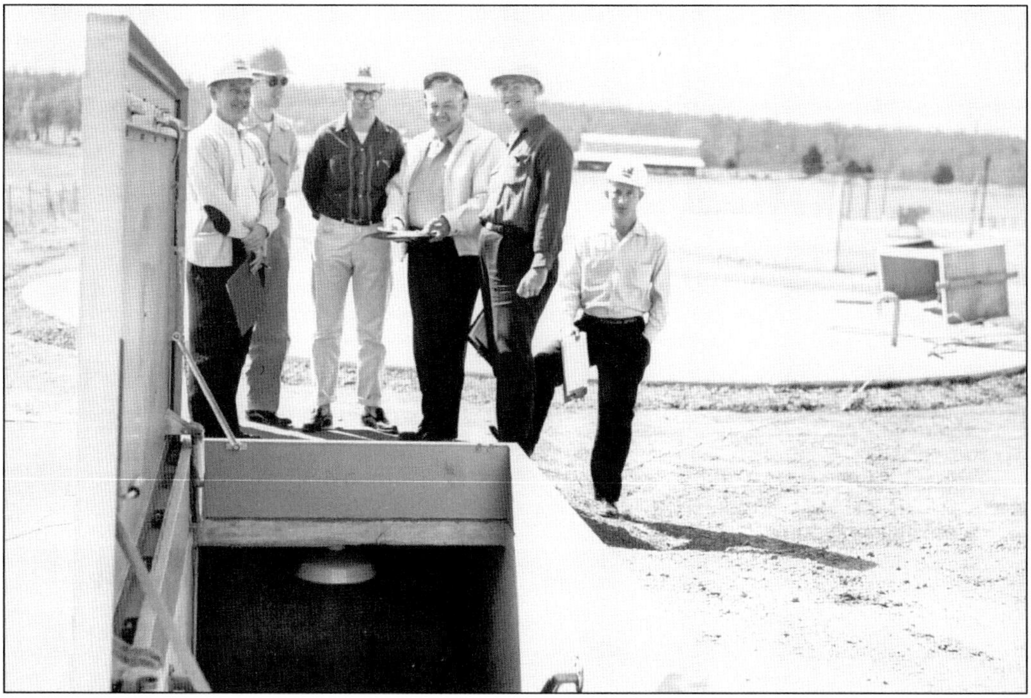

ENTRANCE TO ONE OF FIVE TITAN II UNDERGROUND MISSILE SILOS. The Strategic Air Command in Faulkner County built the underground missile silos in the early 1960s. Silos were built near Mount Vernon, Hamlet, Springhill, Republican, and Guy. Sam Fausett photographed this image. (UCA Archives.)

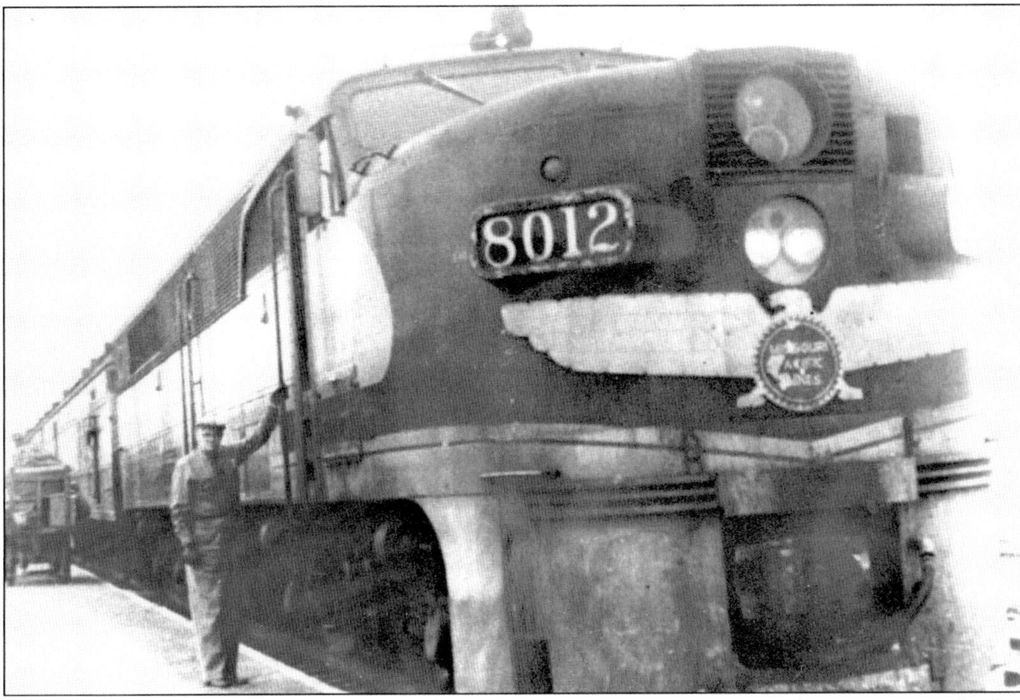

ENGINEER J.R. BERRY WITH HIS ENGINE 8012 ON MARCH 28, 1960. This train was the last northbound passenger train to leave Conway. This signaled the end of passenger service along the railbelt from Little Rock to Kansas City. (UCA Archives.)

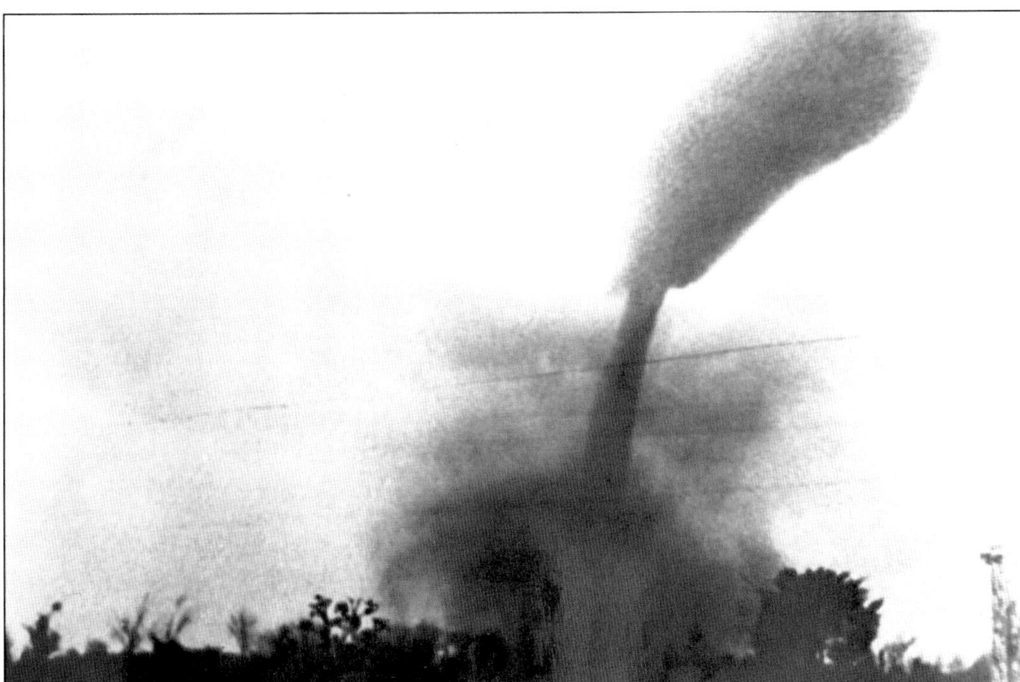

APRIL 10, 1965, TORNADO THAT CUT THROUGH CONWAY. (UCA Archives.)

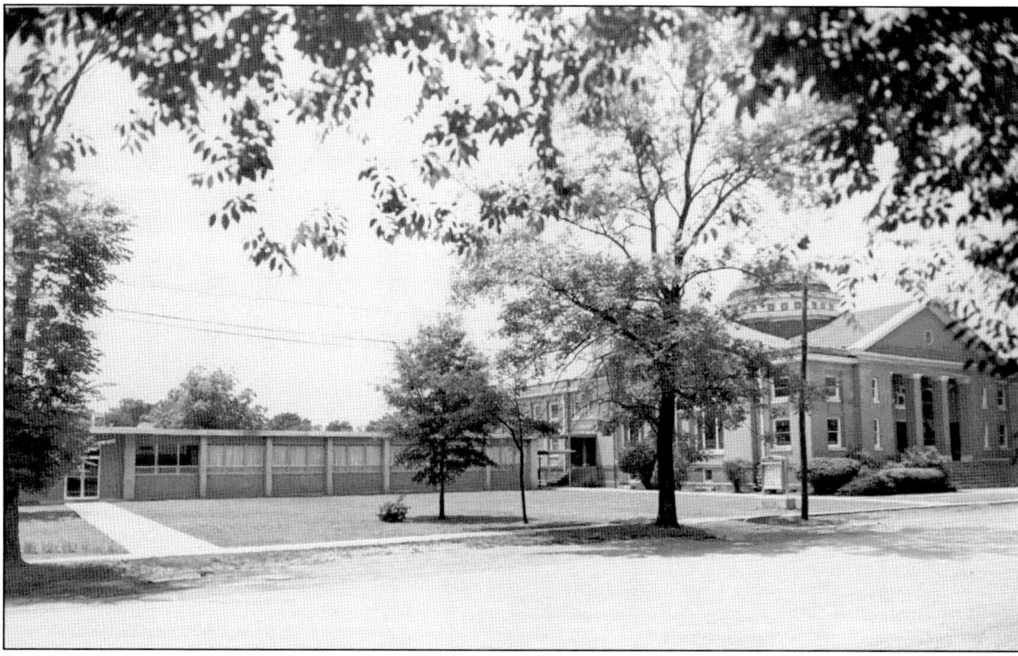

First Methodist Church in Conway, c. 1970. (UCA Archives.)

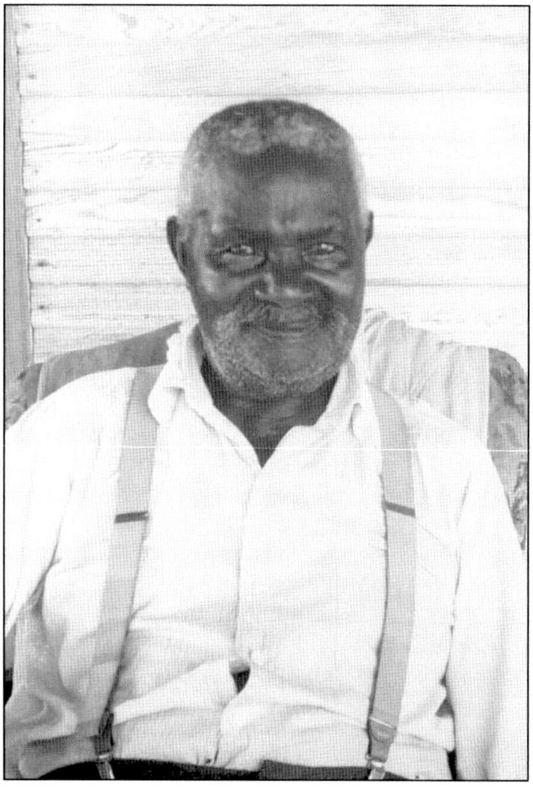

Melton Fields of Conway in the Summer of 1965. He was 91 years young. (UCA Archives.)

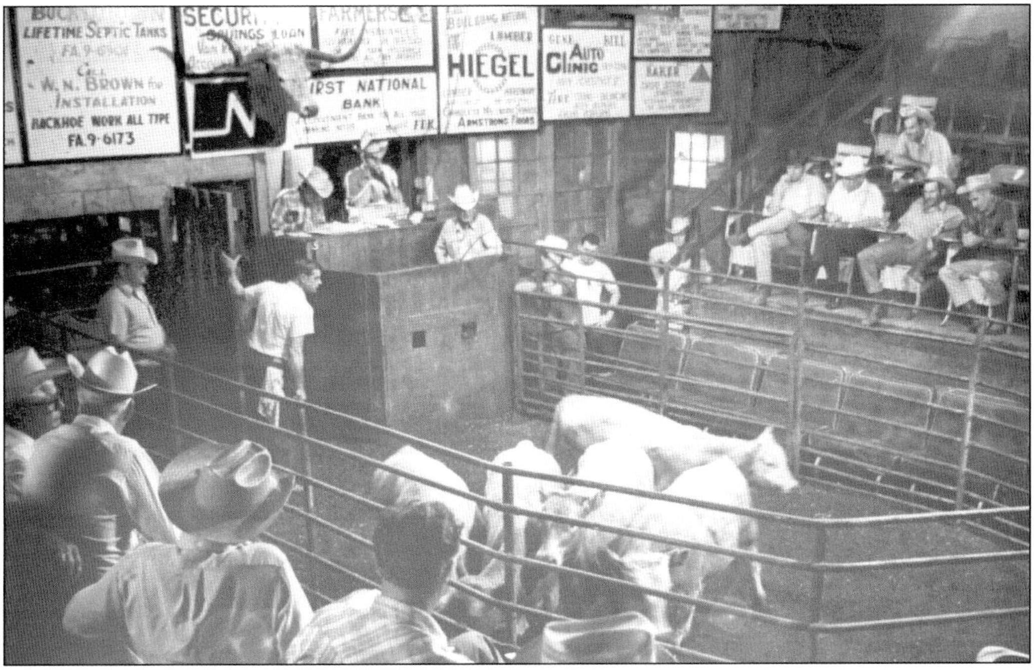

CONWAY CATTLE AUCTION. The old Lewis-Brown Auction Barn was located at Markham and Smith Streets. The top photograph was taken just before the structure was torn down, while the bottom photograph dates from *c.* 1937. This building was razed in 1971 after a new auction barn was built in southeastern Conway along Interstate 40. The above scene was photographed by Paul Faris. (UCA Archives.)

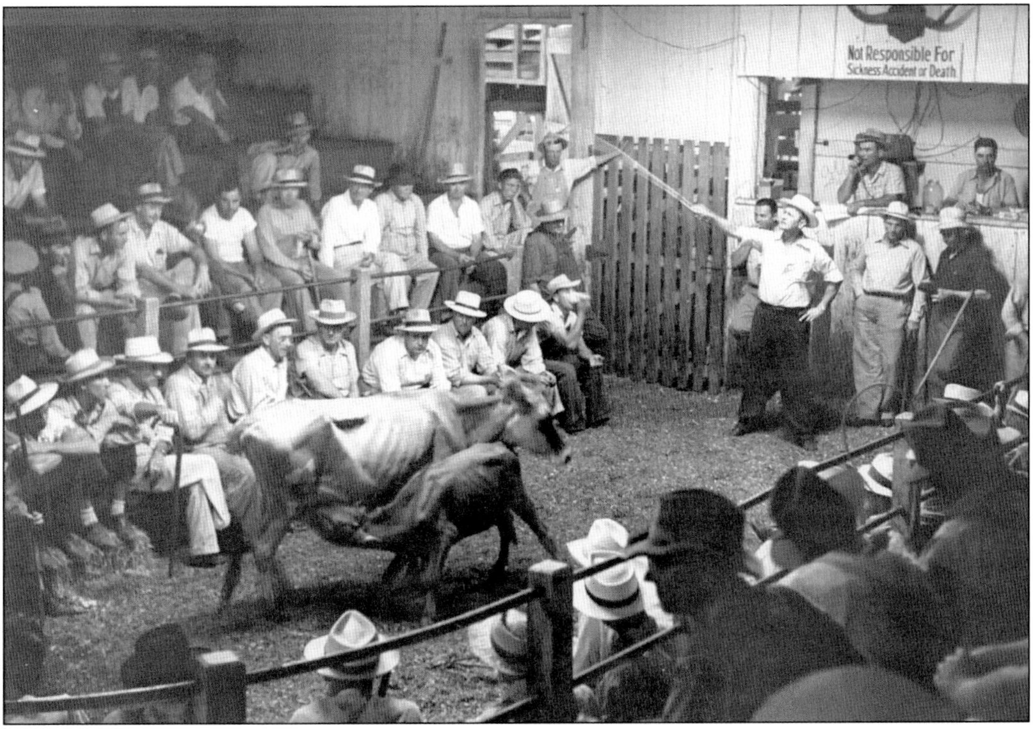

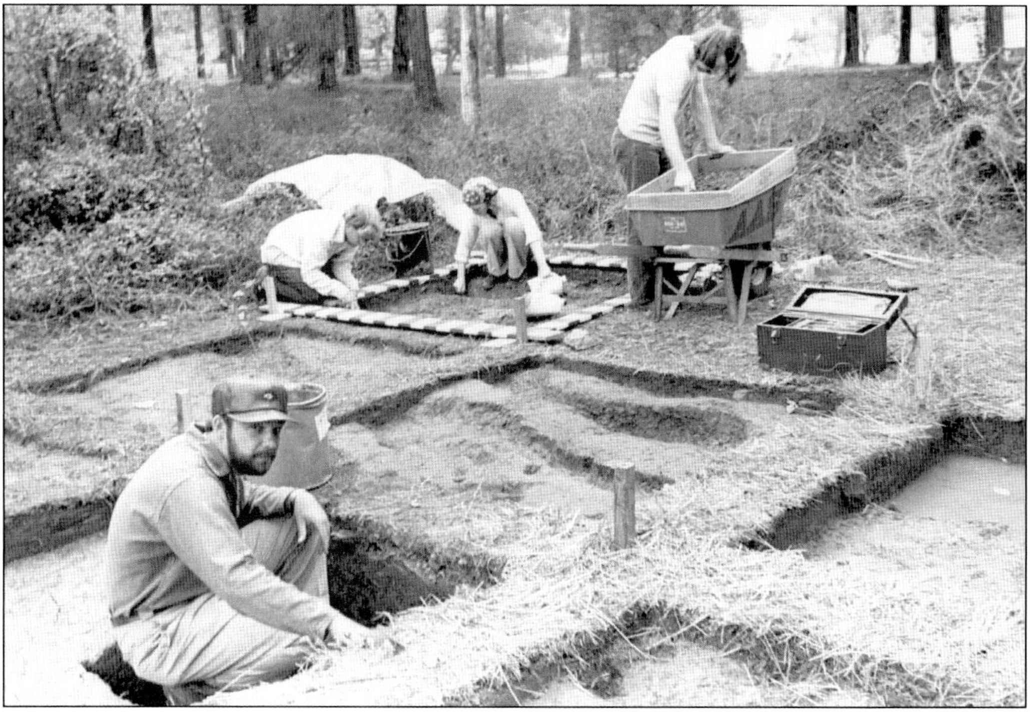

ARCHAEOLOGICAL DIG AT CADRON SETTLEMENT IN THE FALL OF 1973. State archaeologist Sam Smith and his crew discovered many interesting artifacts. Cadron was one of the very first settlements in Arkansas Territory. (UCA Archives.)

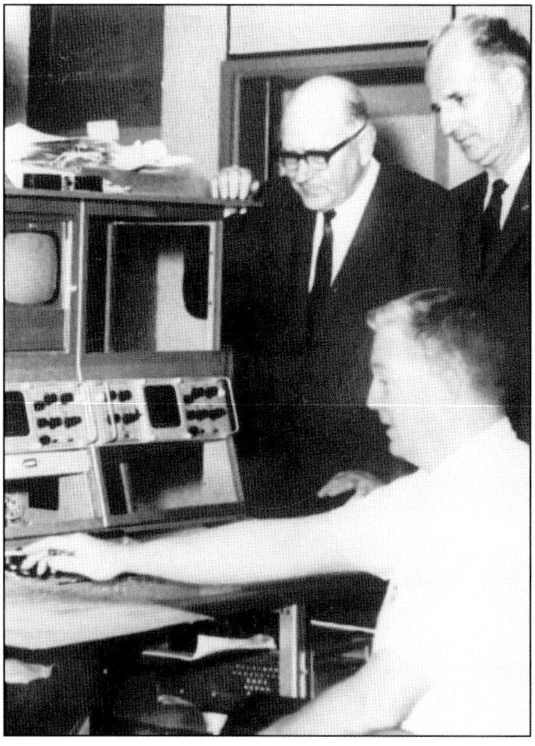

ARKANSAS EDUCATIONAL TELEVISION NETWORK. The public broadcasting station was established in 1964. Seen standing, from left to right, are Lee Reeves (the first director) and Silas Snow. Vern Dillaphone is seated. (UCA Archives.)

CALVIN C. SHOCK AT THE SIMULATED WELL WITH PLAQUE AT THE "GREATHOUSE" HOME. Ann Turney photographed Shock during the Faulkner County Centennial in 1976. His ancestor, John T. Shock, came to Arkansas in 1821 from Virginia. John, in turn, was descended from one of three Bavarian brothers who fought as mercenaries for the British during the Revolutionary War. (UCA Archives.)

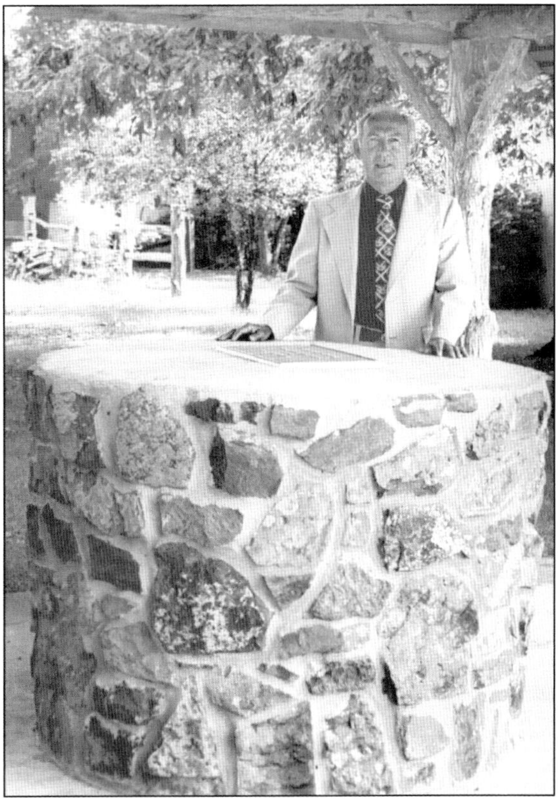

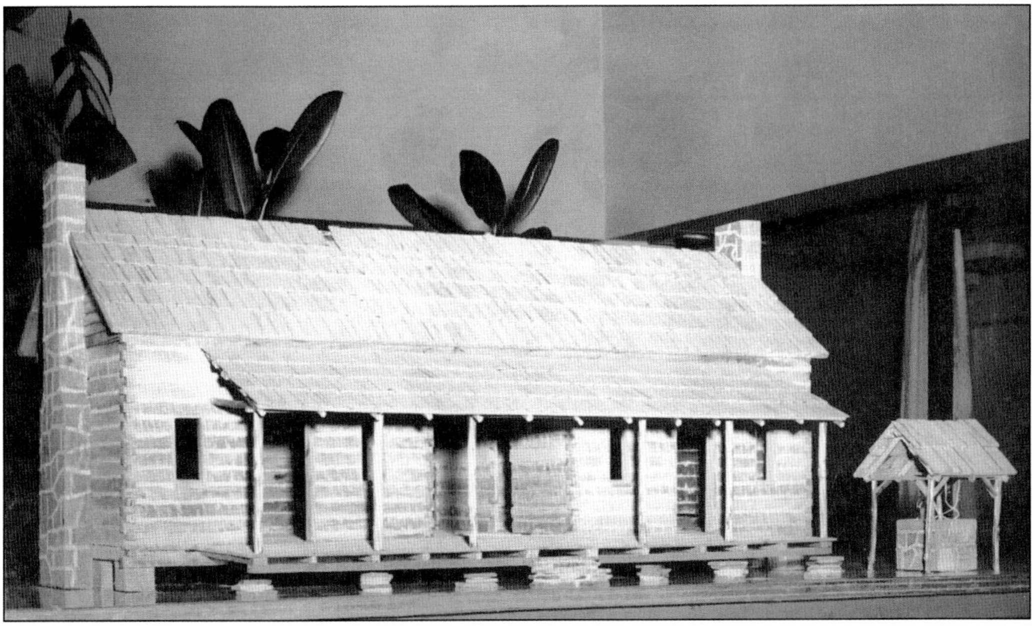

MODEL OF "GREATHOUSE" BY W.E. BAILEY, C. 1970. The original greathouse is an example of an 1830s vintage log dogtrot home that was popular among Arkansas pioneers. (UCA Archives.)

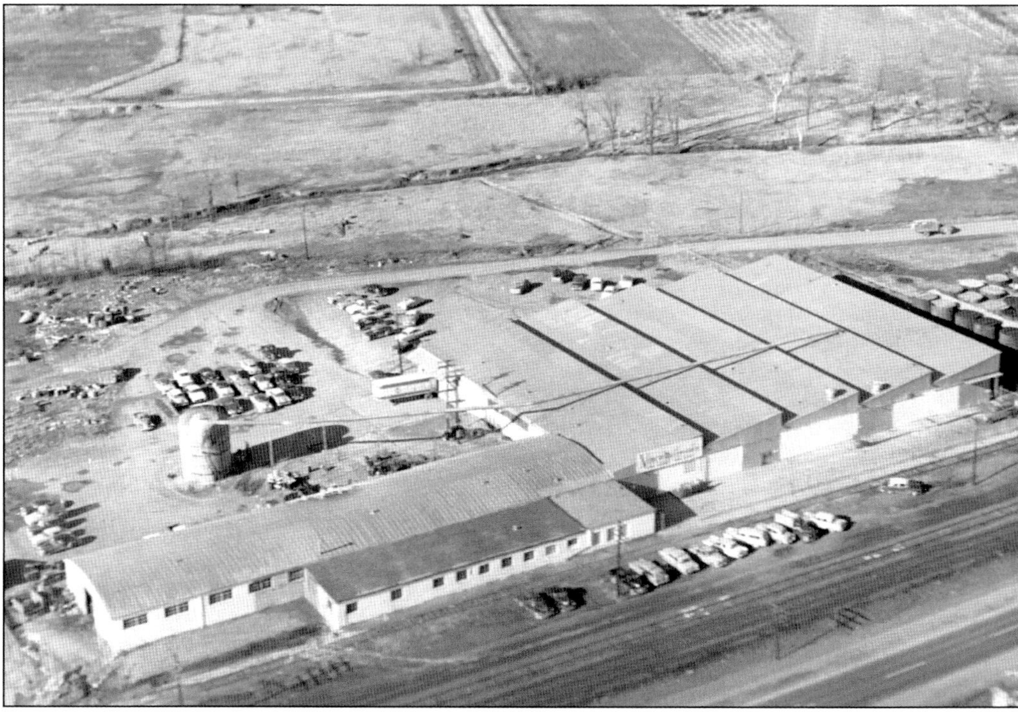

Aerial View of Virco Manufacturing Company on Highway 65 South in Conway, c. Late 1960s. (UCA Archives.)

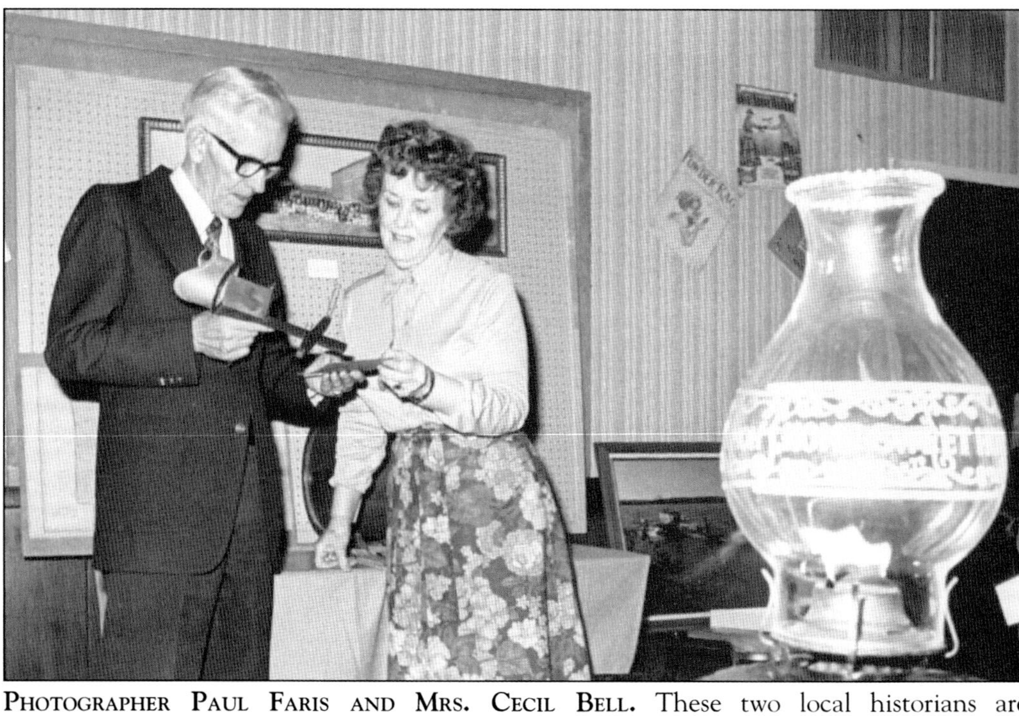

Photographer Paul Faris and Mrs. Cecil Bell. These two local historians are shown attending the 1977 annual dinner meeting of the Faulkner County Historical Society. (UCA Archives.)

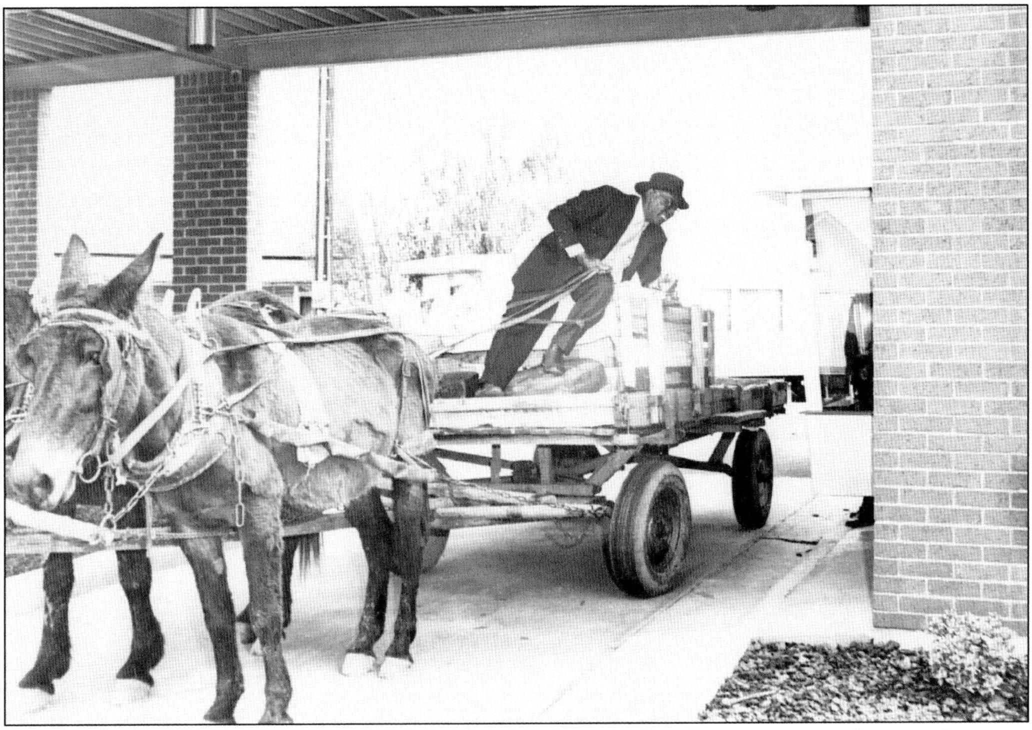

WILLIAM "TOAD SUCK" THOMPSON ON APRIL 15, 1970. Thompson is using the new drive-up window at the First State Bank East at First and State Streets (UCA Archives.)

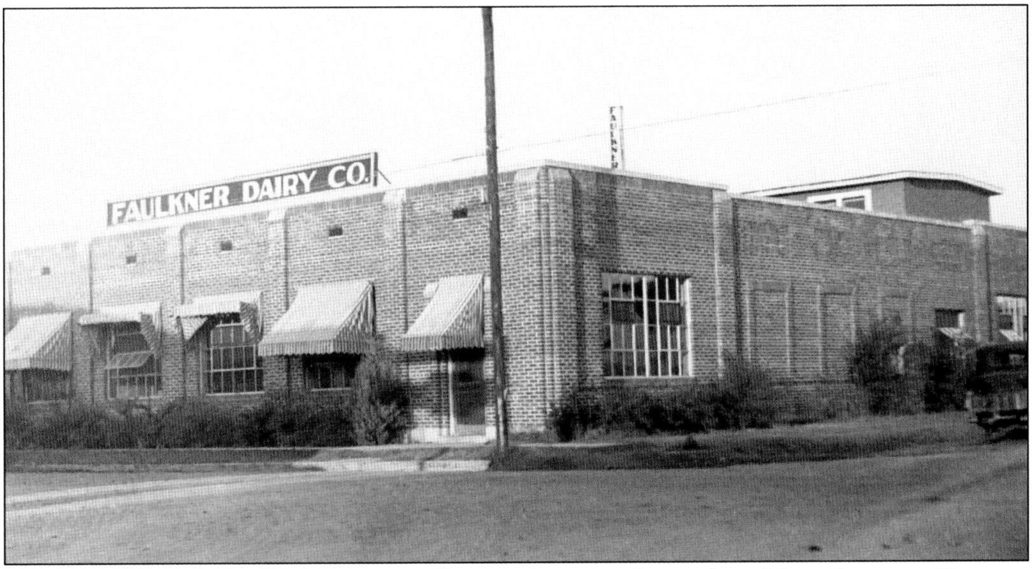

FAULKNER DAIRY COMPANY C. 1978. The company was located on Main Street in Conway. (UCA Archives.)

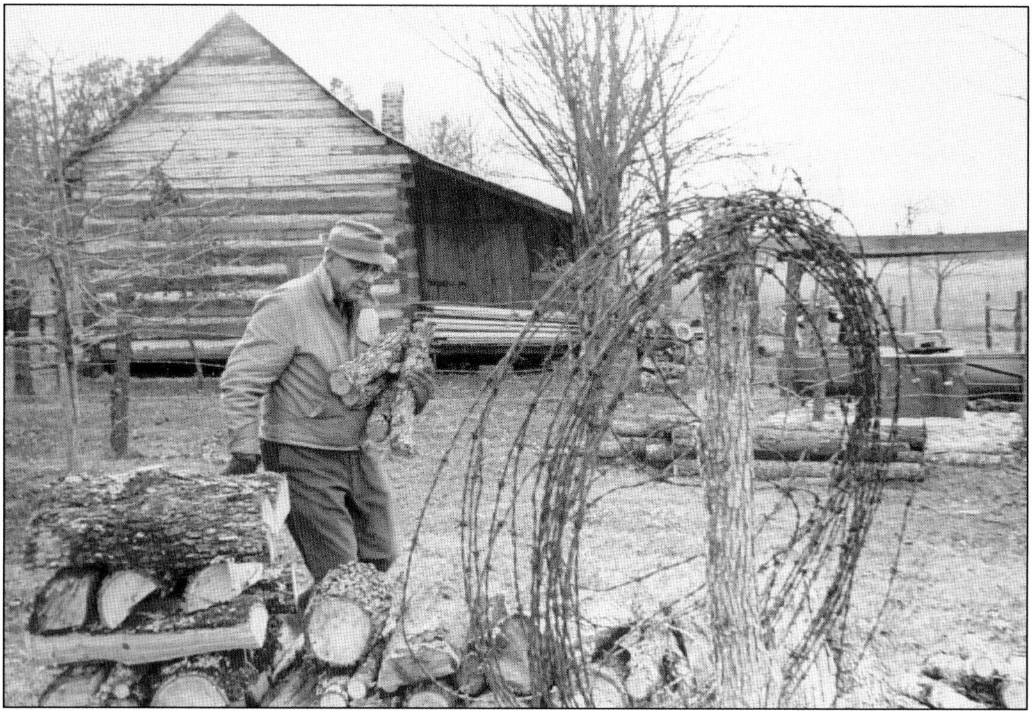

Mary Randall Berry Cabin, North of Beryl. Curtis, seen in this photograph, and Doris Berry Dolon restored this cabin *c.* 1973. The cabin was about 50 years old when Mrs. Henry bought the property in the 1880s. (UCA Archives.)

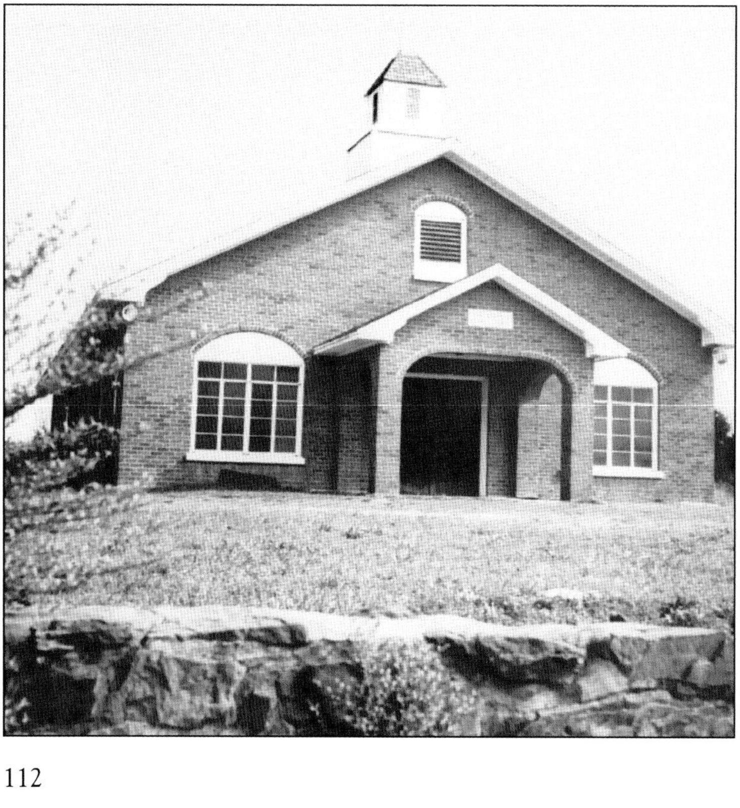

Baptist Church in Mount Vernon, c. 1965. (UCA Archives.)

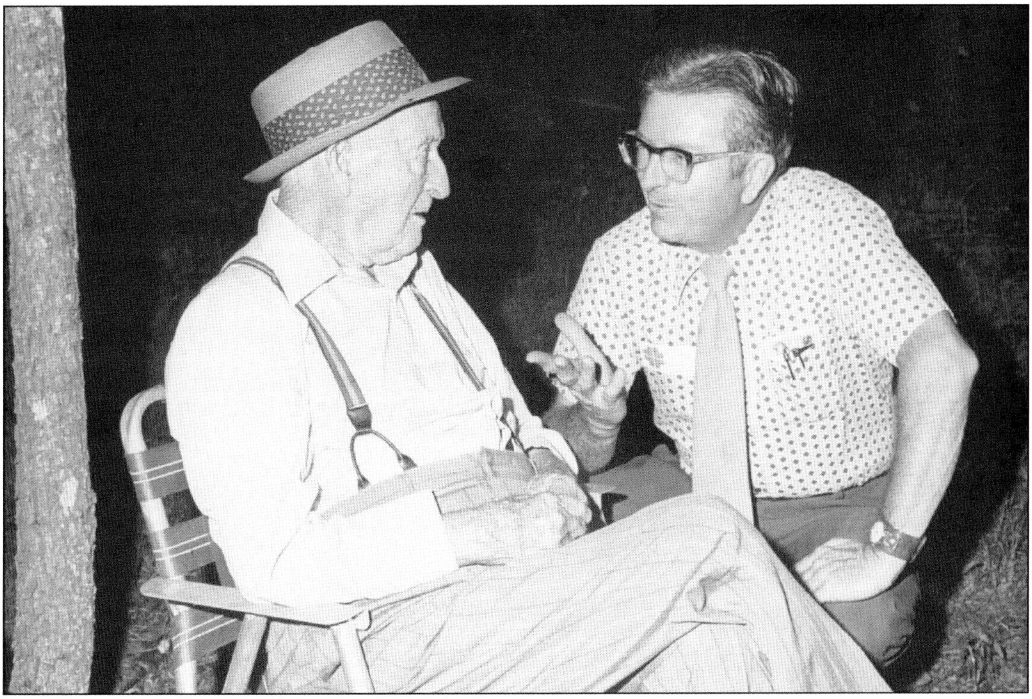

INTERVIEW, SEPTEMBER 19, 1975. Historian Guy Murphy interviews William Thomas Johnson at Woolly Hollow State Park. Johnson turned 95 years old a few weeks later, on November 16. (UCA Archives.)

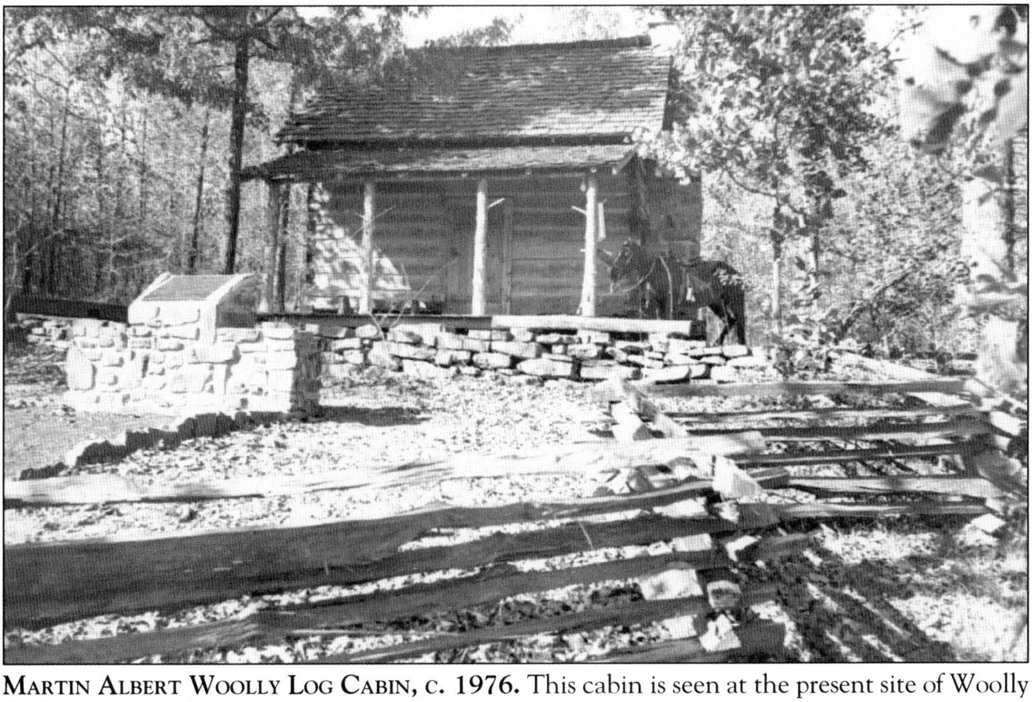

MARTIN ALBERT WOOLLY LOG CABIN, C. 1976. This cabin is seen at the present site of Woolly Hollow State Park. (UCA Archives.)

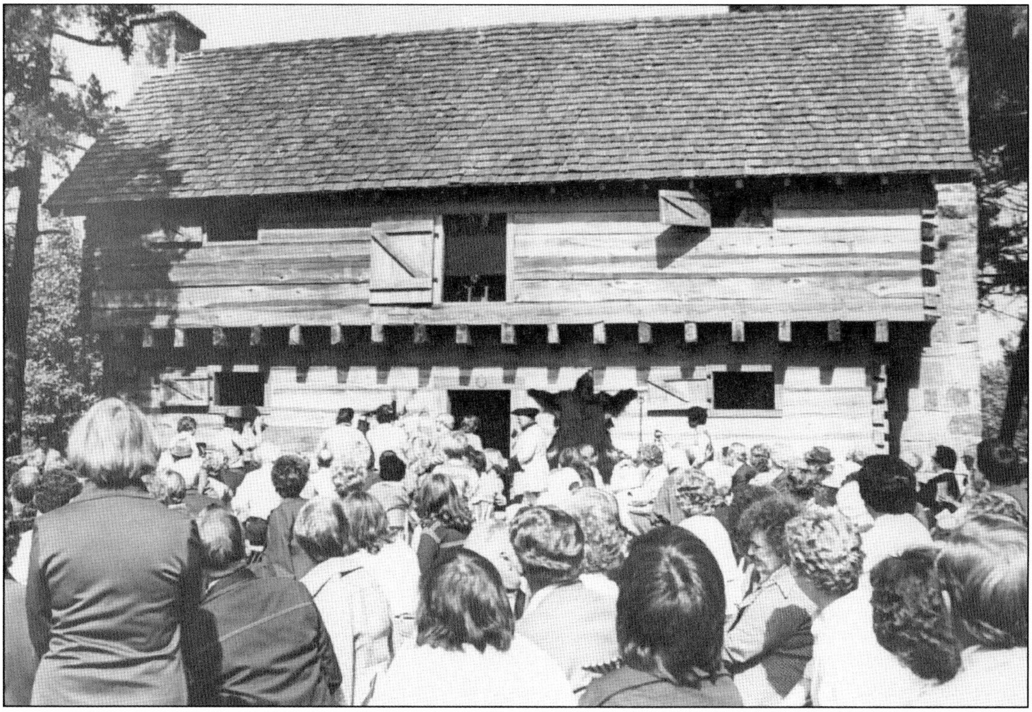

DEDICATION OF BLOCKHOUSE AT CADRON SETTLEMENT PARK IN 1976. (UCA Archives.)

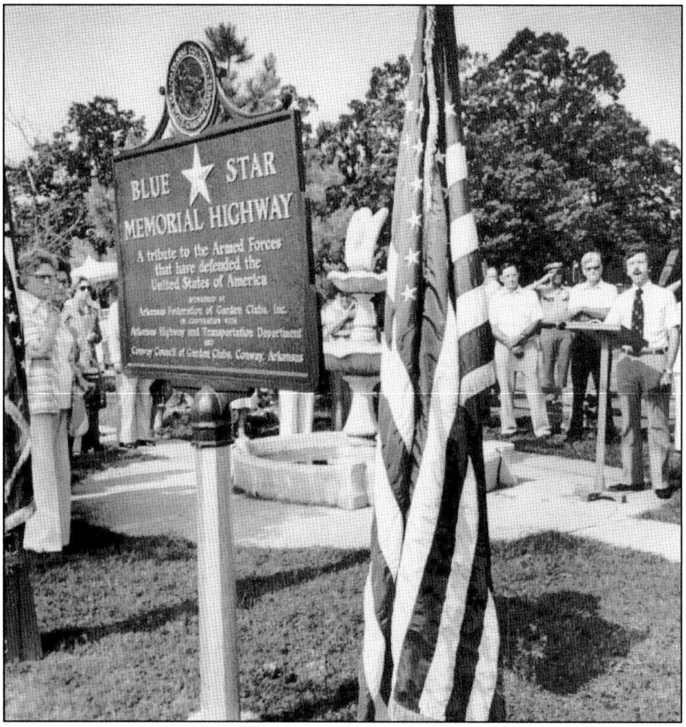

DEDICATION OF BLUE STAR MEMORIAL HIGHWAY MARKER AT MAYFLOWER IN 1975. (UCA Archives.)

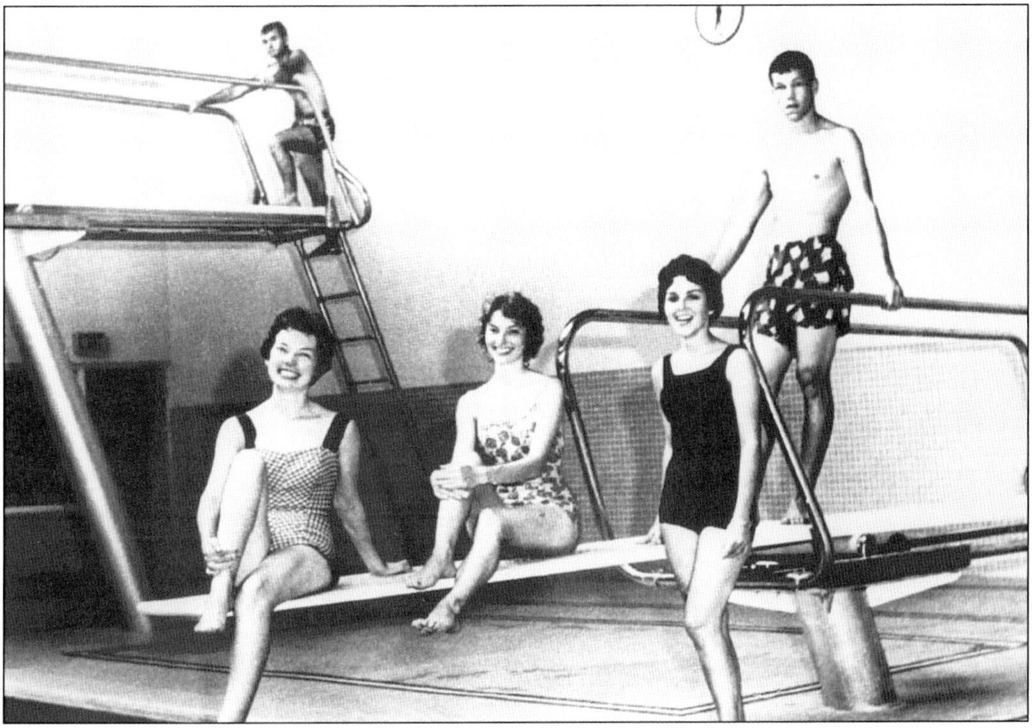

GROVE GYMNASIUM POOL. Thyla Oldham, Kay Lyford, Jackie Witt, and Frank Gibson inaugurate the pool at Hendrix College in 1961. (UCA Archives.)

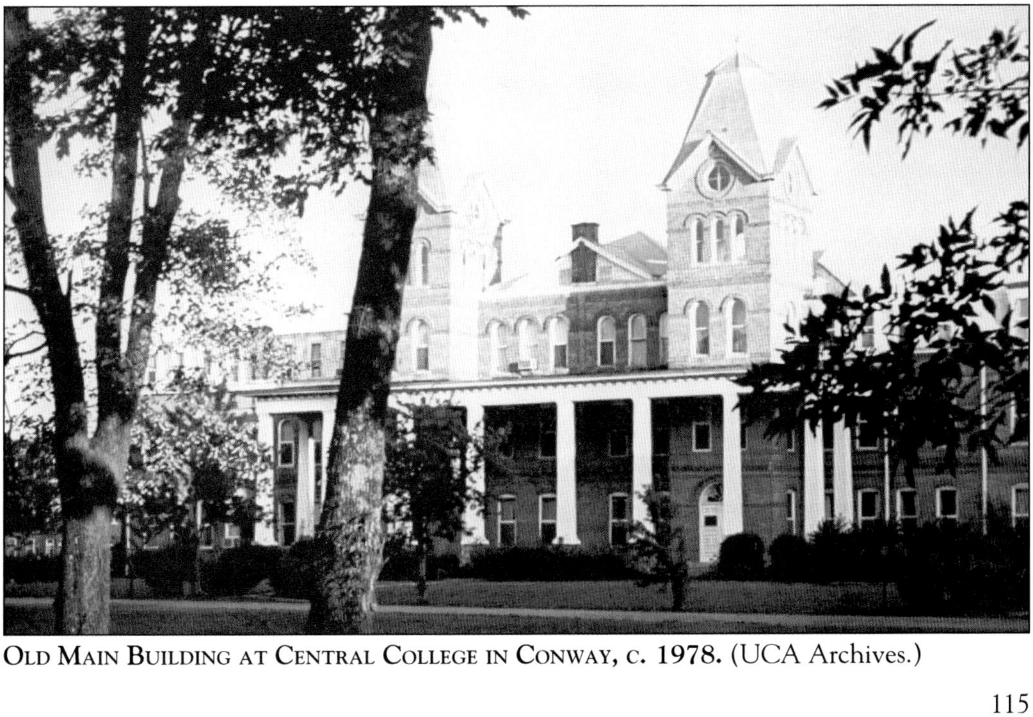

OLD MAIN BUILDING AT CENTRAL COLLEGE IN CONWAY, C. 1978. (UCA Archives.)

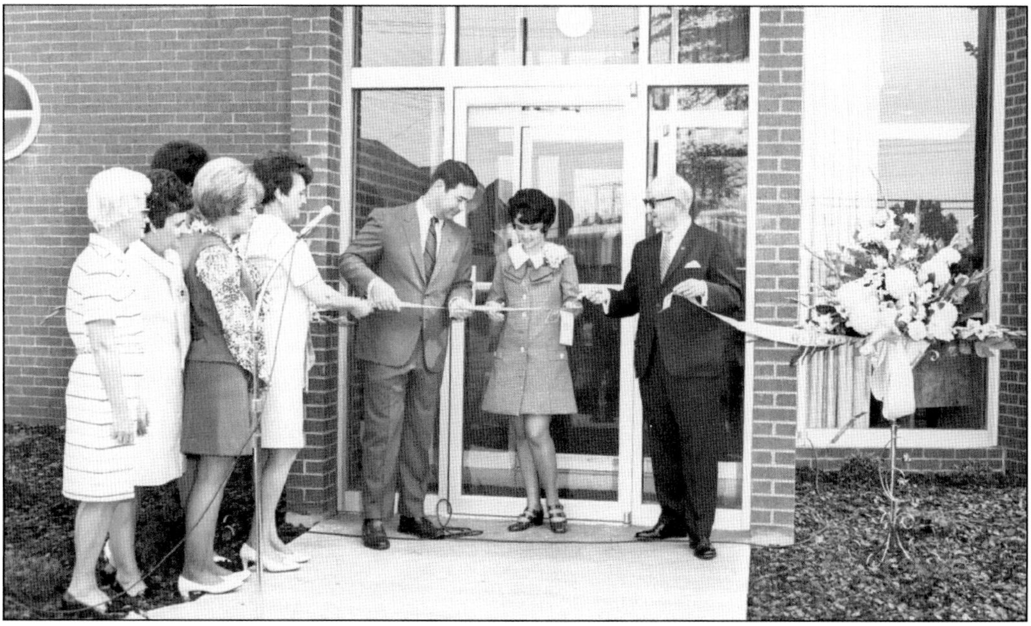

Ribbon-Cutting Ceremony at the New Building for the First State Bank in East Conway, c. 1978. Seen here, from left to right, are as follows: (ladies) Vernetta Nutter, Burnell Terry, Brenda Hester, Kathy Davis, and Mrs. Lyford; (men) Jim Watson and Thomas G. Wilson. Established in 1946, the bank's original location was 908 Front Street. (UCA Archives.)

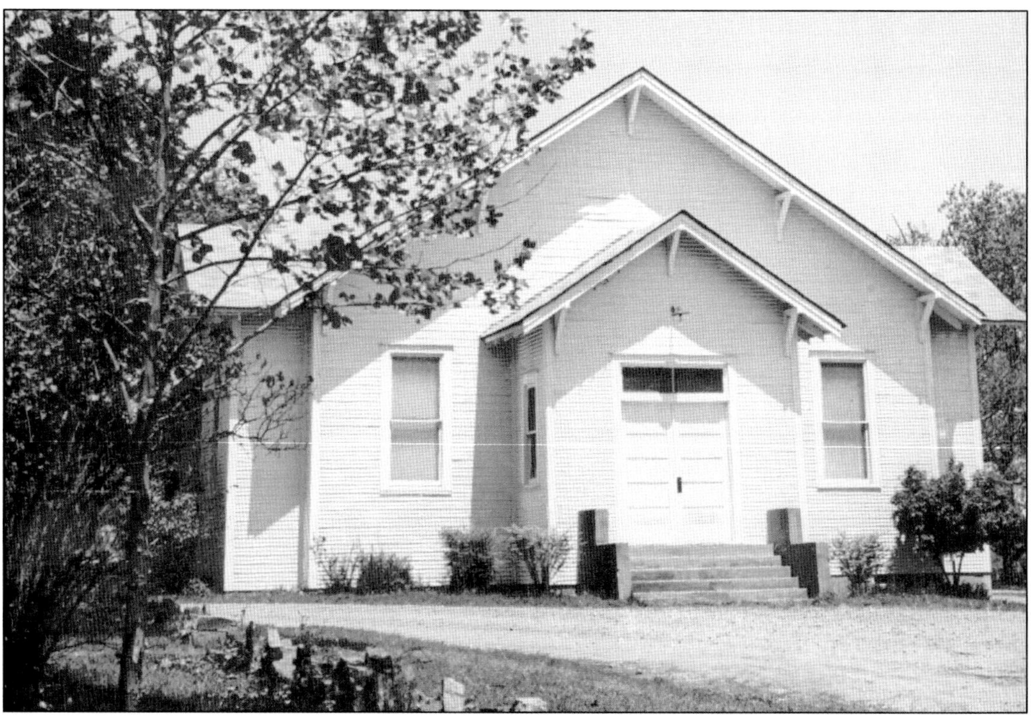

Methodist Church in Quitman. This church was photographed in April 1965. While located in Cleburne County, Quitman has close ties to Faulkner County. (UCA Archives.)

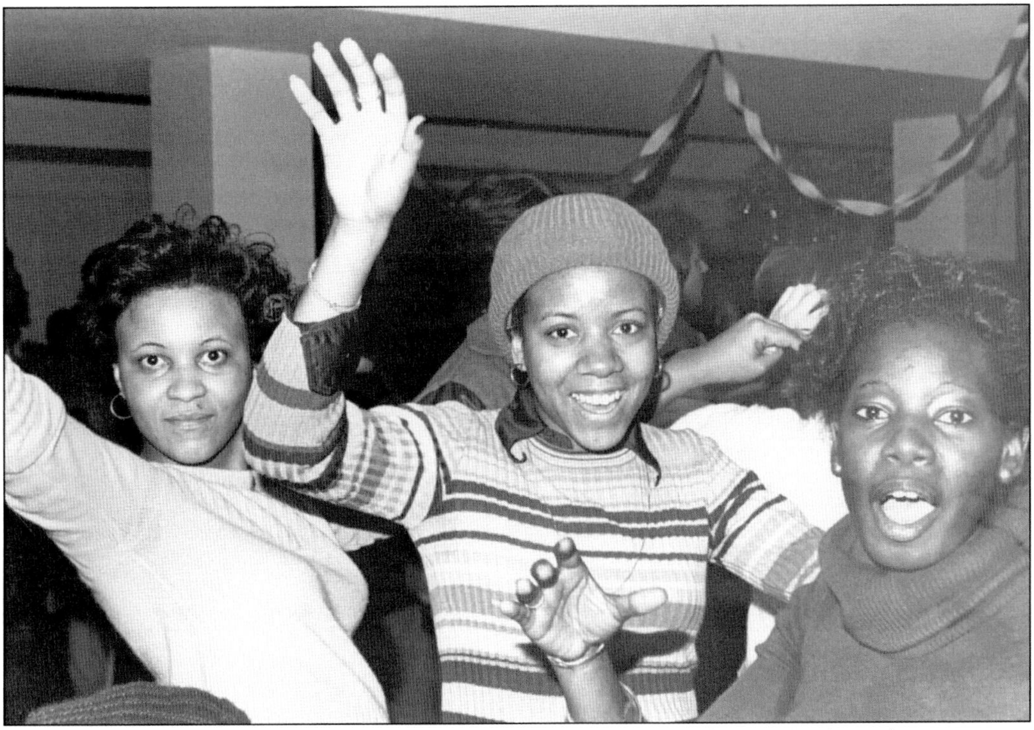

UCA STUDENTS AT HUGHES HALL CHRISTMAS PARTY IN 1977. (UCA Archives.)

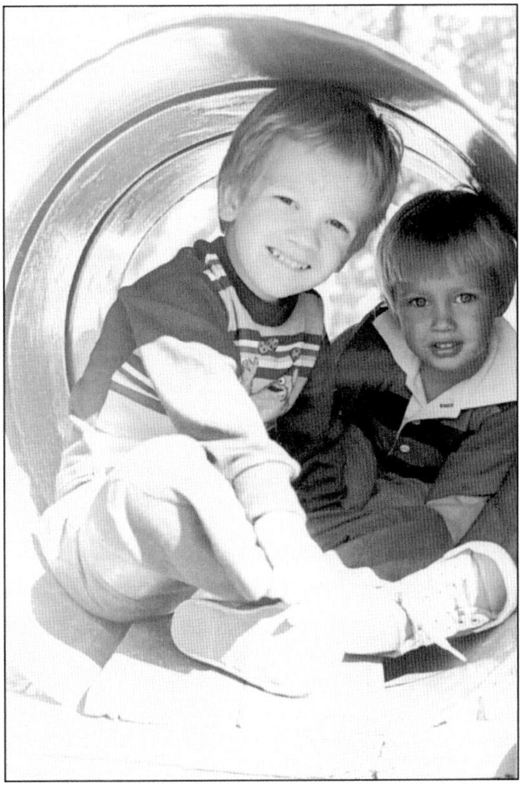

PLAYTIME. These two boys play in a barrel at the Irby Hall nursery school on the UCA campus during the fall of 1977. (UCA Archives.)

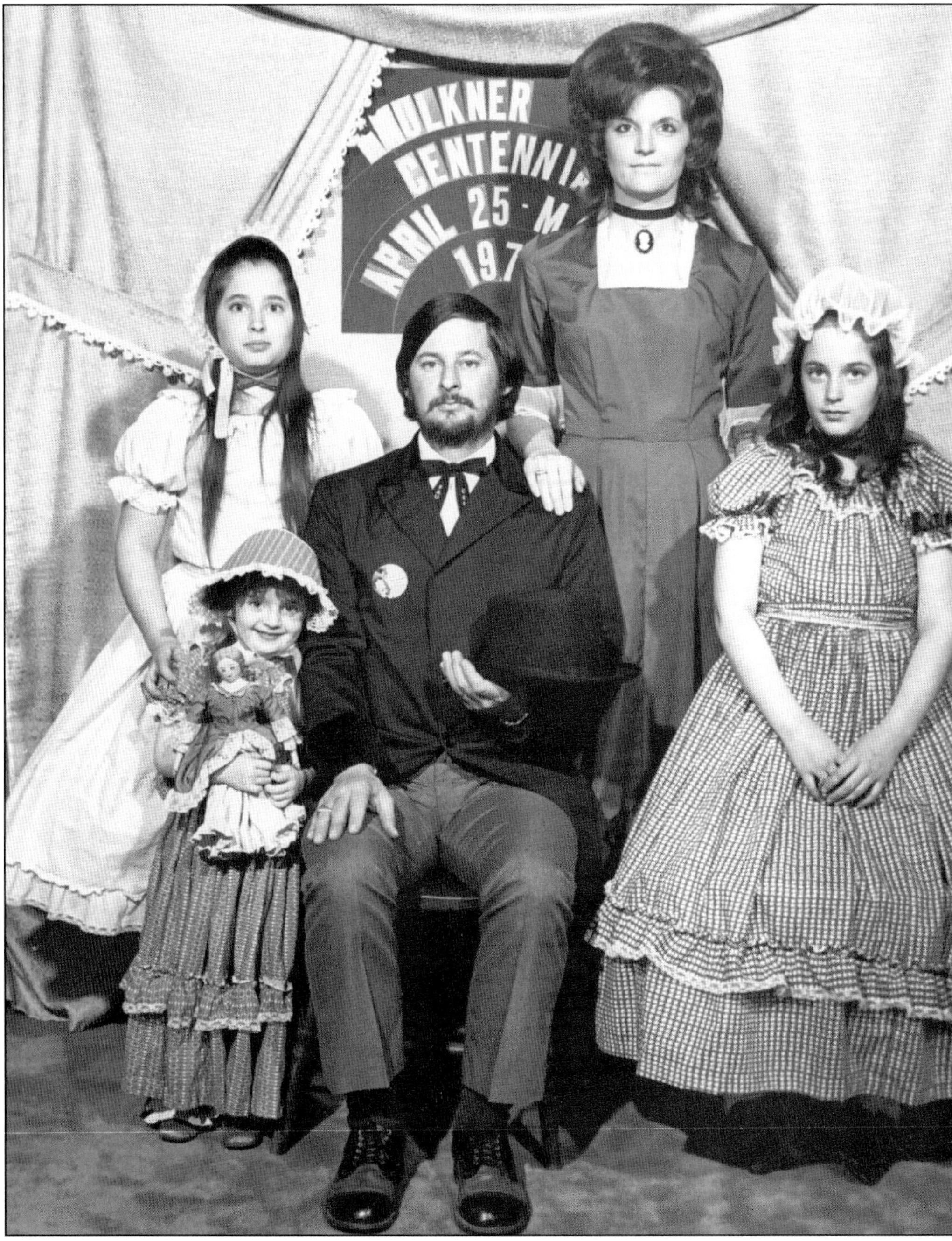

THE JIM BALDUS FAMILY. The photograph shows Jim Baldus, his wife Kay, and their children Theresa Kay (age 11), Lisa (age 10), and Lorri (age 3). The family dressed in period costume for Conway's 1973 centennial celebration. (UCA Archives.)

Seven

A Time of Growth and Optimism

While the first few decades following WW II were a time of significant economic growth and optimism, by the winter of 1981, the economy in Faulkner County was stagnating. John Ward, who was working at the *Log Cabin Democrat* at the time, thought that the county needed a celebration to "entice people out of their doldrums and into the fresh air of a spring day on the banks of the Arkansas River. This, we thought, would cheer people up a little, get them working together on something totally unselfish and genuinely fun."

John Ward bounced the idea off of his brother Bill and Estel Jeffery, and they began fleshing out the concept that weekend. They subsequently approached other people, and the idea gained momentum. By this time, John Ward resolved to somehow fit "Toad Suck" into the moniker for the project, in order to give the celebration local flavor and an attention-getting quality. After trying on countless names for the celebration, the best contender was Toad Suck Days, but that somehow lacked certain panache. "Then, just thinking about it," Ward recalled, "it seemed like 'Daze' would better represent the euphoria we hoped to generate during the celebration, so 'Toad Suck Daze'" was born. The whole area seemed to pitch in. The first Toad Suck Daze was held from April 30 to May 2, 1982. Ward expected 5,000 people, but more than 25,000 showed up. Clearly, this was the right idea at the right time.

Faulkner County's growth reached a critical mass about 1990, when the population seemed to explode. The area has come a very long way since Asa Robinson fell in love with a stretch of prairie along the railroad he was building, since the county was named after a likeable old fiddle player and teller of tall tales, since cotton was king, since Conway became a college town, and since Toad Suck Daze helped revitalize the spirit of Faulkner County residents. The history of Faulkner County is a history of ordinary people making a difference. It is a rich and colorful tapestry that has yet to be completed.

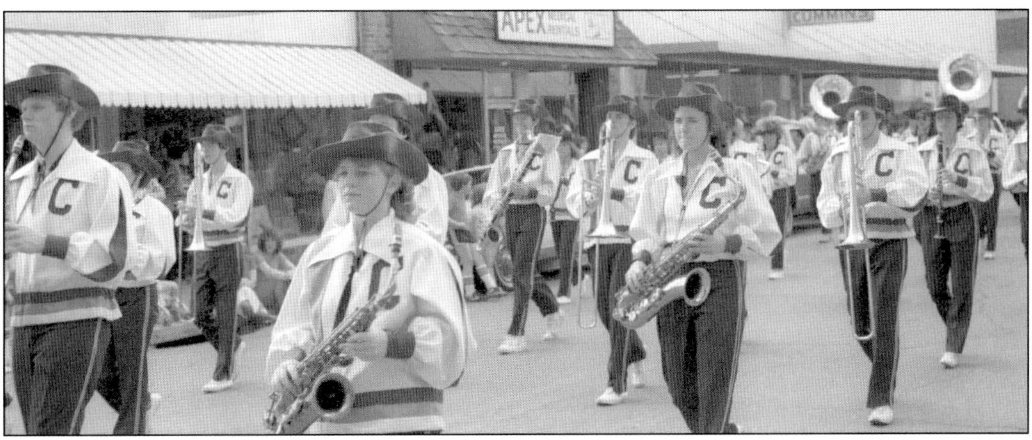

The Conway High School Band. The band marched on Front Street during the 1984 Toad Suck Daze parade in this Desmond Walls Allen photograph.

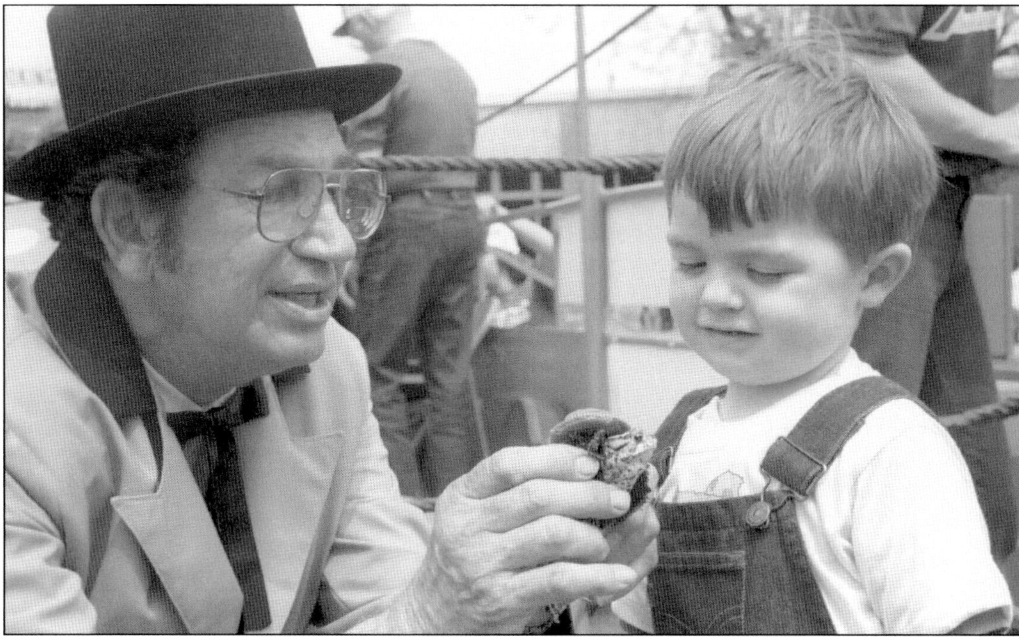

THE OFFICIAL TOAD. In this Desmond Walls Allen photograph, Jim Stone, the first Toadmaster of Toad Suck Daze, shows the official toad to Hadley Hirrill *c.* 1983, the second year of the annual event. The celebration grew year after year, and the nonprofit Toad Suck Daze Council merged with the Conway Area Chamber of Commerce late in 1991. The celebration grew in size and quality, winning the Festival of the Year Award from the Arkansas Festival Association for 1998. By then, attendance had grown to about 125,000 people. Toad Suck Daze has become an integral and exuberant part of county life.

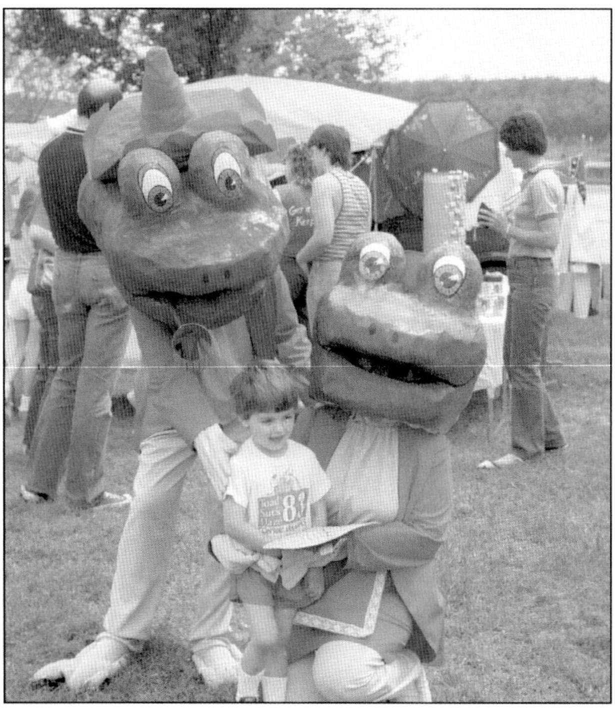

TOAD SUCK DAZE CELEBRATION. Desmond Walls Allen photographed these mascots and a friend on the banks of the Arkansas River in 1984.

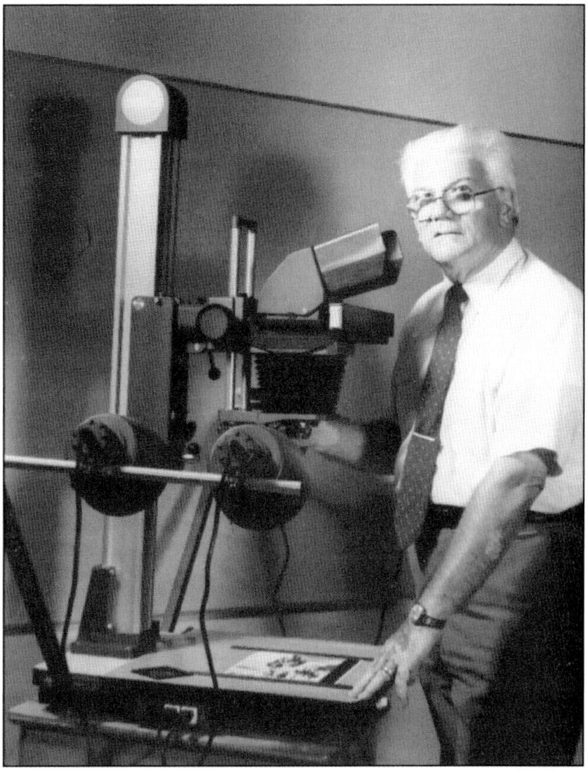

PHOTOGRAPHER OFFIE LITES AT WORK IN HIS CONWAY STUDIO. (UCA Archives.)

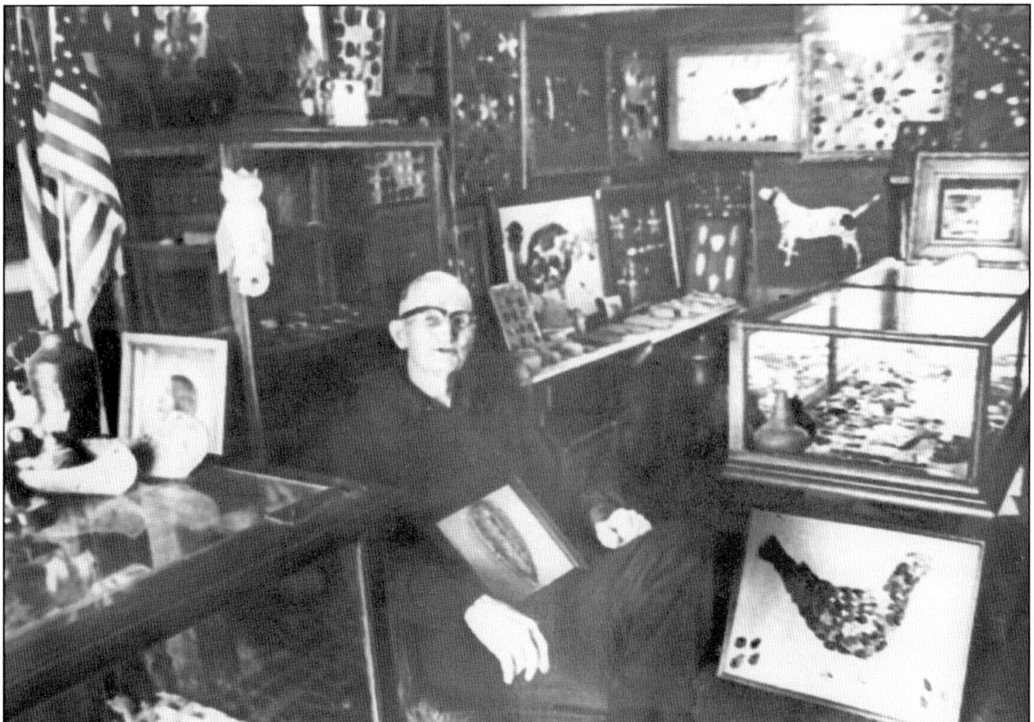

FRED WILSON AT HIS MUSEUM IN GREENBRIER, DATE UNKNOWN. (UCA Archives.)

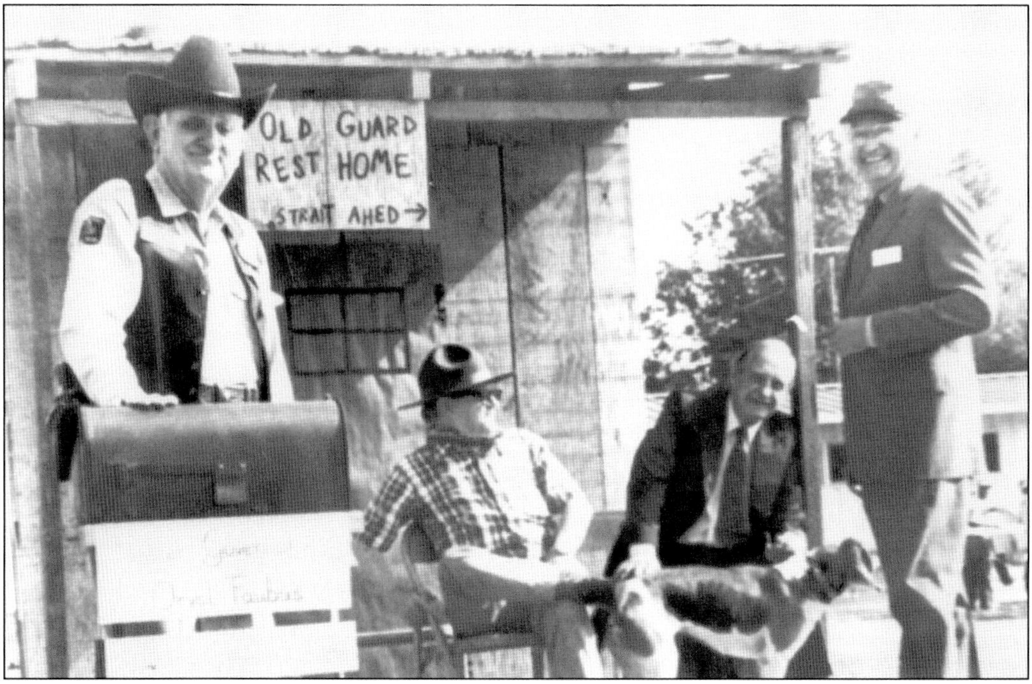

Old Guard Rest Home. Seen here, from left to right, are Sheriff Marlin Hawkins, Senator Guy "Mutt" Jones, former governor Orval E. Faubus, and Justice Jim Johnson. This photograph was taken in Faulkner County in 1985. (UCA Archives.)

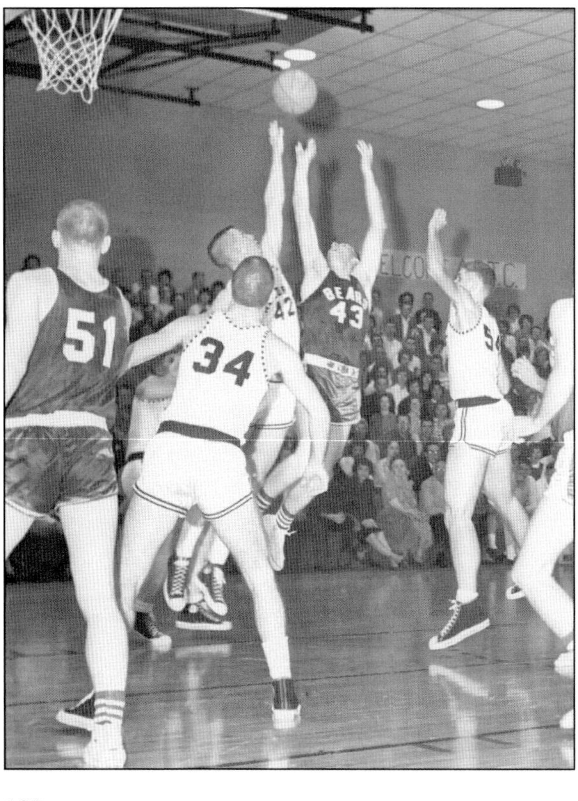

Local Rivals. Arkansas State Teachers College and Hendrix College play against each other in this undated photograph. (UCA Archives.)

HATTIE ANN KELSO AND STELLA CAPEK AT THE CARTER CEMETERY CENSUS. The Faulkner County Historical Society sponsored this event in July 1987. (UCA Archives.)

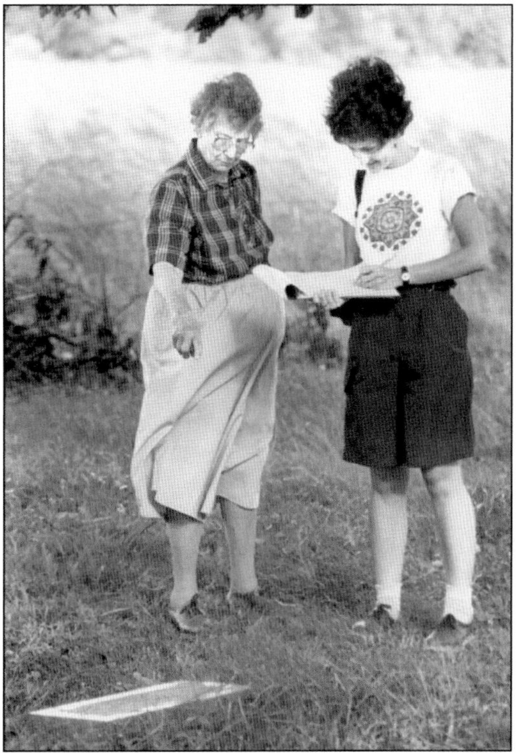

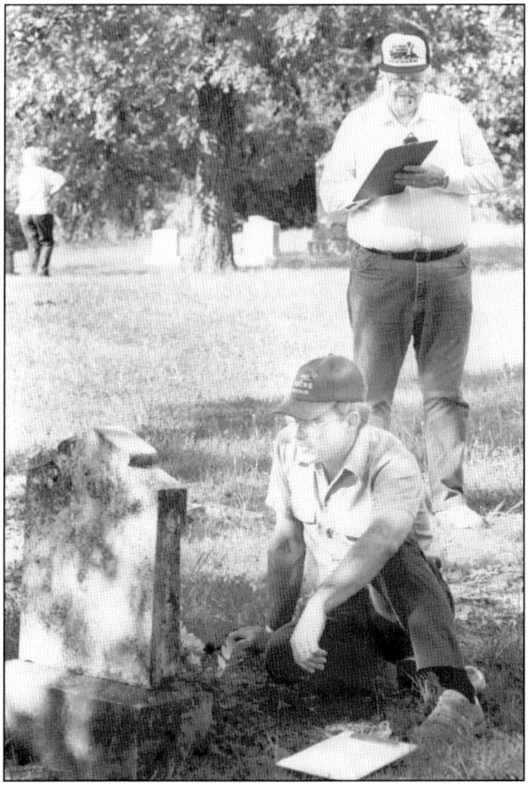

CARTER CEMETERY CENSUS, JULY 1987. Bob Meriwether (standing) and Chris Spatz help with the Carter Cemetery census, which was sponsored by the Faulkner County Historical Society. (UCA Archives.)

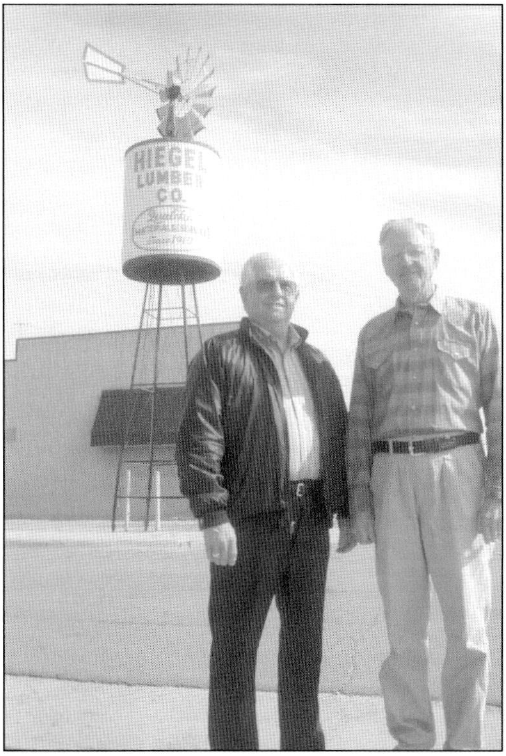

SUSAN ALLEN'S 1998 PHOTOGRAPH OF AL AND PAUL HIEGEL. Nephew of J.J. Hiegel, who founded the Hiegel Lumber Company in 1910, Al Hiegel (right) began managing the company in 1957. His brother Paul (left) became his partner in 1962; the two brothers ran this Conway landmark until it closed its doors 38 years later. It was the last privately owned lumberyard in Conway.

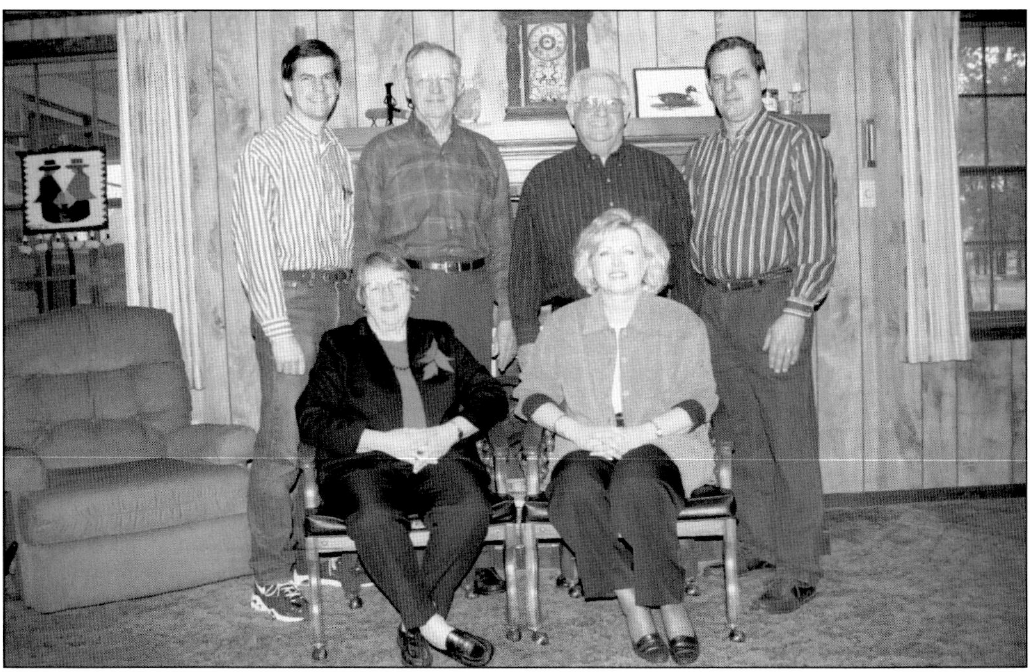

HIEGEL FAMILY PORTRAIT, 1998. Pictured, from left to right, are as follows: (standing) Jerry, Al, Paul, and Philip; (sitting) Mary and Lou. The old Hiegel windmill remains a Conway landmark. It now stands in front of a new plumbing, electrical supply, and hardware store, which is located on Bruce Street and is owned by Al's son Jerry. (Photo by Susan Allen.)

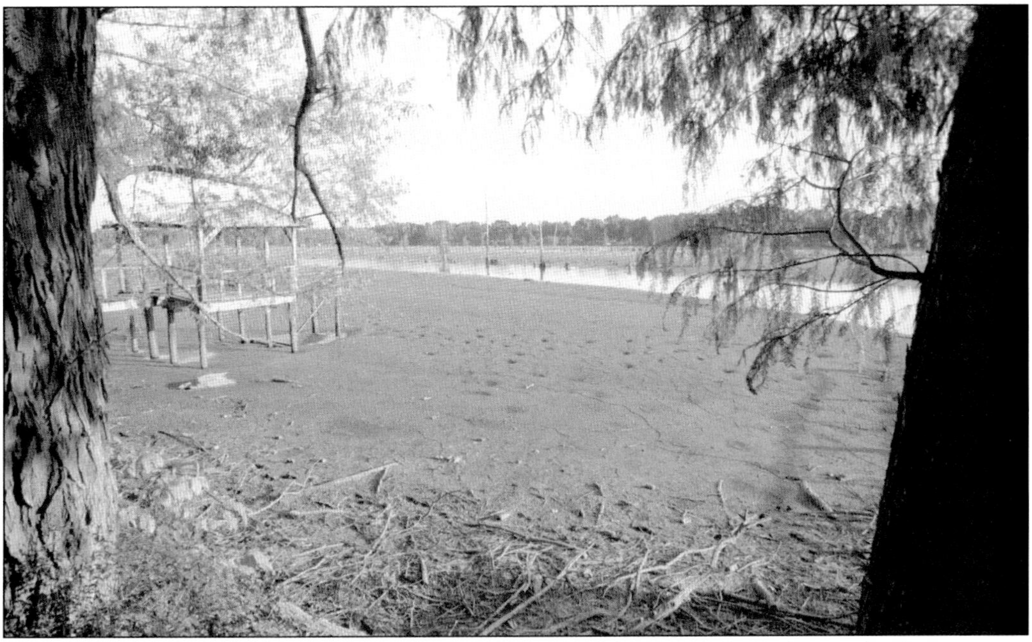

Dam Repair. Lake Conway was drained in 1998 to enable repair of the dam at the downstream end of the lake. Six months after this photograph was taken, water levels had returned to normal. The lake is formed by runoff from Stone Dam Creek, Gold Creek, Palarm Creek, Little Cypress Creek, and Panther Creek. It is the largest man-made lake managed by the Arkansas Department of Game and Fish. (Photograph by Polly Walter.)

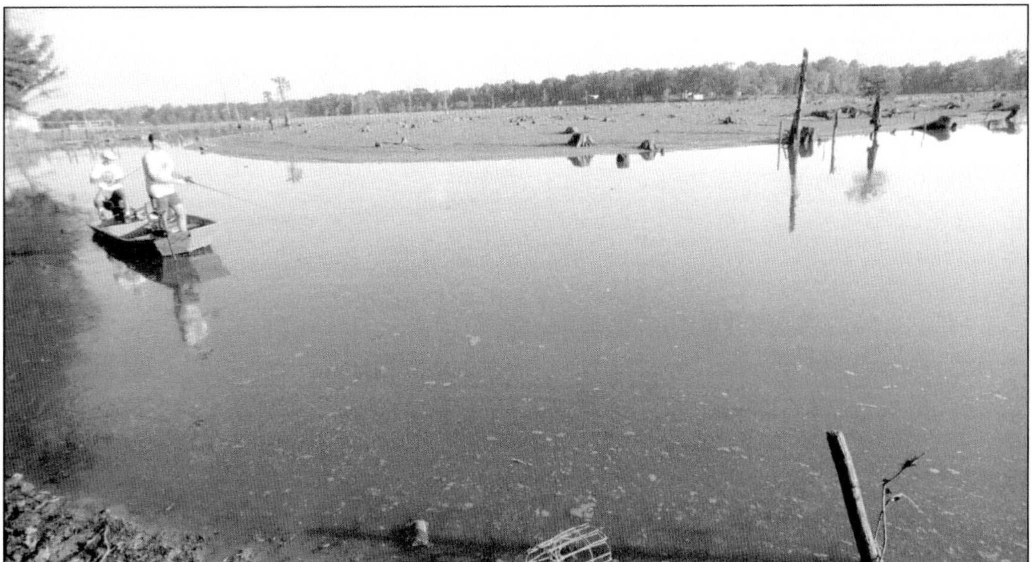

Fisher's Paradise. When the Arkansas Department of Game and Fish temporarily lowered the level of Lake Conway, anglers took advantage of the concentrated population of fish in the remaining waters. In the fall of 1998, Chad Fulmer and Paul Kostecky tried their luck in an old stream bed normally covered by Lake Conway. The 6,700-acre lake is considered one of the state's best places to fish for bluegill, bream, crappie, bass, and catfish. (Photograph by Polly Walter.)

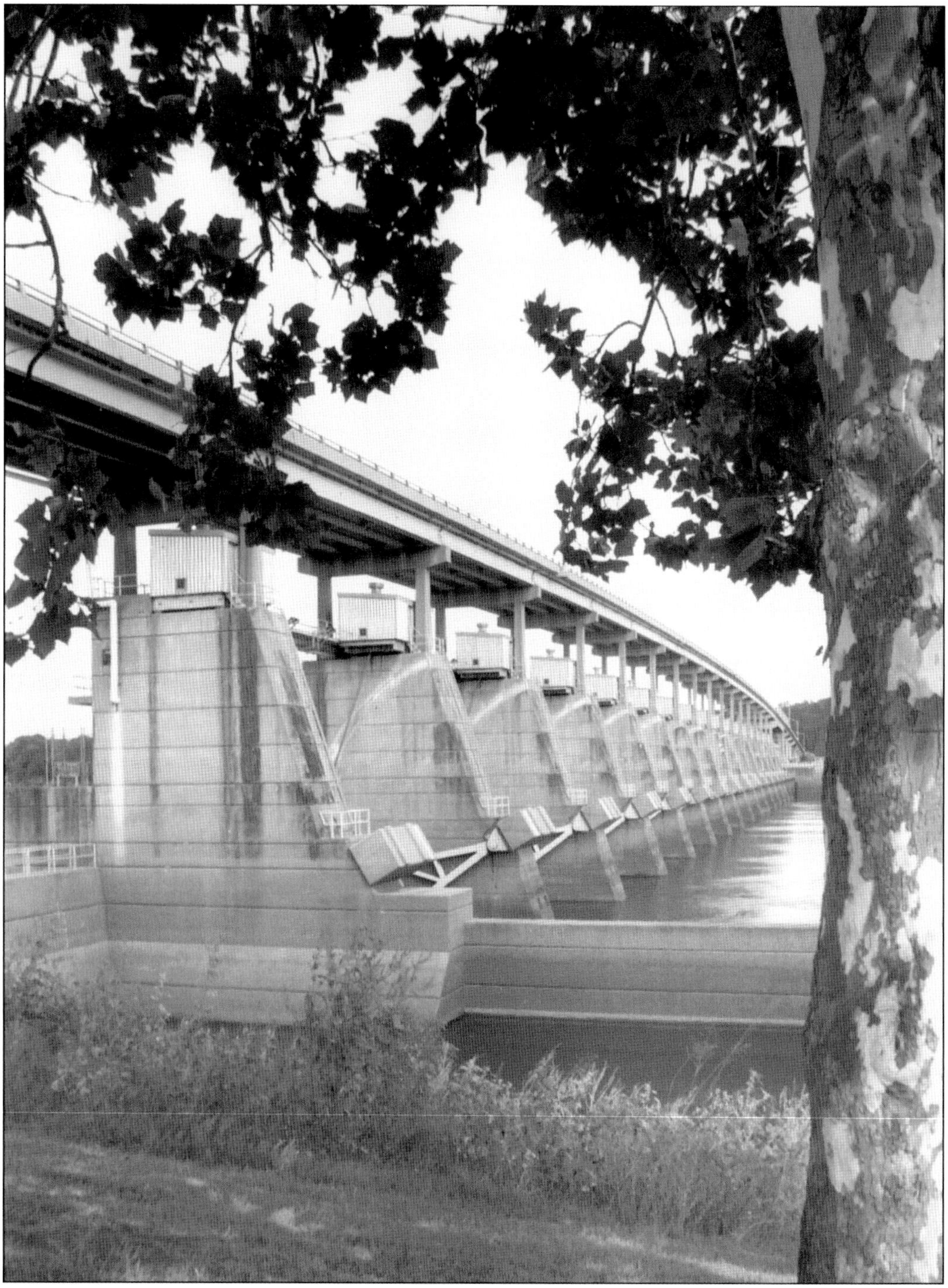

TOAD SUCK FERRY LOCK AND DAM. The lock and dam provide a bridge over the Arkansas River, where privately owned ferries had provided the only means of crossing the river from the 1820s until this lock and dam project was completed in 1969. Present-day Highway 286 crosses the Arkansas River here, taking a similar path to an old postal road established back when the area was known as Arkansas Territory. (Photograph by Henryetta Vanaman.)

Index